D1523835

Church-State Matters

Congress shall make no law respecting an establishment of religion, or prohibiting the free exercise thereof

Church-State Matters

Fighting for Religious Liberty in Our Nation's Capital

J. Brent Walker

Mercer University Press
Macon, Georgia

MUP/H762

First edition.

Books published by Mercer University Press are printed on acid free paper that meets the requirements of American National Standard for Information Sciences—Permanence of Paper for Printed Library Materials.

Library of Congress Cataloging-in-Publication Data

Walker, J. Brent.
Church-state matters : fighting for religious liberty in our nation's capital / J. Brent Walker. -- 1st ed.
p. cm.
Includes bibliographical references and index.
ISBN-13: 978-0-88146-115-2 (hardback : alk. paper)
ISBN-10: 0-88146-115-6 (hardback : alk. paper)
1. Freedom of religion—Washington (D.C.)—History. 2. Church and state—Washington (D.C.)—History. 3. Freedom of religion—United States—History. 4. Church and state—United States—History. 5. Baptist Joint Committee on Public Affairs—History. I. Title.
BR516.W34 2008
323.44'20973--dc22
2008006223

Dedicated to my family
—Nancy, Ryan, Layton and Lucas —
What matters in my life

MERCER
UNIVERSITY PRESS

Endowed by
TOM WATSON BROWN
and
THE WATSON-BROWN FOUNDATION, INC.

Contents

Preface

It is always presumptuous to write a book—all the more when the volume contains mostly previously published, or at least spoken, material.

But that's what you have in your hands. Over the past 18 years as a staff member of the Baptist Joint Committee, I have written close to 200 columns in our flagship publication, *Report from the Capital*; penned numerous articles in other journals; testified orally and filed written testimony before congressional committees nine times; lectured frequently at colleges, seminaries, and law schools; and preached nearly every other Sunday (sometimes Saturdays when worshipping with our Seventh Day Baptist friends).

This book is a collection of some of my columns, articles, testimonies, lectures, and sermons to which many of you have been kind enough to respond with your insight and words of appreciation. I have tried to select representative samples from throughout my nearly two decades of writing and speaking about church and state. Some are historical, others are primarily legal and constitutional, and several deal with specific church-state issues. Some are thoroughly footnoted academic efforts, others are short and sweet *Report from the Capital* columns, and several are sermons written for oral address. They all, however, shed light on the question of how, in the words of the Baptist Joint Committee's mission statement, we seek to "defend and extend God-given religious liberty for all, furthering the Baptist heritage that champions the principle that religion must be freely exercised, neither advanced nor inhibited by government."

This material is not categorized by genre. Nor is it even tightly organized by subject matter. It is loosely arranged by chapters generally addressing Baptist history, the life and ministry of the Baptist Joint Committee, the issues the Baptist Joint Committee deals with daily, the United States Supreme Court and Supreme Court justices, religion's proper place in the public square, and topics of pluralism and religious liberty abroad.

Except for minor editing, I have left the documents as they were originally written or spoken. No attempt has been made to update the material or to revise it, except for an additional footnote here and there and minor editorial changes. Each should be read and understood in the historical context in which it was initially offered. However, feel free to judge and, perhaps, critique what I have written or said in light of subsequent events.

Inasmuch at the Baptist Joint Committee's work has been focused narrowly on religious liberty and the separation of church and state, considerable overlap among the various pieces was inevitable. For example, various testimonies before congressional committees address different issues in the church-state field, but my pitch and rationale are often similar or the same. The five sermons included were preached in many venues and, over time, were revised to address then-current issues and concerns. Moreover, what I might say to a congregation during worship may be the same as what I write about later in a column or in an article. Nevertheless, I have tried to select pieces that maximize breath of coverage, while minimizing points of redundancy.

Why do I deign to publish this body of work? First of all, it provides through primary source documents something of a living history of the Baptist Joint Committee should scholars someday write about its ministry during the final decade of the twentieth century and the first decade of the twenty-first. More than this, I publish the material because it is important. It was when originally written, and it is now.

These church-state matters matter.

I hope readers will agree and will both benefit from and enjoy this book. I trust it also will inspire a renewed commitment to the cause of religious liberty and church-state separation and to the Baptist Joint Committee and its ministry. The Baptist Joint Committee is the only religious body that advocates only for religious liberty. At the risk of sounding immodest, I think we have done a pretty good job of it.

I want to express gratitude to my friends at Mercer University Press, especially Marc Jolley, who came up with the idea of this book. Thanks, too, to the dedicated Baptist Joint Committee staff that helped put this material together, especially Jeff Huett and Phallan Davis, and three interns, Madison McClendon, Allison Collins, and Brad Jackson. Finally, I want to acknowledge a debt of gratitude to former bosses and mentors, James Dunn and Oliver Thomas, who made possible my exciting opportunity of serving the Baptist Joint Committee and the cause of religious liberty for nearly two decades. I stand on their shoulders every day.

J. Brent Walker
Washington, DC
August 2007

History

Congress shall make no law respecting an establishment of religion, or prohibiting the free exercise thereof

Spiritual Roots in Radical Faith:
A Baptist Walk among the Amish[1]

What a peculiar lot they appear to be—a people sent "back to the future" from the late seventeenth century. Actually they are our not-too-distant kinfolk in the family of faith. They can teach us Baptists a lot about how we used to be and serve as a benchmark for judging how much we have changed.

Their men wear dark, natural-fabric sack suits with no lapels, solid-colored shirts (usually white or pale blue), heavy steel-shanked footwear, and a black or straw broad-brimmed hat. Their full beards look a bit truncated because they wear no moustaches. Their women don solid-colored dresses of simple design, with capes and aprons, floor-length skirts, and long sleeves. Their long hair is braided and tucked under bonnets.

They drive gray horse-drawn carriages, some adorned anachronistically with bright orange triangular reflectors on the rear panel. Their fertile farmland is checkerboarded by meticulous rows of crops, dotted with simple white frame houses with green window shades, and squared off with roughly hewn softball diamonds. Mules power their farm equipment, lanterns light their homes, and teachers in one-room schoolhouses educate their children—but only through the eighth grade. They worship God in home meetings, not in church buildings, and in high German, not the more colloquial Pennsylvanian Dutch dialect. Who are these kind, quaint folk? They are the Old Order Amish—sometimes called the "quiet in the land."

I must confess that, until recently, my knowledge of the Amish was rather spotty. I had read about them in law school. (In *Wisconsin v. Yoder*, the Supreme Court ruled that the free exercise rights of the Amish exempted them from compulsory education laws after the eighth grade.[2]) I had seen the movie *Witness*.[3] (I cheered with the rest of the audience when Harrison Ford cold-cocked the unsuspecting town bully in defense of the peaceful

---

[1] *Report from the Capital* 45/4 (April 1990): 4.

[2] *Wisconsin v. Yoder*, 406 US 205 (1972).

[3] *Witness*, directed by Peter Weir, Paramount Pictures, 1985.

Amish.) And, although I had studied in church history about their forebears, it was not until this past November that I learned firsthand about the Amish.

I was asked to lead a youth retreat for the First Baptist Church of Silver Spring, Maryland, to be held in "Amish country"—in Lancaster County, Pennsylvania. One of the topics I was assigned to address was the relationship between the Amish and contemporary Baptists.

What an assignment! No twentieth-century Baptist I knew bore much similarity to the Amish. Quite to the contrary. Neither Rauschenbusch's social gospelism, Fosdick's evangelical liberalism, Norris's narrow fundamentalism, Marney's Christian humanism, King's civil activism, Falwell's moral majoritarianism, nor even the good tobacco farmers and cattle ranchers I pastored in rural Kentucky showed any sign of similarity to the Amish. My work was cut out for me.

I experienced an epiphany. After some study, I found that the Amish and Baptists are ecclesiastical and spiritual relatives—cousins, maybe, if not siblings. The extent of the difference today graphically demonstrates how far Baptists have come (or gone) over the past 350 years.

The Amish trace their lineage back to the radical wing of the Protestant Reformation. Their ancestors sought a more dramatic break with the Catholic Church than did other reformers. Along with church-state separation, their most distinctive belief and practice was believer's baptism. Hence, they came to be known as "Anabaptist," which means to "baptize again."

Anabaptism rose out of the Swiss Reformation in the early 1520s. Conrad Grebel, George Blaurock, Felix Mantz, and others became disenchanted with Ulrich Zwingli's willingness to meld his theological reforms with Zurich city council politics. They also believed that a true New Testament church was composed of regenerate believers who were baptized with water upon their voluntary confession of faith in Christ. In January 1525, these Anabaptists formally broke with Zwingli.

Despite some diversity in belief and practice, the Anabaptists were uniformly the victims of severe persecution. Both Catholics and Protestants (including Zwingli himself) hounded, drowned, burned, and beheaded them. After Grebel died of the plague, Zwingli had Grebel's father beheaded. Mantz, with hands and feet bound and body held in fetal position by a steel rod, was dumped into the icy waters of the river Limmat. Blaurock, holding up his finger as a prearranged sign to his friends that he still followed Christ, was burned at the stake.[4] Most other Anabaptists fared no better, and, understandably, their early antipathy for the merger of church and state was strengthened by the ungodly torture and destruction that the amalgamation of those two realms unleashed.

But obviously many survived, driven into hiding and exile. Remnants managed to immigrate to various parts of Europe, including the Netherlands. In Holland, a Catholic priest, after grappling with doubt over the propriety of infant baptism, eventually came to accept and preach a gospel of repentance and believer's baptism. Impressed by the long-suffering faithfulness of the Anabaptists, he was finally rebaptized and reordained in 1534. His name was Menno Simons.

Menno served as a preacher, missionary, and organizer in Holland for twenty-five years. The authorities sought to kill gentle Menno, but they never succeeded. Although most of the groups spawned by the Anabaptist movement did not weather the persecution or the vicissitudes of history, the followers of Menno Simons—the Mennonites—did. They are the most visible surviving remnant of the radical reformation.

It was from these Mennonites that the Amish came. In the late 1600s, a Swiss Mennonite bishop, named Jacob Amman, lead a retrograde movement within the church. Objecting to what he thought were liberalizing influences within the Mennonite church, he insisted on strict adherence to a confession of faith, particularly the "ban"—the practice of shunning excommunicated members.

The Amish as well as the Mennonites continued to suffer persecution. Both gladly accepted William Penn's invitation to come to Pennsylvania where they could live in peace. The Amish first came to Pennsylvania in the late 1720s and to Lancaster County in the 1760s. The Mennonites settled in Germantown, Pennsylvania, in 1683. Since then, both the Amish and the Mennonites have continued to exist but periodically have split into various conventions, conferences, and sub-denominations.

Contrary to what some believe, Baptists did not originate in the Anabaptists. Nevertheless, the history of Baptists was influenced by and had much in common with the Anabaptist-Mennonite-Amish tradition.

Most historians today trace Baptist roots not to the radical wing of the sixteenth-century reformation (i.e., Anabaptism) but rather to English

---

[4] J. C. Wenger, *How Mennonites Came to Be* (Scottdale PA: Herald Press, 1977) 36–37.

separatism of the seventeenth century. John Smyth, a Cambridge-educated Puritan, pastored a separatist congregation at Gainesborough. Fleeing persecution, he led part of his congregation in 1607 to Holland. (The other Gainesborough remnant became the nucleus of the "Pilgrim Fathers" who took passage to America on the *Mayflower*.)

In Holland, Smyth and his congregation came into contact with a group of Dutch Mennonites. Perhaps as a result of the witness of these Mennonites, Smyth began to question the validity of his separatist church and, more particularly, its practice of infant baptism. Thus, he disbanded his church and started a new one based on a profession of faith in Christ and believer's baptism. Smyth baptized himself and then baptized the others. But Smyth continued to fret over the efficacy even of his self-baptism and entertained notions of joining the Mennonites. Although he never did, after his death a remnant of his followers apparently were rebaptized into the Mennonite fellowship. Another group within the Smyth church, led by layman Thomas Helwys, sailed back to England and established what historians believe to be the first Baptist church on English soil.[5]

Thus, Baptists arose independent of Anabaptism, although Anabaptism may well have affected Baptist faith and practice. Moreover, irrespective of the extent of influence, Anabaptists and early Baptists clearly had much in common, and their beliefs and practices were similar in many ways.

Between sessions during the retreat for FBC Silver Spring, we were given a guided bus tour of Lancaster County by a Mennonite college student. In addition to pointing out sites, she gave a helpful thumbnail lecture on Mennonite-Amish doctrine. She said the basic beliefs and practices could be summed up and easily remembered by the acrostic B-A-S-I-N:

*B*eliever's church. The church is an autonomous gathering of the regenerate believers who decided to be disciples of Jesus Christ. No one becomes a member of a church automatically as a result of birth or cultural heritage. Joining requires a voluntary decision.

*A*dult baptism. As a corollary to their view of church as a gathered community, baptism had to follow an informed, heartfelt commitment to Christ. Early Anabaptists practiced affusion (pouring) or sprinkling instead of dunking. Most contemporary Mennonites-Amish still do.

---

[5] H. Leon McBeth, *The Baptist Heritage* (Nashville: Broadman Press, 1987) 53.

Separation of church and state. This perhaps was the Anabaptists' most far-reaching contribution to the modern world.[6] Their view of church and insistence on a voluntary response compelled this belief. An early Anabaptist saying went "faith is a work of God and not of the heretics' tower."[7] The Anabaptists had learned their lesson well: when the state and the church got mixed up together, the church became perverted and people got hurt.

Involvement. The early Anabaptists believed and the Mennonites-Amish today believe strongly in mutual involvement in each other's lives. Because they have been shunned by the world, they have withdrawn from the world and rely on each other to make their way. Their early evangelistic fervor was tempted by persecution, and today their witness is born mainly through the testimony of their communal lifestyle.

Nonresistance. Most early Anabaptists followed the way of nonviolence and nonresistance. Certainly this is a hallmark of modern Mennonites-Amish. Nonresistance was and is more than pacifism in the limited sense of refusing to fight a war. It involves every aspect of life and carries a positive imperative to be peacemakers.

These Anabaptist tenets are similar to what the early English Baptists believed and how they practiced their beliefs, although few Baptists have ever adopted the extreme pacifism that has typified the Mennonite-Amish tradition.

But how do we stand today? It is always risky to say what a diverse group like Baptists believes and to generalize about how its members practice their faith. Nevertheless, some observations can be made. Most Baptists still adhere to the basic principles that our English Baptist ancestors shared with the Anabaptists. Unfortunately, many of these historic principles are being compromised or repudiated by some Baptists.

The cherished concept of local church autonomy and congregational church governance are often violated with impunity. We now have hierarchically arranged denominational structures that sometimes go beyond *assisting* the local church's ministry and attempt to *dictate* it. Local church decisions to ordain women are met with the withdrawal of fellowship from local associations, and church decisions about commissioning missionaries are stymied by unyielding, denominationally dictated creedalism.

---

[6] William R. Estep, *The Anabaptist Story* (Nashville: Broadman Press, 1963) 189.
[7] Ibid., 193.

Like the Anabaptists and Mennonites, we believe that baptism is an initiatory ordinance that follows a voluntary confession of faith in Christ. But in our rush to succeed in the missionary enterprise, we often practice pedobaptism—baptizing our young before they could possibly appreciate the full gravity of a commitment to Christ.

For some Baptists, the concept of church-state separation is simply a tool to be used to the advantage of a particular theological and political agenda. That is, they want to keep church and state separate when the state seeks to burden the church; all bets are off, however, when the issue of state *support* of the church is discussed. Those Baptists who now support governmental aid to parochial schools and church-run childcare centers are glaring examples of a marked departure from Anabaptist and Baptists distinctives.

The idea of mutual priestly involvement in each other's lives is being lost too. The doctrine of the priesthood of all believers becomes attenuated when interpreted to mean that none of us *needs* a priest instead of meaning, as it should, that each of us *is* a priest to each other. Moreover, the authoritarian leadership model that is so popular today in some Baptist churches and the resolution passed by the Southern Baptists in San Antonio on the priesthood doctrine[8] represent a near revolutionary departure from this hallowed reformation concept.

Finally, unlike the Mennonites-Amish, most Baptists no longer abjure the surrounding culture. We have outgrown our sectarian heritage and dissenting tradition. With this new status we have developed an establishment mentality to the degree that many Baptists now identify more closely with the Puritan John Cotton than the Baptist Roger Williams.[9] Far from the historical tendency of Baptists and Anabaptists to withdraw from and critique culture, Baptists now embrace culture, along with its models of success, leadership, and politics. In a word, as Carlyle Marney once said, Baptists are no longer "pilgrims"; we are now "tribesmen."[10]

By studying the Amish, we Baptists have a rare opportunity to view a rough picture of the way we used to be. Anabaptism has been called the "Dr.

---

[8] On the Priesthood of the Believer (1988), Southern Baptist Annual Convention, resolution no. 5, 131st session, San Antonio, pp. 68–69.

[9] Bill J. Leonard, classroom lecture, Southern Baptist Theological Seminary (SBTS), April, 23 1987.

[10] Dickson Lectures, 1974, quoted in John J. Carey, *Carlyle Marney: A Pilgrim's Progress* (Macon GA: Mercer University Press. 1980) 138.

Pepper of evangelical traditions."[11] I fear that Baptists are becoming decarbonated Coke. There is, of course, no special virtue in tradition, nor is there any particular vice in change. But, as we Baptists grow and evolve, it is helpful constantly to be reminded of our spiritual and ecclesiastical heritage as touchstones for self-evaluation and self-criticism. Frankly, after living among the Amish for a short while and studying their ways, I think our quaint kinfolk may somehow be closer to the Kingdom than we modern Baptists.

---

[11] Rodney Clapp, "The Anabaptist Option," *Christianity Today*, January 15 1990, 61.

The Pulpit and American Independence[1]

The Fourth of July! The mere mention of this popular holiday conjures up thoughts of fireworks, patriotic speeches, and backyard barbecues. It also often engenders an orgy of civil religion, reminding those who revere the Constitution and cherish religious liberty of an age-old dilemma: how to preserve a religiously neutral state while avoiding a separation of God from government; how to protect Mr. Jefferson's Wall of Separation while affirming the absolute relevance of religion to politics. These tensions are highlighted this year as we approach the quadrennial election of the president of the United States.

Nowhere is this more apparent than in America's pulpits. The propriety and shape of political preaching—or at least preaching about public issues—is once again a contentious topic. A number of factors have conspired to up the ante nowadays. Politicians wear their religion on their sleeves as they have perhaps at no other time in recent memory. President Clinton's speeches are laced with Bible verses and rhetorical flourishes reminiscent of Southern Baptist pulpiteers of his boyhood. Senator Dole, a Methodist, takes on Hollywood in a way that reflects the piety, if not the passion, of John Wesley. Pat Buchanan and Alan Keyes rail against abortion and the decline in public morality with righteous indignation. Moreover, churches have been politicized by Christian Coalition voter guides sent to pastors just in time for the Sunday before Tuesday elections, urging them to sermonize in a way that invites a vote for the candidate of a particular (usually Republican) party. Finally, clergy of various stripes boldly push the limits of the federal tax code that, although permitting the discussion of public issues from the pulpit, prohibits endorsing or opposing candidates under pain of losing the church's tax exemption.[2]

Preaching about political issues is not solely a phenomenon of modern American life or a consequence of political muscle-flexing by the radical religious right. The progressive era of the early twentieth century was

---

[1] *Pulpit Digest* 77/540 (July/August 1996): 81.
[2] A bill is pending to permit religious organizations to endorse candidates as long as they spend no more than 5 percent of their budget doing so (HR 2910).

inextricably linked with the social gospel movement of Walter Rauschenbusch. Victories in civil rights cannot be separated from the driving force supplied by the African American churches and Martin Luther King, Jr. The major upheavals of American political life since the 1960s—Vietnam, women's rights, abortion, environment, nuclear disarmament—are closely connected to the prophetic critique leveled by people of religious conviction, including American preachers.

People of faith also played a central role in paving the way for American independence and the adoption of the Constitution and the Bill of Rights. This was not solely the doing of the sons and daughters of the Enlightenment; the children of God played a decisive role, too. Historians commonly point to the fervor of the First Great Awakening as sowing seeds that came to fruition in our break with England half a century later. The experiential, individualistic religion of the Awakening is seen as a precursor to democratic institutions; the rise of nascent, dissenting denominations is viewed as providing the glue for a national cohesion that culminated in the new American body politic.[3] As one scholar has written, "To exaggerate the importance of the Great Awakening would be difficult, not only for religious reasons but also its contributions to American political self-identity and general culture. Some consider the Awakening the real American Revolution."[4]

No less important is the impact that *preaching* in particular had on the political convulsions of the 1780s—not only during the First Great Awakening but also throughout the rest of the eighteenth century. Historian John W. Thornton said it well in 1860: "To the Pulpit, the *Puritan Pulpit*, we owe the moral force which won our independence."[5] Despite periodic strains of anti-clericalism in Colonial life, the American preachers played an important part in formulating political sentiment and shaping a common public ethos.[6]

---

[3] William G. McLoughlin, "Enthusiasm for Liberty: The Great Awakening as the Key to Revolution," in Jack P. Green and William G. McLoughlin, *Preachers & Politicians: Two Essays on the Origins of the American Revolution* (Worchester MA: American Antiquarian Society, 1977) 50, 66-67, 71.

[4] H. Leon McBeth, *The Baptist Heritage: Four Centuries of Baptist Witness* (Nashville: Broadman, 1987) 202.

[5] John W. Thornton, *The Pulpit of the American Revolution* (Boston: D. Lothrop & Co., Publishers, 1860), quoted in Ellis Sandoz, ed., *Political Sermons of the American Founding Era 1730–1805* (Indianapolis: Liberty Fund, 1990) v.

[6] Ibid., xiv–xxiv.

Preach they did. Their homilies were not eighteen-minute, off-the-cuff sermonettes soon to be forgotten by their listeners. Rather, they were prolix, often published discourses on morality, religion, and public philosophy. And these were not just Sabbath affairs. They included election sermons preached annually to the governor and legislature; so-called "artillery sermons" dealing with civic and military matters; Thursday or Fifth-day Lectures, often combined with Market Day to ruminate on social and political matters; as well as sermons delivered on days of prayer, fasting, thanksgiving, and, after 1776, Independence Day.[7]

Support for independence was widespread in American pulpits, including some Anglican ones. Yes, there were many who remained loyal to Great Britain—even among dissenting denominations—and some pacifists who resisted the call to arms, especially in Pennsylvania.[8] However, Colonial preachers mostly embraced the patriot cause with uncritical enthusiasm, using "their pulpits as drums for politics."[9]

Underpinning the support for political independence was a close congruence between civic republicanism and Calvinism that informed much of the preaching of American clergy. The republican tradition and reformed theology both took a pessimistic view of human nature.[10] The former feared the abuse of unchecked power; the latter worried about original sin. The excesses of the British monarchy were proof of both assertions and the fire for revolution. Republican political theory and the theology of the preachers posited the direct relationship between freedom and morality. A central tenet of civic republicanism was the need for the state to promote private and public virtue.[11] Hammering home the themes of virtue, morality, and responsibility, Colonial clergy "helped make sense of revolutionary rhetoric about corruption and evil among English...society."[12] Finally, civic

---

[7] Ibid., xxii–xxiv.

[8] Mark A. Noll, *One Nation Under God? Christian Faith & Political Action in America* (San Francisco: Harper and Row, 1988) 44. See Jon Butler, *Awash in a Sea of Faith: Christianizing the American People* (Cambridge: Harvard, 1990), who depreciates the role of religion in general on the revolutionary ethos (195, 202).

[9] Patricia U. Bonomi, *Under the Cope of Heaven: Religion, Society, and Politics in Colonial America* (New York: Oxford, 1986) 209.

[10] Edmund S. Morgan, *The Birth of a Republic, 1763–1789* (Chicago: University of Chicago Press, 1956) 6.

[11] Michael W. McConnell, "The Origins and Historical Understanding of the Free Exercise of Religion," *Harvard Law Review* 103 (May 1990): 1409, 1441.

[12] Butler, *Awash in a Sea of Faith*, 200-201.

republicanism and the preachers' eschatology expressed a similar view of history and the future. Both saw God's providence working in the destiny of the colonies and their relationship to England to be part and parcel of a cosmic struggle between good and evil.[13]

Colonial preachers often addressed revolutionary politics directly from the pulpit. John Adams observed that ministers in Philadelphia would "thunder and lightning every Sabbath" against British domination, and Thomas Jefferson noticed that pulpit diatribes ran "like a shock of electricity" throughout Virginia.[14] Examples of this kind of preaching include a 1777 sermon delivered by Abraham Keteltas titled "God's Arising and Pleading His People's Cause" in which he portrayed the revolution as a Holy War for "the cause of God"; Jacob Cushing's "Divine Judgments Upon Tyrants," a blistering indictment of the excesses of British soldiers on Lexington Green; and a sermon titled "Defensive Arms Vindicated," often attributed to Stephen Case, describing armed resistance as a positive duty of the people.[15] Indeed, as Patricia Bonomi has written,

> Religious doctrine and rhetoric…contributed in a fundamental way to the coming of the American Revolution and to its final success…. [P]atriotic clergymen told their congregations that a failure to oppose British tyranny would be an offense in the sight of Heaven…. By turning Colonial resistance into a righteous cause, and by crying the message to all ranks in all parts of the colonies, ministers did the work of secular radicalism and did it better: they resolved doubts, overcame inertia, fired the heart, and exalted the soul.[16]

Mark Noll has criticized the widespread, unqualified support of the revolutionary cause from the American pulpits. Noting the "disturbing tendency to employ theological language in the service of the patriot cause," he questions the "unreserved embrace of the cause, the all-or-nothing

---

[13] Noll, *One Nation Under God?*, 42-43; Green and McLoughlin, *Preachers and Politicians*, 62-64.

[14] Bonomi, *Under the Cope of Heaven*, 209-10.

[15] These sermons and more than fifty others are collected in a helpful volume edited by Ellis Sandoz, *Political Sermons of the American Founding Era, 1730–1805* (Indianapolis: Liberty Fund, 1990).

[16] Bonomi, *Under the Cope of Heaven*, 216.

identification of the patriot position as *the* Christian position that strikes the modern observer most forcefully."[17]

But Noll points to others—albeit a minority—who reflected a more discriminating position that resulted in a healthful distance between their preaching and the patriot cause. For example, Ezra Stiles, a minister who later became president of Yale and a proponent of independence, did not allow political topics to seep into his sermons. Stiles feared becoming a dupe "of Politicians without Alliances, Concessions and Connexions dangerous to evangelical Truth and spiritual Liberty."[18] Samuel Hopkins, a Congregational minister in Rhode Island, supported independence, but his patriotism was more measured than those who readily combined their Christian beliefs with the patriot cause: "Hopkins' patriotism was different from that of others who merged their Christianity with their politics.... Though he was a patriot, he was self-consciously first a Christian. As such he was able to separate political and Christian allegiances. And because he did not simply define his Christianity in terms of the patriotic needs, he was able to bring a specifically Christian critique on *American* society."[19]

Other Colonial preachers—mostly evangelical dissenters—stand in this more discerning tradition as a result of their theological and ethical commitment to religious liberty. Although they acknowledged the importance of public morality, they repudiated the notion that it was any of government's business to promote religion.[20] They understood that republican governments could be every bit as hostile to religious liberty as monarchies. For these preachers, the "struggle for religious freedom became the means by which they became patriots."[21]

Two stellar exemplars of these champions of religious liberty are Isaac Backus and John Leland. After an early-life conversion, Backus became a Congregationalist pastor and an itinerant evangelist. He later gradually developed Baptist sentiments and a keen appreciation for the need to ensure religious liberty. In time he became "the most forceful and effective writer

[17] Noll, *One Nation Under God?*, 46-47.

[18] Quoted in Edmond S. Morgan, *The Gentle Puritan: A Life of Ezra Stiles, 1727–1795* (Chapel Hill: University of North Carolina Press, 1962) 262-63.

[19] Noll, *One Nation Under God?*, 50.

[20] McConnell, "Origins and Historical Understanding," 1442.

[21] William R. Estep, *Revolution within the Revolution: The First Amendment in Historical Context* (Grand Rapids: Eerdmans, 1990) xvii.

America produced on behalf of the pietistic or evangelical theory of
separation of church and state."[22]

For Backus, religion was fundamentally a matter between God and
human beings, not to be interfered with by the state. But his was no
privatized Christianity. Backus was sent as an "agent" of the Warren
Association to the 1774 Continental Congress in Philadelphia where he
articulated concerns of New England Baptists in a role that has been
characterized as something like a modern lobbyist.[23] Though an ardent
supporter of the revolution, Backus argued the need to keep the church and
state—even republican governments—separate. His "An Appeal to the
Public for Religious Liberty Against the Oppression of the Present Day"
(1773) is a classic statement of the proper synthesis of political theory and
evangelical theology underpinning his concern for religious liberty and the
separation of the church and state.[24]

John Leland, thirty years younger than Backus, was also a New
Englander who was reared as a Congregationalist but later became a Baptist.
He moved to Virginia where he pastored several churches and preached far
and wide. Leland played an integral role in disestablishing the Anglican
Church in Virginia and lobbied James Madison for a Bill of Rights. Some
scholars claim that, at a legendary meeting near Orange, Virginia, he
threatened to oppose Madison as a candidate for Virginia's ratifying
convention and agreed not to do so only after he extracted a promise that
Madison would pursue explicit protection for religion in the Bill of Rights.[25]
Like Backus, Leland believed in the clear distinction between civil and
ecclesiastical authority because even well-meaning civil authority could not
be trusted. Leland once exclaimed, "[E]xperience…has informed us, that the
fondness of magistrates to foster Christianity, has done it more harm than
all the persecution ever did. Persecution, like a lion, tears the saints to death,
but leaves Christianity pure; state establishment of religion, like a bear, hugs
the saints, but corrupts Christianity…."[26]

[22] William G. McLoughlin, *Isaac Backus on Church, State, and Calvinism: Pamphlets, 1754–1789* (Cambridge: Harvard Press, 1968) 1.
[23] Sandoz, *Political Sermons*, 328.
[24] This sermon is reproduced in Sandoz, *Political Sermons*, 331.
[25] Joseph M. Dawson, *Baptists and the American Republic* (Nashville: Broadman, 1956) 108-109. See also Estep, *Anabaptist Story*, 167.
[26] Edwin S. Gustad, *Sworn on the Altar of God: A Religious Biography of Thomas Jefferson* (Grand Rapids: Eerdmans, 1996) 107.

Summarizing his long life, Leland's nineteenth-century biographer captures an incisive glimpse of this champion of liberty: "Elder Leland sustained, with uniform consistency the two-fold character of the *patriot* and the *Christian*. For his religious creed he acknowledged no directory but the Bible. ...His political creed was based upon the "sufficient truths" of equality, and of the inherent and inalienable rights, recognised by the master spirits of the revolution...."[27]

In sum, preaching during the revolutionary period was not just a religious exercise. It was a political phenomenon. Although most of the Colonial clergy supported the revolution, it was the dissenters—for whom religious liberty was a sacred concern—who spawned what has been called a "revolution within the Revolution."[28]

According to William Estep, what made the American Revolution both unique and lasting was not the political separation from England. It was the Bill of Rights, particularly the protection of our religious liberty in the First Amendment, that brought about the real revolution.

To these Colonial preachers we are indebted for more than our political independence. We are beholden to them for the constitutional prophylaxis that protects our God-given religious freedom. As we celebrate the Fourth of July this year, let us express gratitude for the Colonial pulpits that, in ways no less divided and ambiguous than today, brought their religious convictions to bear on matters of statehood, but, in the end, insisted that government must be forbidden to establish or to disturb humankind's inviolable rights of conscience.

---

[27] L. F. Greene, ed., *The Writings of the Late Elder John Leland* (New York: G. W. Wood, 1845), quoted in Sandoz, *Political Sermons*, 1080.

[28] Estep, *Anabaptist Story*, xvii.

Anniversary a Good Time to Recall Madison's Contributions to Liberty[1]

Last month we celebrated the 250th anniversary of the birth of James Madison—a good time to recall the invaluable contribution he made to the securing of religious liberty in our country.

Our diminutive, soft-spoken fourth president is often eclipsed by his elegant and eloquent collaborator in freedom, Thomas Jefferson. To Jefferson's memory we built a monument on the Tidal Basin, put his visage on the nickel, attribute to him the "wall of separation" metaphor, and trek to his "little mountain" to pay homage. For Madison, there are no monuments, no coins and few rhetorical nuggets, and his modest Montpelier is obscured by the shadow of the neighboring, majestic Monticello.

Yet, arguably, Madison played a greater role in developing the uniquely American tradition of full-orbed religious freedom protected by the separation of church and state. Conventional wisdom suggests that "revolution within the revolution" (to use the late Bill Estep's phrase) was accomplished by an alliance between two very different groups: (1) enlightenment rationalists/religious deists; and (2) dissenting evangelicals—like Baptists, Quakers, and some Presbyterians. In a real sense, Madison stood in and understood both camps. He was uniquely able to express the passion and provide the political acumen necessary to hold together this unlikely alliance in the fight for religious freedom.

Madison certainly can be counted as a scion of the Enlightenment. He studied the classics and the political philosophers of the eighteenth century. But he also read the Bible and studied theology at the College of New Jersey (Princeton)—a bastion of Presbyterian dissent. He witnessed firsthand the dangers of "ecclesiastical establishments" when he happened upon the jailed Baptist preachers in Culpeper, Virginia. His anger piqued, he wrote to a friend, William Bradford, about "that diabolical hell-conceived principle of

---

[1] *Report from the Capital* 56/7 (April 4, 2001): 3.

persecution," asking him to "pray for liberty and Conscience to revive among us."[2]

More than any other founder, Madison was equally committed to both disestablishment and the freedom of religion and conscience. This can be seen in his hard-hitting *Memorial and Remonstrance Against Religious Assessments*. Called by a biographer "the most powerful defense of religious liberty ever written in America,"[3] the *Memorial* challenged Patrick Henry's attempt to provide tax money to pay for the teaching of religion in Virginia. However, the *Memorial* also sounded a clarion call for robust free exercise—dubbing one's obligation to God "precedent, both in order of time and degree of obligation, to the claims of Civil Society."[4]

Two other incidents—one early in his career and one late in life—demonstrate Madison's balanced approach to religious liberty. The original draft of the Virginia Declaration of Rights, written by George Mason, called for religious "toleration." The twenty-five-year-old Madison insisted that the language be changed to the stronger "full and free exercise of religion," a principle that eventually became ensconced in the First Amendment. After retiring from the presidency, the sixty-five-year-old statesman lauded the happy result of disestablishment when he wrote, "the number, industry and morality of the priesthood and the devotion of the people have been manifestly increased by the total separation of church and state."

During his long public service, Madison penned the original draft of the First Amendment, fought and condemned religious bigotry, applauded a "multiplicity of sects," opposed using tax money to pay congressional chaplains, and regretted having issued Thanksgiving proclamations because he regarded them an establishment of religion.

Yes, it is high time we give "Jemmy Madison" his due. He stands taller than any founder—even the towering Jefferson—in acknowledging the God-given rights of conscience of all its citizens and in crafting American governmental institutions to protect them.

Happy birthday, Mr. Madison!

---

[2] Letter written on January 24, 1774.

[3] Irving Brant, *James Madison, the President, 1809–1812* (Indianapolis: Bobbs-Merrill Publishing, 1956).

[4] James Madison, "Memorial and Remonstrance against Religious Assessments" (1785), repr. in Ronald Floweres, *That Godless Court?*, 2nd ed. (Louisville: Westminster John Knox Press, 2005) 187–192.

Nation's Founders, Early Baptists Supported Principle of Separation[5]

In a book titled *Separation of Church and State*, Philip Hamburger tries to debunk what he calls the "modern myth" of church-state separation.[6] He peddles the wrong-headed thesis that our nation's founders and early religious dissenters consciously avoided using the word "separation" and never intended to ensconce even the concept of separation in the First Amendment. Rather, he contends separation was popularized in the nineteenth and twentieth centuries as an anti-Catholic polemic and as a tool of secularists to segregate religion from public life. Hamburger concludes that this view of separation has militated against the full flowering of religious liberty in this country.

Hamburger could not be more wrong.

While Roger Williams advocated for the "wall of separation between the garden of the church and the wilderness of the world," the words "separation of church and state" were not widely used or well known during the seventeenth and eighteenth centuries.[7] It is also true that eighteenth-century Baptists, like Isaac Backus and John Leland, probably did not use the word "separation." But they certainly supported the principle. Backus, for example, argued that church and state should "never be confounded together," and Leland opined that attempts by "the magistrate to foster Christianity has done it more harm than all the persecution ever did."[8] They both fervently opposed the use of taxes to support the advancement of religion.

Although there is no evidence that Thomas Jefferson or James Madison used the word "separation" in the eighteenth century, how could anyone

---

[5] *Report from the Capital* 57/16 (August 7, 2002): 3.
[6] Philip Hamburger, *Separation of Church and State* (Cambridge MA: Harvard University Press, 2002).
[7] In Edwin S. Gaustad, *Liberty of Conscience: Roger Williams in America* (Grand Rapids MI: William B. Eerdmans, 1991) 207.
[8] C. F. Green, ed., *The Writings of the Late Elder John Leland* (New York: Arno Press 1970) 278.

read Jefferson's "Bill Establishing Religious Freedom" in Virginia and Madison's *Memorial and Remonstrance Against Religious Assessments* without concluding that they unequivocally supported the concept? They both used the word explicitly in the early nineteenth century.[9]

The fact that the separation of church and state has been supported by some who exhibited an anti-Catholic animus or a secularist bent does not impugn the validity of the principle. Champions of religious liberty have argued for the separation of church and state for reasons having nothing to do with anti-Catholicism or desire for a secular culture. Of course, separationists have opposed the Catholic Church when it has sought to tap into the public till to support its parochial schools or to argue for on-campus released time in the public schools, but that principled debate on the issues does not support a charge of religious bigotry.

Hamburger's gravest error comes when he creates a straw man of his caricatured view of church-state separation—one in which religion is segregated from public life. In his view, "separation" harms religious liberty, when a proper understanding of the concept suggests the opposite.

For some of us, religious liberty is bound up in the notion of "soul freedom" that all receive as a gift of God; for others, it is intimately tied to freedom of conscience. Church-state separation is only the political/constitutional means of protecting the end of religious liberty.

Moreover, the separation of church and state serves both religion clauses in the First Amendment. It operates not only to insist upon non-establishment, but also to ensure the free exercise of religion. In fact, the Supreme Court's first use of the words "separation of church and state" came in a free exercise case in 1879. Properly understood, separation calls for "neutrality"—even, to use Chief Justice Warren Burger's words, "benevolent neutrality"—toward religion, not in any sense hostility.[10]

Finally, the separation of church and state does not require a segregation of religion from public life. In fact, even Leland and Backus, for all of their insistence upon the principle of separation, were thoroughly involved in public policy debates and attempts to influence legislation in their day. I know of few separationists today who would endorse Hamburger's hard-edged characterization of separation as hostile to religion.

---

[9] Madison, "Memorial and Remonstrance," in *That Godless Court?*, 187–192.
[10] *Walz v. Tax Commission* 397 US 664 (1969).

Separation has been good for both church and state. For each to do its work, there must always be a decent distance between the two—some "swingin' room," to use Gardner Taylor's phrase. The institutional and functional separation of church and state has resulted in a vibrant religion, a plush pluralism, and a vital democracy. History teaches and contemporary geo-politics reveals that nations that abjure a healthy separation of church and state wind up with tepid, attenuated, majoritarian religion at best, or a theocracy at worst.

I, for one, will cast my lot with my Baptist forebears Williams, Leland, and Backus, and founders like Jefferson and Madison, not with misguided historical revisionism.

Jefferson's Wall
and Cheshire Cheese[1]

Baptists and all supporters of church-state separation celebrated two bicentennials last month.

I'm sure most readers of this periodical know about one—Thomas Jefferson's January 1, 1802, letter to the Danbury Connecticut Baptist Association in which he popularized the metaphor of the wall of separation. Jefferson wrote in response to a letter of congratulations and encouragement from the Danbury Baptists, who, chafing under the heavy hand of an established church (Congregational), were grateful for Jefferson's support of the rights of conscience.

Using his reply as an occasion to "[sow] useful truths and principles among the people, which might germinate and become rooted in their political tenets," Jefferson penned these immortal words: "I contemplate with sovereign reverence that act of the whole American people which declared that their legislature should make no law respecting an establishment of religion, or prohibiting the free exercise thereof, thus building a wall of separation between church and state."[2]

We celebrated another bicentennial last month, occurring on the same day in 1802. Daniel Dreisbach, in a recent essay published in *Journal of Church and State*, reminds us of a lesser-known gift from another group of admiring New England Baptists.[3] John Leland—the itinerant evangelist who fought for religious liberty in Virginia in the 1780s—had returned to his home in the Berkshire Hills of western Massachusetts. Under Leland's leadership, the citizens of Cheshire, Massachusetts, made and delivered to Jefferson a mammoth round of cheese. It was said to have been more than 4 feet in diameter and weighed more than 1,200 pounds. Eyewitnesses reported that the cheese bore the slogan, "Rebellion to tyrants is obedience

---

[1] *Report from the Capital* 57/3 (February 6, 2002): 3.
[2] Thomas Jefferson to Danbury Baptist Association, January 1, 1802.
[3] Daniel L. Dreisbach, "Mr. Jefferson, a Mammoth Cheese, and the 'Wall of Separation Between Church & State': A Bicentennial Commemoration," *Journal of Church and State* 43/4 (Autumn 2001): 725–745.

to God." As with their Baptist cousins in Danbury, Dreisbach points out that the "cheese-makers of Cheshire were both a religious and a political minority subject to legal discrimination in a commonwealth dominated by a Congregationalist-Federalist establishment."[4] They, too, were grateful for Jefferson's strong stand against state establishment of religion.

The commemoration of these two incidents reminds us of the integral part that dissenters in general and Baptists in particular played in the fight for religious liberty in this country. As the late William Estep so persuasively pointed out in his *Revolution within the Revolution*, born-again evangelicals, as much as the sons of the Enlightenment, argued for the First Amendment's religion clauses and supported politically those who would champion their cause.[5]

According to Professor Michael McConnell,

> This explains why the more fervent evangelicals, including the Baptists, tended to become Jeffersonians, notwithstanding the deism of Jefferson and the piety of his opponents. Religion, the evangelicals believed, is vital to civic harmony. But voluntary religious societies—not the state—are the best and only legitimate institutions for the transmission of religious faith and, with it, virtue. The only support that churches can legitimately expect from the government...is protection and non-interference.[6]

Where do we stand two centuries later? Nobody remembers the huge hunk of Cheshire cheese—other than maybe a handful of historians. Dreisbach opines that remnants of the cheese lasted for two or more years after which the "decaying, maggot-infested remains were unceremoniously dumped into the Potomac River."[7]

But the Connecticut Baptist-inspired metaphor of the wall of separation between church and state indeed has become "rooted in [our] political tenets" as Jefferson had hoped. It continues to remind us that the

---

[4] Ibid., 726.

[5] William R. Estep, *Revolution within the Revolution: The First Amendment in Historical Context, 1612–1789* (Grand Rapids MI: William B. Eerdmans, 1990).

[6] Michael W. McConnell, "The Origins and Historical Understanding of Free Exercise of Religion," *Harvard Law Review* 103/7 (May 1990): 1409–1517.

[7] Dreisback, "Mr. Jefferson," 744.

church and the state are both better off—and religious liberty is best protected—when neither tries to do the job of the other.

Happy bicentennial, Mr. Jefferson and Elder John Leland. Thank you both for your legacy of liberty.

Timeless Roger Williams Treatise
Knocks Civil Coercion in Religion[1]

I've been rereading some pretty good Baptist theology lately—Roger Williams's classic work, *The Bloudy Tenent of Persecution for Cause of Conscience*, originally printed in 1644 in London. (Truth be known, I am reading it for the first time straight through; I tasted bits and pieces of this treatise in seminary.)

I have a new edition, made far more readable by the good editorship of Richard Groves, pastor of the Wake Forest Baptist Church in Winston-Salem, North Carolina. It contains a wonderful foreword by Walter Shurden and a helpful "Historical Introduction" by Edwin Gaustad. Mercer University Press published this improved edition in 2001. You should pick up a copy.[2] There is no longer any excuse for shying away from Williams's sometimes arcane prose.

Williams's no-holds-barred defense of the cause of conscience and opposition to any form of civil coercion in religion is introduced by a short list of what Groves calls "Twelve Theses"—something of a syllabus for Williams's entire work.

These twelve points, some slightly paraphrased by me, go like this:

1. Religious warfare is "not required or accepted by Jesus Christ the Prince of Peace."

2. The Scriptures and sound argumentation belie "the doctrine of persecution for the cause of conscience."

3. Those who might support the doctrine of persecution for the cause of conscience—like John Calvin and John Cotton—must be answered forcefully.

4. "The doctrine of persecution for the cause of conscience is proved guilty of all the blood of the souls crying for vengeance under the altar."

---

[1] *Report from the Capital* 57/19 (September 25, 2002): 3.
[2] Roger Williams, *The Bloudy Tenent of Persecution for Cause of Conscience*, ed. Richard Groves (Macon GA: Mercer University Press, 2001).

5. Governments and magistrates discharge an essential civil function, but are not "judges, governors, or defenders of the spiritual."

6. Since the coming of Jesus, God has given permission to even "the most paganish...or anti-Christian consciences and worship," and they should be answered only by "the sword of God's Spirit, the word of God."

7. The theocracy of Israel is "proved figurative and ceremonial, and no pattern nor precedent for any kingdom or civil state in the world to follow."

8. God does not require religious conformity enforced by the civil state. Any such attempt is "the greatest occasion of civil war, ravishing of conscience, persecution of Christ Jesus in his servants, and of the hypocrisy and destruction of millions of souls."

9. Forced conformity by the civil state makes evangelism more difficult, not easier.

10. Compelled conformity of religion in the civil state "confounds the civil and religious, denies the principles of Christianity and civility, and that Jesus Christ is come in the flesh."

11. Full religious liberty will result in a "firm and lasting peace; good assurance of being taken, according to the wisdom of the civil state, for uniformity of civil obedience from all sorts."

12. "True civility and Christianity may both flourish in a state or kingdom," even where consciences are protected and differing opinions allowed to be entertained.

These were true in the seventeenth century and are still true today. When you are finished reading *The Bloudy Tenent*, give it away to someone—maybe a politician who supports vouchers, charitable choice, state-sponsored prayer, and civil religion. It might do some good.

Freedom-loving Baptists Should Remember John Clarke's Contributions[1]

We freedom-loving Baptists hold up Roger Williams as our all-time all-star. And properly so. But we should not forget the contributions of others, such as John Clarke. True, Williams coined the phrase "wall of separation" and founded the First Baptist Church in America. But he did not stay a Baptist for long. His contemporary, John Clarke, a physician and lay minister, remained a lifelong Baptist. In 1639 Clarke founded the town of Newport, Rhode Island, and became the pastor of the local Baptist congregation. Clarke traveled with Williams to London to secure a new charter for Rhode Island colony in 1663, which granted permission to continue a "lively experiment" of religious liberty.

Clarke also penned what might be the first Baptist confession in New England. In 1651 Clarke, along with two other Baptists, John Crandall and Obadiah Holmes, traveled to Lynn, Massachusetts, to conduct a worship service (including the Lord's Supper and baptism) in the private home of a blind Baptist named William Witter. That "illegal" act earned them arrest and imprisonment. Their sentence? A fine or public flogging. Clarke managed to pay his fine, but Holmes was "well-whipped" with thirty lashes. So outraged was Clarke by what he called this "tragicall story" that he published an account of the Lynn persecutions titled *Ill Newes from New-England: Or a Narrative of New-England's Persecution.*[2]

In that powerful treatise, Clarke articulated four "conclusions" that summarized the pith of his Baptist convictions. I have slightly paraphrased for modern readers what Clarke wrote:

1. Jesus is the Christ, the Anointed Priest, Prophet, and King of Saints. Christ is also the Lord of his Church in point of ruling and ordering them with respect to the worship of God (the Lordship of Jesus Christ).

---

[1] *Report from the Capital* 57/19 (September 25, 2002): 3.
[2] Reproduced in *Colonial Baptists: Massachusetts and Rhode Island* (New York: Arno Press, 1980).

2. Baptism is one of the commandments of Christ and will continue until he comes again. Believers are the proper subjects of baptism. They are to wait for the promise of the Spirit, as with the presence of Christ (Believers' Baptism and the Gathered Church).

3. Every believer ought to improve his talent both in and out of the Congregation (the Ministry of Laity and the Priesthood of Every Believer).

4. No servant of Jesus has any authority from him to force upon others either the faith or the order of the Gospel of Christ (Religious Freedom and the Rights of Conscience).

Clarke went on to elaborate this final point concerning the rights of conscience: "no such believer, or servant of Christ Jesus, has any liberty, much less authority from his Lord, to smite his fellow servant, nor yet with outward force, or arm of flesh, to constrain or restrain his Conscience, no nor yet his outward man for Conscience sake, or worship of his God, where injury is not offered to the person, name, or estate of others...."[3]

The astute reader will see in these words about the liberty of conscience the seeds of the modern First Amendment doctrine that government is permitted to burden the exercise of religion only where it has a "compelling state interest." Although no one is permitted, according to Clarke, to "constrain or restrain Conscience," regulation of religious conduct (i.e., "his outward man for Conscience sake") can be justified only in cases where injury is "offered to the person, name, or estate of others." Clarke understood a principle that five members of the US Supreme Court abjured in their 1990 decision *Employment Division v. Smith*[4]: government should restrict religious exercise only when such practices threaten the life, safety, or welfare of others and only if it adopts the least restrictive means available to ensure those ends.

Modern Baptists would do well to read and heed their history, including writings such as *Ill Newes*. We must also take responsibility for reminding our culture and Supreme Court of these precious principles. If we fail to do so, the signal achievement of John Clarke and the "lively experiment" will not long survive.

---

[3] In *Colonial Baptists*, 37.
[4] *Employment Division v. Smith*, 494 US 872 (1990).

Experiencing Baptists' Roots
and Fruit in England[1]

Attending the Baptist World Centenary Congress in Birmingham, England, this summer made me proud to be Baptist.

Here in the States we tend to think that all Baptists look and think like us. Spending several days with 13,000 Baptists from around the globe reminds one that Baptists come in all shapes, sizes, and colors. For me, Jimmy Carter's powerful call for unity among our amazing diversity was the highlight of the meeting.

My two weeks in Birmingham and traveling through the Cotswolds helped me get in touch with my Baptist roots. Baptists originated as an outgrowth from English Separatists in the early seventeenth century. One group, under the leadership of John Smyth and Thomas Helwys, went to Holland in 1609 where they formed a Baptist church. Some of them became involved with and absorbed by Dutch Anabaptists, while others, led by Helwys, came back to Spittalfield, near London, and formed the first Baptist church on English soil.

Helwys authored a cutting-edge treatise on religious liberty titled *A Short Declaration of the Mystery of Iniquity (1611/1612)*.[2] In his inscription to the copy he sent to King James I were the audacious words that the king is a mortal man, not God, and has no power over the immortal souls of his subjects. For his trouble, Helwys and his wife Jane were thrown into Newgate Prison in London where they later died.

On a side trip to Regents Park College at Oxford University, our tour group (ably led by premiere Baptist historian Buddy Shurden and Georgia Baptist leader Drayton Sanders) had the opportunity to view one of the four known extant first-edition copies of *The Mystery of Iniquity*. What a powerful link with the past and a tangible connection to the first Baptist martyr for freedom.

---

[1] *Report from the Capital* 60/8 (September 2005): 3.
[2] Thomas Helwys, *A Short Declaration of the Mystery of Iniquity (1611/1612)* (Macon GA: Mercer, 1998).

We also traveled to Kettering to visit the Fuller Baptist Church. The church is named for one of its early pastors, Andrew Fuller (1754–1815). A strong strain of hyper-Calvinism resulted in an anti-missionary mentality among eighteenth- and early nineteenth-century Baptists. Fuller was the theologian who broke the back of hyper-Calvinism and cast the theological vision for the modern missionary movement. It was thrilling to step into Fuller's pulpit and to visit his grave behind the church.

We then traveled a short distance to Moulton to see the Carey Baptist Church, named for William Carey (1761–1834). A cobbler and school-teacher by trade, Carey served as pastor in Moulton and was instrumental in forming the Baptist Missionary Society in 1792. If Fuller was the theologian of the modern missionary movement, Carey was the leading missionary. He traveled to India in 1793 and spent more than forty years—the rest of his life—in mission work there. The connection with this ordinary man who accomplished extraordinary things was overwhelming as we toured Carey's small, one-room schoolhouse and stood in his humble pulpit.

While in England I also experienced the fruit of our Baptist beginnings. Helwys's fight for religious liberty and the missionary enterprise spawned by Fuller and Carey have resulted in a worldwide Baptist diaspora. Baptists from more than 100 countries and more than 200 unions worshiped, studied, and had fellowship together.

I participated in an insightful focus-group session led by British Baptist Frederick George on persecution and religious liberty. Baptists from Germany, Lebanon, Sri Lanka, Georgia, Indonesia, and Latvia all told stories of religious persecution in their countries and regions. I was struck by how, in just shy of 400 years, we could come from persecuting early Baptists to electing one president of the United States while Baptists continue to be persecuted in other parts of the world.

I found particularly striking the common thread among nearly every story from all these countries: the boot heel of persecution came not so much from the forces of hostile atheism as from the oppressive policies of established or semi-established state churches. The rights of conscience and the free exercise of religion have been denied throughout history and are denied today as much by people of faith seeking to impose their brand of religion as by people of no faith seeking to deprive us of ours.

These stories from around the world reminded me of the crucial importance of the two protections for religious liberty in the Bill of Rights—one prohibiting the interference of the free exercise of religion but the other keeping government from trying to establish religion. Without either one of these, religious liberty is endangered. In a word, my trip to England encouraged me to bless my roots and to redouble my efforts to preserve the fruit of religious liberty for everyone in the world.

Religious Liberty:
A Continuing Struggle[1]

Genesis 1:26-27; Matthew 22:17-21; Galatians 5:1
I.
*"I will make them conform themselves, or I will harrie them out
of the land."[2]*

Who spoke these words? King James I of England—the man whose name appears on some of your Bibles. Whom was he talking about? They were seventeenth-century religious weirdos—nonconformists who objected to the oppressive state religion. They chafed under the heavy hand of the Anglican church and the English state that had merged a century earlier when King Henry VIII broke with Rome and declared himself to be at once king and head of the English church. These radical Christians believed in a newfangled idea of religious liberty that viewed the true church as separate from the civil state.

Religious liberty is well grounded in Scripture. Its taproot runs deep into the creation accounts in Genesis. God's decision to "make human beings in his image" necessarily implies the freedom to say yes or no—to choose for or against a relationship with God (Gen. 1:27). Jesus foreshadowed the modern idea of the separation of church and state when he said, "Give therefore to the emperor the things that are emperor's, and to God the things that are God's" (Matt 22:17). And who is not thrilled by the apostle Paul's bold declaration that "For freedom Christ has set us free. Stand firm, therefore, and do not submit again to a yoke of slavery" (Gal 5:1).

Despite these biblical roots—or because of them—the idea of religious liberty was dangerous stuff, King James must have thought. For centuries,

---

[1] An early version of this sermon appears in Walter B. Shurden, ed., *Proclaiming the Baptist Witness Religious Liberty* (Macon GA: Smyth and Helwys Publisher, 1997) 101.

[2] John A. Armstrong, "Restless for Religious Liberty," *Report from the Capital* 44/5 (May 1989): 4.

the church and state had operated as something of a joint venture. Most thought society would come apart if the state did not support the church and the church did not prop up the state. Indeed, this understanding was made explicit during the Reformation in the Peace of Augsburg in 1555, which held that the people of a certain territory were required to adhere to the beliefs of the prince. Yes! King James was bound and determined to stop the heresy of religious liberty and resist the divorce of church and state by whatever means available.[3]

II.

To escape this kind of intolerance a young, rough-and-tumble Puritan preacher came to Massachusetts Bay Colony in 1631. Roger Williams, called by some the "apostle of religious liberty," came preaching and teaching "soul freedom." Williams insisted that faith could not be dictated by any church or government authority, but must be nurtured freely and expressed directly to God without human interference. Picking up on Jesus' warning about rendering to Caesar and anticipating the American notion of church and state separation that would bear fruit a century and a half later, Williams advocated a "hedge or wall of separation between the garden of the church and the wilderness of the world."[4]

Roger Williams was not bashful about speaking his mind. The Puritan theocrats in Massachusetts were no more amused by this crazy talk than was King James. So they kicked Roger Williams out of the colony. They sent him packing. He settled in what would become Rhode Island and founded a town he dubbed "Providence," because (as a thoroughgoing Calvinist) he believed that God had led him there. Williams began what he liked to call the "livlie experiment" of religious liberty and founded the first Baptist church on North American soil.

Over the ensuing centuries, Baptists championed soul freedom and religious liberty with unrelenting vigor and asserted the absolute importance of the separation of church and state to protect that precious liberty. Isaac Backus, an eighteenth-century Congregationalist pastor and itinerant evangelist, developed Baptist sentiments and a keen appreciation for the

---

[3] Ibid.

[4] Edwin S. Gaustad, *Liberty of Conscience: Roger Williams in America* (Grand Rapids MI: Eerdmans, 1991) 207.

need to assure religious liberty. For Backus, religion was fundamentally a matter between God and human beings, not to be interfered with by the state. John Leland from Massachusetts, who came to Virginia during that heady decade of the 1780s, boldly advocated religious liberty and church-state separation. He also played a pivotal role in convincing James Madison, the father of the Constitution, that the guarantees for religious liberty must be written down and made explicit. The original Constitution, of course, had no Bill of Rights—no provision calling for religious liberty. Madison was a candidate for the convention called to ratify the new Constitution; Leland was thinking about running. Legend has it that one day, in the shade of a great oak tree near Orange, Virginia, Madison and Leland met and cut a deal. Leland agreed not to run if Madison would promise to pursue a Bill of Rights containing a guarantee of religious freedom.[5] Two years later the Bill of Rights was adopted.

J. M. Dawson, the first executive director of the Baptist Joint Committee, once said, "If [historians] were to be asked who was most responsible for the American guaranty of religious liberty, their prompt reply would be 'James Madison'; but if James Madison might answer, he would as quickly reply, 'John Leland and the Baptists.'"[6]

III.

Despite the urging of these and other Baptists, complete religious liberty was slow in coming—even in America. Centuries of religious intolerance were firmly ingrained, and old habits died hard. All but four states (Rhode Island, Pennsylvania, Delaware, and New Jersey) had officially established churches and varying degrees of persecution and intolerance. All but two states (Virginia and Rhode Island) had religious qualifications for public office; five denied basic civil rights to Catholics; and in Vermont, blasphemy was a capital offense.[7]

But our wise founders had a different vision for the new country. They took the bold, radical step of separating church and state in civil society,

---

[5] Herschel Hobbs and E. Y. Mullins, *The Axioms of Religion* (Nashville: Broadman Press, 1978) 44.

[6] J. M. Dawson, *Baptists and the American Republic* (Nashville: Broadman Press, 196) 117.

[7] Douglas Laycock, "Nonpreferential Aid to Religion: A False Claim about Original Intent," *Wm. & Mary L. Rev* 27 (1986): 875, 916.

much to the delight of Baptists like Leland. They provided in Article VI of the new Constitution that there would be no religious test or requirement for public office. Not only did the religion of the prince not bind the rest of the country, but the prince could not even be required to have a religion! One's status in the civil community simply would not depend on a willingness to espouse any religious confession. These Baptist-inspired architects of the new nation decided that the federal government would not be permitted to make any law "respecting an establishment of religion, or prohibiting the free exercise thereof."

These initial words of the Bill of Rights erected twin pillars in our constitutional architecture protecting the freedom of religion and upholding the wall of separation between church and state. These two clauses—no establishment and free exercise—require government to remain neutral toward religion, and, turning it loose, leaving it to flourish or flounder on its own.

For the first time in human history, a nation denied to itself the right to become involved in religious matters or violate the rights of conscience.

IV.

With just a few lapses here and there over the past two centuries, we have done a pretty good job of preserving our rights of conscience and ensuring the separation of church and state—at least when compared with the track record of other nations. But, unfortunately, today this tradition is not universally accepted, even among some who call themselves Baptist. Many are threatened by unbridled freedom. Many want government to get into the act. A recent poll shows that about one half of those surveyed think separation between church and state is either a bogus concept or has been applied too rigorously. Twenty percent think an official state church would be okay. Our Baptist birthright is weathering a withering assault from left and right, and its preservation demands a continuing struggle.

The Baptist Joint Committee, now seventy years old, continues to lead that struggle! A quick look at some pressing church-state issues confirms the need to redouble our efforts to turn our heritage into a legacy.

• The United States Supreme Court ruled that religion is not entitled to any special constitutional protection against governmental regulation.[8]

---

[8] *Employment Division v. Smith*, 494 US 872 (1990).

Five members of the Court wrote that strong protection for religious liberty is a "luxury" that we can no longer afford as a society. It took an act of Congress—the Religious Freedom Restoration Act of 1993 (RFRA)—to restore robust protections to the free exercise of religion. Then the other shoe dropped. The Supreme Court declared portions of this act unconstitutional as applied to state and local governments.[9] Not only is our "first freedom" no longer first, it is barely a freedom at all!

• The administration continues to try to funnel tax money directly to churches to help finance their ministries and allow them to discriminate on the basis of religion in federally funded projects. The Baptist Joint Committee has opposed "charitable choice" on constitutional grounds and to keep churches and religious organizations free from the governmental regulation that would inevitably accompany such government giveaways.

• Many in Congress support a bill to allow churches (but not secular nonprofits) to endorse candidates from the pulpit. This misguided measure would be extremely divisive and coercive. It would politicize our houses of worship and turn our pulpit prophets into political puppets.

• Some politicians have arrogated to themselves the role of a "secular high priest" by posting the Ten Commandments, thereby endorsing one religion and selecting preferred Scripture passages, making theological judgments all the while. Indeed, James Dunn has declared, "How strange to create a graven image out of a document that says we are not supposed to have any."

• Many pundits and politicians are quick to badmouth so-called activist judges, claiming a war on Christianity. Some in Congress are seeking to pass laws to strip federal courts of jurisdiction to decide their disfavored constitutional issue de jure. A bill recently passed the House of Representatives that would eliminate attorneys' fees for even successful establishment clause challenges—virtually gutting one of the two First Amendment religion clauses. I don't always agree with the courts, including the Supreme Court, but these outlandish diatribes and court-stripping measures do nothing to advance the commonweal and surely will precipitate a constitutional train wreck over the separation of powers.

These are but a few instances of the constant, pervasive, unremitting threats to our religious liberty. Roger Williams, Isaac Backus, John Leland: where are you today?

---

[9] *City of Boerne v. Flores*, 521 US 507 (1997).

V.

It is high time for us to teach our children and remind our adults about the great Baptist heritage of religious freedom and the separation of church and state. Let the clear cry be heard again. We believe in free souls. As Bill Moyers has said, "We are all grown ups before God." competent to determine our own spiritual destinies. We believe in free churches—autonomous and able to worship and practice their faith without governmental meddling, interference, or even help. We believe in a free state where the "god of the majority" is never forced on the consciences of the minority. The First Amendment protects Buddhists as much as Baptists; Moonies as much as Methodists; Latter-day Saints as much as Seventh-day Adventists. If anyone's religious liberty is denied, everyone's religious liberty is threatened.

I fear we are on the verge of giving up our freedom more than having it taken away. We all say we want freedom, but talk is easy and cheap. Choosing is scary, and deciding is frightening. It is tough to make hard choices, to live in a morally ambiguous culture, to tolerate religious differences in a free state. Sometimes many Baptists, no less than others in this post 9-11 world, are willing to trade in their liberty in exchange for sought-after security.

In his letter to the Galatians, Paul was dealing with those in his day who were trying to escape from freedom: Christians who were trying to crawl back under the security blanket of the law. But the apostle sounded a clarion call to those Galatians who shirked the freedom of Christ's gospel and lusted after the legalism of the Jewish cultus. Paul called it nothing less than slavery.

It is my prayer and the focus of the ministry of the Baptist Joint Committee that we not forget our heritage. We must remember our forebears like Roger Williams, Isaac Backus, and John Leland—and the principles of soul freedom, religious liberty, and church-state separation that they and others worked so tirelessly to advance. Where are "they"—Williams, Backus, Leland? They are here—you, me, and all freedom-loving Baptists; they are at this church; they are at the Baptist Joint Committee; they are at the Baptist World Alliance; they are at the Cooperative Baptist Fellowship. Will you join us in the fight? To take the heritage of freedom our forebears have left us and turn it into a legacy for future generations and say to them, along with the apostle Paul, "stand firm, and do not submit again to a yoke of slavery."

The Baptist Joint Committee

Congress shall make no law respecting an establishment of religion, or prohibiting the free exercise thereof

Three Reasons We Should
Care About Religious Liberty[1]

Recently I had the privilege of speaking at the First Baptist Church of Dalton, Georgia. It was part of an eight-week Sunday evening series on a variety of topics. Each presenter was asked to speak on "Why I Should Care About...?" My topic, of course, was religious liberty. This was a good exercise for me. We often assume the importance of religious liberty and then barge ahead to analyze the church-state issue de jure. It's helpful, however, to go back and examine exactly why we value religious liberty in the first place.

What would you say to a skeptic who doesn't accept your a priori assumptions in order to convince him or her of religious liberty's importance? These are the arguments I would present.

It is not too facile to say up front that we should care about religious liberty because so few do nowadays. Many, including Baptists who ought to know better, take their own religious liberty for granted. Even those who care about their own often do not care about the liberty of others. No one should be able to claim religious liberty for himself or herself unless he or she is equally concerned about the liberty of everyone else.

In light of this, we should care about religious liberty for three reasons. First, it is the right thing to do. Liberty is precious, primal, and prescient. It is based on who we are as humans and who God is as our sovereign. It has to do with "soul freedom"—a God-given freedom of conscience that we enjoy not because we are Baptists or Christians, but simply by virtue of our basic humanity. God has made us all free agents—free to say yes, free to say no, and free not even to make up our minds. To be sure, our faith is nurtured in the womb of the church, but our decision is something each of us has to make for ourselves. Religious freedom, as Baptists throughout history have reminded us, does not result from any act of toleration on the part of the state. Religious freedom is not just a warmed-up leftover from the Enlightenment. It has theological import. The fight for religious liberty is

---

[1] *Report from the Capital* 61/4 (April 2006): 3.

an effort to ensure against others doing, the church doing, or the state doing what God will not do: violate conscience or force faith.

Second, it is the fair thing to do. Religious liberty goes beyond its theological moorings; it has ethical import. It often has to do with simple fairness, common sense, and good citizenship. What we wish for ourselves and our families, we should wish for everybody else. Concern for religious liberty requires us to heed what Charles Haynes and Os Guinness commonly refer to as the three R's of civic life: rights, responsibility, and respect.[2] We must treasure the rights God has given us, take seriously our responsibility to exercise them wisely, and respect those who have a different point of view about our religious beliefs. In the long run, the rights I enjoy are no stronger than your willingness to stand up for them, and your rights are no more secure than my courage to defend them.

Another way to talk about this concept is to couch it in terms of a golden rule. The sheer reasonableness of the golden rule is acknowledged by almost everyone—people of faith and people of no faith. The golden rule of religious liberty goes something like this: "I must not ask government to promote my religion if I don't want government to promote somebody else's religion. I must not permit government to harm somebody else's religion if I don't want government to harm my religion." How much better off we would all be—in the United States and abroad—if everyone or even most of us would adhere to this time-honored principle of fairness.

Third, it is the expedient thing to do. In addition to fundamental rightness and demonstrable fairness, raw self-interest should impel us to care about religious liberty. Even if one is successful in obtaining official governmental sanction for one's own religion, it's still playing with fire. Once you establish the precedent of knocking down the wall of separation for your own benefit, it's hard to deny it to somebody else when they take over or gain control. One day it might be somebody else's religion. Just consider the fast-growing religious groups: Mormonism, Islam, and various others. While these religious traditions deserve our respect, the idea of a theocracy governed by the president of the LDS Church or even a moderate Imam is not something most Baptists would welcome.

Even if that never happens—or in the meantime before it happens—it's still a bad idea. Experience has demonstrated that the merger of church and

---

[2] C. Haynes and O. Thomas, *Finding Common Ground: A Guide to Religious Liberty in Public Schools* (Nashville: First Amendment Center, 2001) 62.

state, even in the hands of a benevolent government, waters down religion and robs it of vitality. This in part explains why some western European democracies, where religion is replete in the public school and square but church pews are empty, are talking seriously about disestablishing their privileged churches.

So this was my best shot at it—three reasons why we should care about religious liberty. You may think of others. If you do, let me know.

Coalitions a Necessity to Get Things Done in Washington[1]

One of the guiding principles of life in Washington is that to get things done, one must work in coalition with others who pursue the same goal. Those who try to go it alone are simply not very effective. The Baptist Joint Committee often works with a number of groups and persons with whom we share a common goal, even though we may disagree about certain aspects of theology and other public policy issues. The Baptist Joint Committee has been and is purposefully inclusive in our work as we seek to ensure religious liberty for all.

This then invites the question, are there any limits to this kind of coalition work? Would we for instance become allied with Larry Flynt to fight a church-state battle? After all, we are "known by the company we keep," aren't we? But on the other hand, fair-minded people routinely decry attempts to assign "guilt by association." Where does one draw the line between acceptable and unacceptable coalition partners?

It really depends on the nature of the relationship. If it is more like a marriage partnership or formal alliance—such as the relationship we have with participating Baptist bodies—then we insist upon a confluence of beliefs, values, and assumptions. However, where the relationship is more of a transitory network or single-issue coalition, then with rare exception all that we insist upon is an agreement on goals.

For example, when we both endorse the same religious liberty bill, I want to work with the American Civil Liberties Union. Those of us on the Baptist Joint Committee may disagree with the ACLU's position on *other* issues with which we are not dealing directly. We may also disagree about the values and benefits that inform our devotion to religious freedom. We say that religious liberty is a gift from God. It is not merely the result of toleration on the part of the state; the state is simply called upon to protect what is already there. Others might believe that religious liberty is not God-given or even deny the existence of God, but recognize the importance of

---

[1] *Report from the Capital* 53/20 (October 13, 1998): 3.

religious liberty as a fundamental human right. We can still work together
to achieve the greatest protection for religious freedom, whatever its source.

Indeed, the First Amendment was passed primarily because colonial
free churchmen formed a powerful political alliance with Enlightenment
rationalists and deists. If John Leland had been snooty about working with
Thomas Jefferson, who knows whether or when our first freedom would
have been ensconced in the First Amendment.

This strategy is not only a sound tactic, but it is theologically well
grounded. The Great Commission compels us to go into *all* the world—not
just to people who believe and behave as we do. Jesus urged us in the
Sermon on the Mount to be "salt of the earth" and "light of the world."
This means at least that we rub shoulders with those with whom we
disagree. Jesus showed us how to do it, too. He ate and drank with sinners,
stayed in the house of Zaccheus, and associated with women caught in
adultery.

The stark reality that "all have sinned," including BJC staffers, leaves
us with no choice but to work with fallen humanity. We do this all the time
as we seek to advance the Baptist Joint Committee's mission: "To defend
and extend God-given religious liberty for all, bringing a uniquely Baptist
witness to the principle that religion must be freely exercised, neither
advanced nor inhibited by government."[2]

Even so, don't look for the Baptist Joint Committee ever to find
common league with *Hustler* magazine.

---

[2] The mission statement of the Baptist Joint Committee subsequently was
changed to "The mission of the Baptist Joint Committee for Religious Liberty is to
defend and extend God-given religious liberty for all, furthering the Baptist heritage
that champions the principle that religion must be freely exercised, neither advanced
nor inhibited by government."

Sticks and Stones[1]

Ever feel like you are walking a tightrope with people on both sides trying to push you off in opposite directions? I had that feeling last week.

On church-state issues, the Baptist Joint Committee is seen as a centrist organization. We often play a bridge role between groups on both sides of the spectrum as we seek to build viable coalitions. Witness the Equal Access and the Religious Freedom Restoration Act coalitions.

Recently, the BJC participated in such a project. Along with thirty-five other groups, we helped craft a document called *Religion in the Public Schools: A Joint Statement of Current Law*. In this document, we briefly identified the many ways in which public school students can pray and express their religious convictions in the public school setting under present law. We hope this statement will help educate the American people about where the proper line should be drawn, as well as provide a common baseline for debate when the constitutional amendment on school prayer is introduced. Even some groups that support an amendment (i.e., National Association of Evangelicals and Christian Legal Society) joined in the statement.

We are proud of this statement and our involvement in its preparation. But, as often happens, we drew fire from both sides. The ironic twist here is that the sticks and stones came from members of the same family whose names are synonymous with both corpse-cold secularism and religious fundamentalism.

Give up? It's Madalyn Murray O'Hair and her son, William J. Murray.

First, William (not to be confused with Jon Garth who still works with Madalyn). At age fourteen, William was the named plaintiff in the famous 1963 Supreme Court case concerning devotional Bible reading in the public schools. As you may know, he became a Christian in 1980 and apparently is trying to make up for the sins of his mother. William wrote me that "the document *A Joint Statement of Current Law* is full of lies." He then charged that "those who associate themselves with this document are just plain liars." He lamented that the BJC "represents the liberal political agenda," working with suspect characters on this project who, according to Murray, are mostly

---

[1] *Report from the Capital* 50/13 (June 27, 1995): 3.

"pro-abortion and anti-the Christian faith." (Never mind that the National Association of Evangelicals and Christian Legal Society are decidedly Christian and actively anti-abortion.)

Enter Mama. In her "American Atheist Newsletter" that I received several days later, Madalyn excoriated the signers of the document for selling out to the religious right. She berated the many "Jewish organizations" that participated, lambasted the "liberals" for caving, and then wondered about the "strange bedfellows" (including the BJC) who joined in. Wrote O'Hair, "With extraordinary alacrity, the nation's so-called defenders of state-church separation capitulated to the Christian Coalition's not-yet-named specific demands for the intrusion of religion into the public schools." With the floodgates open, she went on to prognosticate that the "next concession will be that the mythological J.C. may be depicted as a historical person, with his resurrection and ascendance into 'heaven' presented as recorded fact." She concluded that "the public schools should be 'religion-free,' secular institutions of learning."

There you have it. The BJC is comprised of a bunch of leftwing, anti-Christian liars and weak-kneed, fundamentalist-appeasing dupes at the same time. Just ask O'Hair and Murray. If groups are defined by who their opponents are, I take heart. We must be right on.

Be Prepared to Fend Off Beanballs If You Favor Church-State Separation[1]

You think baseball is the national pastime? From my spot on the field it appears the favorite sport of many both within and outside Baptist life is hurling beanballs at the BJC. Strong advocacy for religious liberty and the separation of church and state always seems to make some people lose sight of the proverbial strike zone.

In an article in the June issue of Focus on the Family's *Citizen* magazine, the author chronicles the attempt by a Baptist layman to end his Baptist body's support of the BJC, alleging a variety of indiscretions on our part.[2] The article contains a number of half-truths and guilt-by-association allegations. I wish the author had bothered to call me to discuss the charges before publishing them.

Then, the Southern Baptist Convention's Baptist Press, which rarely passes up a chance to sucker punch the BJC, wrote a "news story" about the *Citizen* magazine article.[3] The author includes a litany of tired, Roger Moran-inspired accusations against the BJC. Needless to say, neither the Baptist Press writer nor the editors bothered to call me.

The accusations in both articles gravitate toward three points. Each one fails to cross the plate.

1. *The Baptist Joint Committee cares more about no establishment than it does free exercise.* Not true. For sixty-five years, the BJC has pursued a balanced, sensibly centrist position on church-state issues affirming *both* the no establishment and free exercise clauses in the First Amendment as essential guarantors of our God-given religious freedom. Let me highlight a few recent examples. We chaired a broad coalition to seek passage of the historic Religious Land Use and Institutionalized Persons Act of 2000 to strengthen the hand of churches in dealing with unreasonable zoning laws and iron-fisted land use regulators. We filed a brief in the US Supreme

---

[1] *Report from the Capital* 56/11 (May 30, 2001): 3.
[2] Matt Kaufman, "Not with My Tithe You Don't," *Citizen* 15/6 (June 2001).
[3] http://www.bpnews.net/bpnews.asp?ID=10927.

Court defending the right of the Good News Club to meet in elementary schools after class to provide the children with moral instruction from a religious viewpoint. We wrote a short book outlining how churches can cooperate with government—even accept money for social services—in a way that is constitutionally permissible and protects the churches' autonomy. Just last week on national television, I defended Attorney General John Ashcroft's right to hold Bible studies and prayer meetings with Justice Department personnel before work in his office.[4]

2. *The Baptist Joint Committee is too partisan.* Not true. We work with Democrats and Republicans, meting out criticism to politicians in both parties when they run roughshod over our "first freedom." We advocate positions on *issues*; we do not support or oppose *politicians*. In criticizing President Bush's "charitable choice" proposal, I have repeatedly lauded the president's goal of helping the poor. We simply believe that "charitable choice" is the wrong way to do right. When Al Gore endorsed "charitable choice" during the last election campaign, my predecessor, James Dunn, wrote an open letter to Mr. Gore telling him that he had ripped his britches. We worked with Sen. Kennedy and Sen. Hatch in passing the Religious Freedom Restoration Act and chided three Baptist senators of both parties for opposing it. In short, we are equal-opportunity critics when public officials cross the line.

3. *The Baptist Joint Committee is aligned with objectionable left-wing organizations.* Not true. We always maintain our independence and take positions on church-state issues consistent with our mission statement and historic Baptist principles. Yes, we work with various organizations—Left and Right—who agree with *our* positions on church-state issues; no, we do not thereby endorse positions that *they* take on other issues.

But get this. At the very moment I sat in my office reading the *Citizen* and BP articles, Holly Hollman, the BJC general counsel, and Mandy Tyler, her assistant, were meeting in *our* conference room with representatives of both the Focus on the Family-spawned Family Research Council and the Southern Baptist Convention's Ethics & Religious Liberty Commission. They were developing strategy for encouraging states to adopt religious liberty bills! Even as we were being nailed by unfair press reports delivered by Focus on the Family and the SBC's Baptist Press, we were meeting with *their* public policy advocates to promote religious liberty.

---

[4] "Prayer in the Workplace," *Religion & Ethics Newsweekly*, May 18, 2001, ep. 438.

The Baptist Joint Committee has been extremely successful in its sixty-five-year history. We have been effective precisely because we value stringent enforcement of both religion clauses, work with and criticize members of both political parties, and form coalitions with groups that agree with *us* when expedient to do so.

No organization is above criticism, and we are always looking for ways to improve how we do our work. But we will not cower, and we trust you will not be misled by one-sided attacks from those who would tear down the wall separating church and state.

We will continue our mission to "defend and extend God-given religious liberty for all, bringing a uniquely Baptist witness to the principle that religion must be freely exercised, neither advanced nor inhibited by government."

Batter up.

BJC Better Defined by Its Record
Than by "Strict Separationist" Label[1]

The views and record of the Baptist Joint Committee continue to be misconstrued and distorted. In his recent book titled *Uneasy in Babylon: Southern Baptist Conservatives and American Culture*, my friend Barry Hankins writes a history of the fundamentalist takeover and domination of the Southern Baptist Convention.[2] Much of Hankins's work is based on extensive interviews with current SBC leaders. While it is helpful to listen to their unadorned reflections, Hankins's methodology has severe limitations. It allows for plenty of spin, self-serving statements, and largely unchallenged characterizations of supposed opponents, such as Southern Baptist moderates.

Hankins details how Richard Land, president of the SBC's Ethics & Religious Liberty Commission, seeks to position his agency in the center of the church-state landscape. Land tries to put distance between the ERLC and so-called "neo-establishment majoritarians" (proponents of a Christian nation and Christian Reconstructionism) on one side, and "strict separationists" (secular extremists who allegedly want to scour religion from the public square) on the other. He then lumps moderate Baptists in general and the Baptist Joint Committee in particular in the "strict separationist" camp.

This sleight of hand completely distorts the church-state landscape and the position of the Baptist Joint Committee. We are not strict separationists in the way the phrase is often used.

Strict separationists typically camp hard on "no establishment" principles to the neglect of "free exercise." The BJC believes both are equally important First Amendment principles; both are vital to protecting religious liberty. Our leadership in efforts to pass free-exercise legislation, defend the constitutionality of religious accommodations, and uphold equal access for student Bible clubs all demonstrate a commitment to free-exercise values.

---

[1] *Report from the Capital* 58/6 (March 19, 2003): 3.

[2] Barry Hankins, *Uneasy in Babylon: Southern Baptist Conservatives and American Culture* (Tuscaloosa: Alabama University Press, 2002).

Strict separationists often resist efforts by government to accommodate religion when not required to do so by the Free Exercise Clause. Heaven knows that is not us. We support many legislative accommodations of religion when permitted by the Establishment Clause. The Baptist Joint Committee has long defended, for example, tax exemptions for churches, housing allowance for clergy, and exemptions for the churches from the nondiscrimination in employment provisions of the civil rights laws—even though these accommodations have never been held to be required by the Free Exercise Clause.

Strict separationists sometimes believe that religion is a private affair that should have little, if any, influence on public policy and are often skittish about a public conversation concerning religion in political campaigns and public life. That is not where we are. We applauded the public discussion about religion in the presidential elections of 2000. We have never contended that our dedication to church-state separation implies a walling off of religion from politics. Yes, there is always the potential for misuse of religion by politicians who want to baptize their political ambitions in the water of sacred approval. We should speak out against such abuse of religion, but it is wrong summarily to relegate public religious expression to second-class speech.

The Baptist Joint Committee is something else entirely. Carl Esbeck, in his five-fold typology for church-state relations, puts the Baptist Joint Committee in what he calls the "pluralistic separationist" category.[3] According to this typology, pluralistic separationists want a neutral state, not a hostile one. They want all religious traditions—in the pluralism of America's religious landscape—to get a fair shake under the First Amendment. They emphasize religion's prophetic role in the public square. Their motto is "a free church in a free state." Certainly, we would endorse these views.

Actually, the Baptist Joint Committee might find an even more comfortable home in Esbeck's "institutional separationist" camp.[4] These separationists think that government neutrality should err on the "benevolent" rather than the hostile side. Both institutions—the church and the state—are subject to the reign of God, but each with different roles and

---

[3] Carl H. Esbeck, "Five Views of Church-State Relations in Contemporary American Thought," *BYU Law Review* (1986): 385.

[4] Ibid., 389.

tasks to perform. A certain amount of careful cooperation between church and state is inevitable and, in some cases, desirable. But neither the church nor the state should control, dominate, or become entangled with the other.

This sounds a lot like us, too. Truth be known, we are probably a blend of the pluralistic and institutional separation typology. Certainly we are not strict separationists in the sense described above.

Hankins concludes that Land's attempt to place his organization between "neo-establishment majoritarians" on the right and "strict separationists" on the left "while attempting to be a culture warrior himself has been self-defeating."[5] When forced to choose a side in the debate over Rep. Ernest Istook's proposed constitutional amendment on school prayer, Land chose a position consistent with his cultural view that minimized establishment clause principles. Similarly, Land's effort to stake out a centrist position is undercut by his support for school vouchers, the Houses of Worship Political Speech Protection Act (a bill to allow churches to endorse candidates), religious exercises at commencement and athletic events, and, in Land's words, "a consummation of the marriage" between the religious right and the Republican Party.

I'll leave it to the reader to judge which organizations best occupy the sensible center.

---

[5] Hankins, *Uneasy in Babylon*, 163.

Ham and Eggs Law[1]

The Baptist Joint Committee has filed three briefs in the 1993 term in the US Supreme Court and is spearheading a coalition of groups urging Congress to pass the Religious Freedom Restoration Act. That's not all we have been doing. In addition to the lofty tasks of filing briefs in the Supreme Court and drafting legislation, we also are involved in day-to-day church-state problems on behalf of Baptist constituents and others—what that lawyer-turned-novelist John Grisham calls "ham and eggs" law. We give advice and guidance, write letters and make phone calls, and sometimes actually intervene in disputes.

These are just a few of the diputes that we have dealt with recently and in some cases routinely:

Tax exemption. A church starts to fill out the thick Form 1023 application for tax exemption and gets fed up with that burden, or the IRS presses for disclosure of delicate information about the church's donors or average attendance at worship service. The pastor gets nervous and gives us a call about what to do. We usually say stop what you are doing and do nothing. Churches and religious organizations are presumptively exempt from federal taxation. There is no need to *apply for* the exemption. Most Baptist churches are covered by the group exemption letter that their denomination has obtained anyway.

We also get a lot of questions about the extent to which churches and religious organizations can engage in what appear to be commercial enterprises on the side. A church that regularly carries on a trade or business that is not substantially related to its exempt purpose may be required to pay unrelated business income tax (UBIT) on the proceeds even when otherwise tax exempt.

Two such churches have come to our attention recently: one church wants to use its fellowship hall to serve meals to outside tax-exempt groups on a weekly basis where the church hostess will make a small profit, and a second church wants to rent excess educational space during the week to a

---

[1] *Report from the Capital* 48/4 (April 1993): 3.

private school. The first church is probably exempt; the latter one may have to pay UBIT.

Students' rights. We got a call from a high school student in California who was prevented from performing a song that he wrote titled "Jesus" at an after-hours drama club talent show. He even offered to change the name to "My Best Friend," but that wouldn't satisfy the principal. Ultimately the student was given permission to only to play the accompaniment. But he then pulled a fast one. When he finished, he referred the audience to copies of the words at the rear of the auditorium if they cared to look at them as they left. The school was clearly out of line, and the principal recanted.

A hot topic nowadays, in light of last summer's Supreme Court decision in *Lee v. Weisman* (the Rhode Island middle school graduation prayer case),[2] is how properly to do graduation—commencement ceremonies and baccalaureate services. Our general advice is not to have prayer at the graduation service, but to hold a church-sponsored, voluntary baccalaureate service (in addition to graduation services) where praying and worship can be done with impunity and without limitation.

Employment issues. We get many questions about the operation of Title VII of the Civil Rights Act of 1964 concerning employment discrimination. These usually revolve around two areas: (1) Church as employer. A church is entitled to discriminate on the basis of religion under Title VII. A Virginia church recently called concerning a complaint that had been filed by a disappointed Muslim applicant for a day-care job who had been turned down because she was not Christian. The investigation is being dismissed. (2) Discrimination against church members. Religious people are often discriminated against in their secular jobs where the employer refuses to accommodate their religious exercise. The US Postal Service refused to allow a Baptist in Western New York off work to worship on Sundays. Apparently, the local supervisor let Jews off on Saturday almost without exception, but not Christians on Sunday. The matter is being pursued in an effort to work out the dispute before Equal Employment Opportunity Commissions proceedings are begun.

We recently were able to intervene successfully on behalf of a Seventh-day Adventist woman javelin thrower at the University of Tennessee who would have missed both the SEC meet and the NCAA nationals because her event was scheduled either on Friday evening or on Saturday. She also

---

[2] *Lee v. Weisman*, 505 US 577 (1992).

would have lost a major part of her scholarship. With our intervention, along with others, the events were switched so that she could compete.

Extinguishing rumors. We spend a lot of time trying to counter demagoguery. The best example of this is the infamous Madalyn Murray O'Hair FCC petition that has cropped up periodically for the last fifteen years. It says that Madalyn Murray O'Hair has petitioned the FCC to discontinue religious broadcasting and urges the reader to write the FCC and complain. This is utterly false, but you wouldn't know it from the 22 million letters received by the FCC since 1974.

A more recent rumor has to do with a flyer titled "Could the Federal Government Close Down Your Church?" This is a diatribe against various gay rights bills that have been introduced in Congress. It goes on to say that these bills would prevent churches from discriminating against homosexuals in hiring, require churches to perform marriages for gay couples, subject churches to mandatory hiring quotas, and even shut churches down. Of course, all of this is false. We are seeking exemptions for churches and religious organizations from the gay rights bills. Even if we are not successful, however, the law could still not be used to force churches to hire homosexuals as ministers or perform tasks that are essentially religious in nature.

I could mention many other examples from church discipline to child sexual abuse, from questions about the American flag in the sanctuary to immigration law, from intervening to preserve the clergy-communicant privilege in the face of a federal subpoena to testify at a murder case to helping a church obtain a zoning variance to build a steeple to a desired height.

I urge you to give us a call if you have a church-state problem no matter how mundane it seems to be. We might be able to help. If not, we will not feel bashful about saying, "I don't know." But if we don't know the answer, we usually find someone who does. We are here to help. Please call on us.

The Legacy of Dawson and
Dunn, Then and Now[1]

Earlier this month, the Baptist Joint Committee co-hosted the annual meeting of the Baptist History & Heritage Society at the First Baptist Church of the City of Washington, DC. The meeting's theme was "The Contributions of Baptist Public Figures in America." I had the privilege of delivering the keynote address, titled "BJC=JMD[2]: The Contributions of Joseph M. Dawson and James M. Dunn to the Baptist Joint Committee."

In that speech I outlined the general approach to church-state issues exhibited by the BJC's first and fourth executive directors. I then discussed what I thought were their top ten contributions (five each) to the preservation of religious liberty generally and to the BJC in particular.

These are summaries of my top ten:

1. Early in Dawson's seven-year tenure, the BJC filed briefs in two seminal Supreme Court cases dealing with public funding of religion (*Everson v. Board of Education*[2]) and religion in the public schools (*McCollum v. Board of Education*[3]), thus initiating the practice of filing friend-of-the-court briefs, which the BJC has done more than 100 times since then.

2. Dawson established the publication *Report from the Capital*, built the BJC coalition of Baptist bodies, and helped found Protestants and Other Americans United for Separation of Church and State (now Americans United for Separation of Church and State).

3. Dawson spoke prolifically and prophetically and wrote *three important books* on church and state and Baptist distinctives.[4]

4. Dawson fought attempts to appoint an ambassador to the Vatican and, in the process, sacrificed an otherwise cordial relationship with a Baptist president and fellow worshiper, Harry Truman.

---

[1] *Report from the Capital* 61/6 (June 2006): 3.

[2] *Everson v. Board of Education*, 330 US 1 (1947).

[3] *McCollum v. Board of Education*, 333 US 203 (1948).

[4] J. M. Dawson, *Baptists and the American Republic* (Nashville: Broadman, 1956); Dawson, *America's Way in Church, State, and Society* (New York: MacMillan Co., 1953); Dawson, *Separate Church and State Now* (New York: Richard R. Smith, 1948).

5. Dawson was instrumental in causing a guarantee for religious liberty to be included in the Universal Declaration of Human Rights adopted by the United Nations General Assembly.

6. Early in his nineteen-year tenure, Dunn spoke out against the Reagan school prayer amendment; he also led the fight to convince Congress to pass the Equal Access Act of 1984. These efforts said "no" to state-sponsored religion and "yes" to constitutionally permissible accommodations of student religious exercise.

7. Dunn worked to restore protections for free exercise of religion through the passage of the Religious Freedom Restoration Act in 1993, and his lawyers defended its constitutionality in the Supreme Court.

8. The BJC led various religious organizations in consulting with the IRS in an effort to maintain churches' tax-exempt status and otherwise to guard their autonomy against intrusive governmental regulation.

9. Dunn fought for human rights internationally on many fronts. Amendments were sought and obtained to the International Religious Freedom Act (1997) to ensure the rights of conscience for all, not just for Christians.

10. In what was perhaps Dunn's most significant legacy, he successfully guided the BJC through the Southern Baptist controversy and caused it to emerge a healthy agency.

James Dunn was in the audience as I spoke. At the end of the speech, he was asked to critique my selection of accomplishments. Although he did not disagree with my choices, he waxed eloquently about another aspect of his leadership of which he was particularly proud—the BJC internship program. He said that his personal relationships with and the encouragement of young people through the internship program was arguably his most significant and enduring contribution.

I cannot disagree. Over the past 25 years, we have hosted more than 150 interns. Most have gone on to achieve success in law, ministry, teaching, and other leadership roles in Baptist and American life. One notable example is Bill Underwood, a 1981 BJC intern, who has been tapped as the next president of Mercer University.

The internship program continues full force. This year we will enjoy the service of nine interns.

Our internship program increases the effectiveness of our ministry, gives young people an experience of working and living in Washington, and develops an "alumni association" for the BJC that only colleges and seminaries usually enjoy. Simply put, former interns make wonderful ambassadors for the BJC and the most effective advocates for religious liberty throughout the country and around the world.

Thank you, James and Joe, for showing us the way.

Balcony People[1]

Isaiah 51:1–2; Hebrews 12:1–2; Galatians 5:1, 13–14

We are urged by the prophet in Isaiah 51 to "look unto the rock from which you are hewn, and to the quarry from which you were dug"—the writer's colorful way of saying "look to your past and those from whom you come, those rock-solid ancestors (like Abraham and Sarah) who went before and showed you the way."

The writer of Hebrews in the New Testament does the same thing, referring to these folks as "a cloud of witnesses"—from Abel to Jesus. I am originally from Tampa, Florida—the "lightning capital of the world." I remember well those big, black, boisterous thunderheads rolling in from the Gulf of Mexico accompanied by a frightful display of lightning. It's hard for me to think of our forebears sitting up in those clouds.

I prefer a metaphor coined by Carlyle Marney. He calls our faith ancestors "balcony people"—exemplars, role models, heroes—who from their lofty perch on the balcony of our lives watch over, encourage, and teach us and lift us up to greater heights.[2]

How important it is to look to the great heroes of the Christian faith and our Baptist heritage—whether we call them the rocks from which we are chipped, a great cloud of witnesses, or balcony people.

This is particularly important when it comes to our heritage of freedom, especially with some today questioning the notion of "soul freedom"—that God-infused freedom of conscience—and others repudiating altogether the "separation of church and state." If we are to be able to stand firm in our conviction that freedom is fundamental, and "not submit to that yolk of slavery" that Paul condemned in Galatians 5, we need to take an occasional look up at that balcony. That's what I aim to do this morning,

---

[1] Unpublished sermon.
[2] From an oral presentation.

I.

From jail cells in England to stockades in Massachusetts Bay to whipping posts in Virginia, Baptists suffered and paid the price for religious liberty. Along with believers' baptism, there was nothing more important to our Baptist forebears than soul freedom, religious liberty, and separation of church and state. We honor our Baptist heroes—and preserve these distinctives—by retelling their stories over and over again.

I see Thomas Helwys up on that balcony! After establishing the first Baptist church on English soil, Helwys authored a cutting-edge treatise on religious liberty called *A Short Declaration of the Mystery of Iniquity*[3] and sent a copy to King James I. In his inscription, he wrote these audacious words: "You, King, are a mortal man, not God, and have no power over the immortal souls of your subjects." For his trouble, Helwys, along with his wife Joan, were thrown into jail. Helwys later died in Newgate Prison.

I spy on the balcony a young, rough-and-tumble Puritan preacher who migrated from England to Massachusetts in 1631. Roger Williams, often called the apostle of religious liberty, insisted that faith could not be dictated by any church or government authority, but must be nurtured freely and expressed directly to God without human interference. Williams advocated a "hedge or wall of separation between the garden of Church and the wilderness of the World,"[4] thus coining the "wall" metaphor more than 150 years before Thomas Jefferson wrote about it in a letter to the Danbury Connecticut Baptist Association in 1802 and 350 years before some revisionists of history insisted it is the invention of latter-day secular humanists.

The Puritan theocrats in Massachusetts were not amused by this kind of crazy talk. They had come to these shores seeking religious freedom, but what they gained for themselves they denied to others. So they kicked Roger Williams out of the colony. Traipsing through snow and surviving the bone-chilling New England winter only with the help of friendly Indians, he settled in what would become Rhode Island and founded a town he dubbed Providence because he believed God's providence had led him there.

---

[3] Thomas Helwys, *A Short Declaration of the Mystery of Iniquity (1611/1612)* (Macon GA: Mercer, 1998).

[4] In Edwin S. Gaustad, *Liberty of Conscience: Roger Williams in America* (Grand Rapids MI: William B. Eerdmans, 1991).

Williams began what he liked to call the "livlie experiment" of religious liberty and established the first Baptist church on North American soil.

I can see Elder John Leland, an evangelist from Massachusetts who preached in Virginia during that heady decade of the 1780s, boldly advocating religious liberty and separation of church and state. He reminded us that "the fondness of magistrates to foster Christianity has caused it more harm than all the persecutions ever did. Persecution is like a lion, it tears the saints to death, but leaves Christianity pure; state established religion is like a bear, it hugs the saints, but corrupts Christianity."[5]

Leland played a pivotal role in convincing James Madison of the need for a spelled-out constitutional guarantee protecting religious freedom. Madison was a candidate for the convention called to ratify the new Constitution; John Leland was thinking about running, too. Tradition has it that one day, in the shade of a great oak tree near Orange, Virginia, Madison and Leland met and cut a deal. Leland agreed not to run if Madison would promise to pursue a Bill of Rights containing a guarantee for religious freedom. Two years later the Bill of Rights was adopted. The first sixteen words are as follows: "Congress shall make no law respecting an establishment of religion, or prohibiting the free exercise thereof."

I also see on the balcony twentieth-century Baptist heroes like George W. Truett, pastor of the First Baptist Church of Dallas, Texas, for nearly fifty years. To an estimated crowd of some 10,000 on the east steps of our nation's capitol eighty-five years ago (May 1920), Truett preached his eloquent sermon titled "Baptists and Religious Liberty."[6] In that sermon, he delivered a powerful defense of and justification for religious freedom and separation of church and state.

It's good for us to hear some of what Truett said eight decades ago. Listen now to his words, paraphrased slightly for modern ears.

> Baptists have one consistent record concerning liberty throughout all their long and eventful history. They have never been a party to oppression of conscience. They have forever been the unwavering champions of liberty, both religious and civil. Their contention now is, and has been, and must ever be, that it is the

---

[5] Ibid., 344. Cf. Green, ed., *The Writings of the Late Elder John Leland* (New York: Arno Press, 1970) 278.

[6] BJC website, www.bjconline.org/resources/pubs/pub_truett_address.htm.

natural and fundamental right of every human being to worship God or not, according to the dictates of conscience, and, as long as this does not infringe upon the rights of others, they are to be held accountable alone to God for all religious beliefs and practices. Our contention is not for mere toleration, but for absolute liberty. There is a wide difference between toleration and liberty. Toleration implies that somebody falsely claims the right to tolerate. Toleration is a concession, but liberty is a right. Toleration is a matter of expediency, while liberty is a matter of principle. Toleration is a gift from government, while liberty is a gift from God. It is the consistent and insistent contention of Baptist people…that religion must be forever voluntary and uncoerced, and that it is not the prerogative of any power…to compel conformity to any religious creed or form of worship, or to pay taxes for the support of a religious organization…. God wants free worshipers and no other kind.

***

That utterance of Jesus, "Render unto Caesar the things which are Caesar's, and unto God the things that are God's," is one of the most revolutionary…utterances that ever fell from those lips divine. That utterance, once for all, marked the divorcement of church and state. It marked a new era for creeds and deeds. It was the sunrise gun of a new day, the echoes of which are to go on and on until in every land, whether great or small, the doctrine shall have absolute supremacy everywhere of a free church in a free state.

We cannot help but spy on that collective balcony Dr. Martin Luther King Jr., perhaps the most prophetic voice in Baptist (and American) life of the twentieth century. King understood that the separation of church and state by no means divorces religious ethics from public life or mutes religion's prophetic witness in society. In a 1963 sermon, he proclaimed, "The church is not the master or servant of the state, but rather the conscience of the state. It must be the guide and the critic of the state, and never its tool. If the church does not recapture its prophetic zeal, it will become an irrelevant social club without moral or spiritual authority."[7]

---

[7] Martin Luther King Jr., "Strength to Love," 1963, Atlanta GA.

King was never willing to squander that authority by relying on Caesar to do Christ's bidding. Ambassador Andrew Young recounts the story of Robert Kennedy trying his best to give King federal money to pay for a voter registration drive. King respectfully declined, fearing the consequences of an all-too-close entanglement with government. He instead set up an independent voter registration project—separate from the Southern Christian Leadership Conference—to work directly with the government on that all-important enterprise. King would not barter his spiritual authority for a mess of government money!

The Baptist World Alliance was founded 100 years ago last Sunday. We must honor those who have made the BWA what it is—a beacon for religious liberty and human rights around the world. Leaders like E. Y. Mullins (president of Southern Baptist Theological Seminary) in Stockholm (1923), Oscar Johnson (pastor of Third Baptist Church—St. Louis) in Cleveland (1950), and Herbert Gezork (president of Andover-Newton Theological Seminary) in London (1955) never backed down from threats to human rights and rights of conscience. Significantly, in Toronto (1980), the 14th World Congress adopted a Declaration on Human Rights. It reminds us that such rights are not only freedom of and freedom from something, but freedom for others as well as ourselves. "Because we are being set free by the power of God through faith in Christ Jesus as Lord, we pledge to use our freedom responsibly to help free others. Individually as well as through our churches and institutions we promise to pray and work for the defense of human rights, to strive to avoid violating the rights of others, and to serve him from whom all human rights come, the only One who is Righteous, Just, and Merciful, the Father of our Lord Jesus Christ."[8]

Helwys, Williams, Leland, Truett, King, BWA leaders—what a balcony we have!

II.

The Baptist Joint Committee, now nearly seventy years old, continues to lead the struggle for freedom on behalf of millions of Baptists and continues to be faithful today as these have been faithful in the past. We stand at the intersection of church and state and, literally, hold forth from the

---

[8] Walter B. Shurden, *The Life of Baptists in the Life of the World* (Nashville: Broadman Press, 1985) 247.

intersection of Second Street and Constitution Avenue (across the street from the Supreme Court building) that soul freedom is universal, religious liberty is non-negotiable, and church-state separation is indispensable.

I look forward to a day when, if someone says, "God has been kicked out of the public schools," people won't get mad; instead, they will laugh because they know that God Almighty has a perfect attendance record. And they will catalogue the dozens of ways that religion can properly be included in the school day (Bible clubs, "See You at the Pole" prayer meetings, character education, teaching about religion, voluntary student prayer anytime, etc.). What we don't need is state-sponsored religion in the public schools.

I look forward to a day when, if someone says, "This is a Christian nation," Christians (not just Muslims and Jews) will stand and say, "No it is not. It is not a Christian theocracy but a constitutional democracy dedicated to real religious liberty for everyone, not just Christians," and Baptists will quote John Leland's admonition that "the notion of a Christian Commonwealth must be exploded forever."[9] There must be no second-class citizens in the USA—especially when based on religion.

I look forward to a day when, if someone asks what is wrong with the government doling out tax money to churches to finance their ministries, Baptists all over the land will stand and retort with George Truett's truism that "Christ's" religion needs no prop of any kind from any worldly source, and to the degree it is thus supported a millstone is hanged about its neck."[10] What government funds, government always regulates. When the church depends on government for sustenance, its prophetic witness becomes muted, as Martin Luther King Jr. knew in his guts.

I look forward to a day when, if zoning officials try to ban house churches in residential neighborhoods, people will stand and say, "If you can have Super Bowl parties, Final Four parties, reality TV parties, and Longaberger basket parties, we can certainly assemble to worship God in this neighborhood." Or, if they say we can worship in the church house but cannot feed the hungry and shelter the homeless during the week, we will say, "How dare you deign to tell us we can praise God on Sunday but not

---

[9] John Leland, "A Chronicle of His Time in Virginia," as cited in Forrest Church, ed., *The Separation of Church and State* (Boston: Beacon Press, 2004) 92.

[10] From sermon, "Baptists and Religious Liberty," delivered by George W. Truett from the east steps of the US Capitol on May 16, 1920, www.bjconline.org/resources/pubs/pub_truett_address.htm.

follow Jesus on Monday?" The BJC led the way in 2000 to convince Congress to pass a federal religious land-use bill to strengthen the hand of churches when dealing with unreasonable zoning authorities and filed a brief in the Supreme Court defending its constitutionality.

I look forward to a day when, if some judge, late at night, places a two-and-one-half-ton rock bearing holy scripture in the middle of a courthouse, people of faith will proclaim, "The question is not whether the Ten Commandments embody the right *teachings*, but who is the right *teacher*—politicians or parents, government officials or pastors and rabbis, congressional committees or churches and synagogues," and then, taking a page from the prophet Jeremiah, say we should write the Commandments "on our hearts" to provide a living witness to those teachings.

I look forward to a day when seductive talk about "religious equality" will be exposed for the lie that it is. Yes, all religions should be treated equally one with another, but we do not want religion to be treated the same as secular activities. Religion is special and it is different. It must be treated differently—sometimes receiving special concessions (tax exemptions and exceptions from other laws needed to lift burdens on exercise of religion) and sometimes special constraints (no taxes to subsidize religion; no state-sponsored religious exercises in public schools). All this talk about religious equality demeans religion and weakens religious freedom.

I look forward to a day when both religion clauses in the First Amendment—no establishment and free exercise, twin pillars of our constitutional architecture erected by James Madison—are again taken seriously and robustly enforced by the courts to keep government from stepping on our "first freedom." In terms of the no establishment clause, four justices of the Supreme Court have clearly signaled their willingness to approve virtually any plan to subsidize even pervasively religious bodies like houses of worship and a majority of five okayed school vouchers to finance teaching of religion. Another five have an astonishingly pinched notion of the protections afforded by the free exercise clause. They think strong protection for everyone is a "luxury" we can no longer afford. Wrong! It's not a luxury we can no longer afford; it's a right we cannot afford to live without.

I long for the day when all of these things will be a reality.

III.

My prayer and the focus of the ministry of the Baptist Joint Committee is that we Baptists not forget our heritage; that we look to the rock from which we are chipped as we take seriously Paul's admonition to stand fast in the spirit of Christ's freedom. Let us regularly visit our balcony people like Thomas Helwys, Roger Williams, John Leland, George Truett, M. L. King Jr., and BWA leaders, and remember the principles of soul freedom, religious liberty, and church-state separation that they and others worked so tirelessly to advance.

These heroes of faith have done their part, and we are here today to enjoy their bequest of freedom and do our part to pass it on as a legacy to the future. Won't you join hands with us at the BJC? Help us proclaim this wonderful message of freedom to the world. Help us defend and extend religious liberty for all God's children. God willing, maybe someday we'll climb up on that balcony to inspire and lift up generations to come!

Directing Traffic at the
Intersection of Church and State

Congress shall make no law respecting an establishment of religion, or prohibiting the free exercise thereof

Testimony on "Charitable Choice"[1]

Thank you, Mr. Chairman and Members of the Subcommittee, for this opportunity to speak to you on a matter as important as religious liberty.

I am J. Brent Walker, executive director of the Baptist Joint Committee on Public Affairs (BJC). I am an ordained Baptist minister. I also serve as an adjunct professor of law at Georgetown University Law Center, where I teach an advanced seminar in church-state law. I speak today, however, only on behalf of the BJC.

The BJC serves fourteen Baptist bodies, focusing exclusively on public policy issues concerning religious liberty and its constitutional corollary, the separation of church and state. For sixty-five years, the BJC has adopted a well-balanced and sensibly centrist approach to church-state issues. We take seriously both religion clauses in the First Amendment—no establishment and free exercise—as essential guarantors of God-given religious liberty.

No principle is more important to Baptists and the BJC than religious liberty and separation of church and state. At our best, we embrace the words of John Leland, a Virginia Baptist evangelist, who said more than 200 years ago, "the fondness of Magistrates to foster Christianity has caused it more harm that all the persecution ever did."[2] This is why for the last five years the BJC has fought "charitable choice" proposals to allow government to fund religious ministries.

The Problems with "Charitable Choice"
"Charitable choice"—a specific legislative provision that allows pervasively religious organizations, such as houses of worship, to receive government funds to subsidize social services—was first codified in 1996 as part of the

---

[1] Testimony before the Subcommittee on the Constitution of the Committee on the Judiciary, United States House of Representatives, regarding state and local implementation of existing "charitable choice" programs, April 24, 2001.

[2] Cf. Green, ed., *The Writings of the Late Elder John Leland* (New York: Arno Press, 1970) 278.

welfare reform law.[3] Since then, Congress has passed three additional pieces of legislation containing "charitable choice" provisions.[4]

For the first time since its inception five years ago, "charitable choice" has attracted national attention and scrutiny in the last few months.[5] Today's hearing—the first ever on the topic of "charitable choice"—further attests to that fact. The cause of the focused attention on this important topic is undeniably the attention given to "faith-based initiatives" by President George W. Bush. President Bush opened six federal offices of Faith-based and Community Initiatives during his second week in office and has listed faith-based proposals, including the expansion of "charitable choice," as one of his top domestic priorities for his administration's first year.

We join others in applauding President Bush's recognition of religion's vital role in addressing social ills, but we believe religion will be harmed, not helped, by directing government money to fund pervasively religious enterprises.

So we oppose "charitable choice"—not because we are against faith-based social ministries, but because of our desire to protect religious freedom.

As the BJC has said for several years, "charitable choice" is the wrong way to do right.[6] The problems with "charitable choice" are many.

First, "charitable choice" is unconstitutional. "Charitable choice" promotes religion in ways that breach the wall of separation between church and state. The United States Supreme Court has long said that governmental financial aid to pervasively religious organizations, even for ostensibly secular purposes, violates the establishment clause of the First

---

[3] *Personal Responsibility and Work Opportunity Reconciliation Act*, Public Law 104-193 (1996).

[4] *Community Services Block Grant Act*, Public Law 105-285 (1998); *Children's Health Act of 2000*, Public Law 106-310 (2000); and *New Markets Venture Capital Program Act*, Public Law 106-554 (2000).

[5] Contrary to some strains of popular opinion, cooperation between government and religion in the provision of social services is not a new idea. It predates this administration's "faith-based initiatives" and even the 1996 "charitable choice" provision. This cooperation—often between government and religiously affiliated organizations that are not pervasively religious—demonstrates the right way for religions and government to partner in providing social service to those in need.

[6] Indeed, the BJC Board adopted a "Resolution on the Charitable Choice Provision in the New Welfare Act" as early as October 8, 1996.

Amendment.[7] Pervasively religious entities (like houses of worship or parochial schools)—ones that are so fundamentally religious that they cannot or will not separate secular and religious functions—should be disqualified from receiving government grants because to fund them is to fund religion.

In a pervasively religious institution, the money that goes into one pocket goes into all pockets. Proponents of "charitable choice" who claim that the provision does not violate separation of church and state point to a provision that bars government funds from paying for "sectarian worship, instruction or proselytization." However, this so-called "protection" is illusory since privately funded sectarian worship, instruction, or proselytization may operate throughout the tax-funded program. Even if one purports to pay for only the soup and sandwich through a government grant, these funds will necessarily free up other money to pay the preacher to bless the meal and deliver a sermon after dinner. In short, "charitable choice" unconstitutionally funds government services that are delivered in a thoroughly religious environment.

Second, "charitable choice" violates the rights of taxpayers. Just as funding pervasively religious organizations violates the First Amendment's Establishment Clause, taking my taxes to pay for your religious organization, or vice versa, violates the First Amendment's free exercise principles. Although the Supreme Court has never ruled that taxpayers have standing to assert a free exercise challenge to a funding scheme, I believe this is exactly what Thomas Jefferson had in mind when he said that "to compel a man to furnish contributions of money for the propagation of opinion which he disbelieves and abhors, is sinful and tyrannical."[8] It was true more than 200 years ago, and it is today. Government should not be allowed to use your tax money to promote my religion.

Third, "charitable choice" results in excessive entanglement between government and religion. It is an iron law of American politics that government regulates what it funds. This is what a Virginia pastor friend of mine meant when he asked government not to give us any "pats on the

---

[7] See *Bowen v. Kendrick*, 487 US 589 (1988); *Roemer v. Board of Public Works*, 426 US 736 (1976); *Hunt v. McNair*, 413 US 734 (1973); and *Tilton v. Richardson*, 403 US 672 (1971).

[8] "A Bill for Establishing Religious Freedom," Virginia Assembly, presented June 1779.

back." For all too often a friendly pat by Uncle Sam turns into a hostile shove by Big Brother.

Some regulation is outlined in the "charitable choice" legislation itself. As already mentioned, religious organizations that receive grants must make sure that the tax money is not used to pay for "sectarian worship, instruction or proselytization." It is a mystery how this legislative language will be enforced without a government officer standing in the sanctuary or poring over the church books, all while making razor-thin theological judgments about what amounts to worship, instruction, or proselytization. The "charitable choice" provision also requires religious organizations to be audited. If funds are segregated, then the audit would be limited to that funding. If the funds are not so segregated, then government will be able to review all of the church's books.

The regulations set forth in the statute, however, are just the beginning. Other federal and state laws and regulations are triggered by the expenditure of federal tax money.[9] Even in cases where the religious organization agrees with the purpose of those laws and regulations, putting itself in a position to prove the compliance itself may be inimical to the autonomy of religious organizations. Ensuring compliance with rules and regulations will also drain the already overtaxed resources of the religious organizations providing services. I agree with the recent observation that churches will spend "more time reading the *Federal Register* than the Bible."[10]

Fourth, "charitable choice" dampens religion's prophetic voice. Religion has historically stood outside of government's control, serving as a critic of government. How can religion continue to raise a prophetic fist against government when it has the other hand open to receive a government handout? It cannot.

Dr. Martin Luther King Jr., arguably the twentieth century's best example of religion's prophetic voice, warned, "Thus church must be reminded that it is not the master or the servant of the state, but rather the conscience of the state. It must be the guide and the critic of the state, and

---

[9] See generally, Melissa Rogers, "The Wrong Way to Do Right: Charitable Choice and Churches," in *Welfare Reform and Faith-based Organizations*, ed. Derek Davis and Barry Hankins (Baylor University, Waco: J.M. Dawson Institute of Church-State Studies, 1999) 64-67.

[10] Michael Tanner, in "Corrupting Charity: Why Government Should Not Fund Faith-Based Charities," CATO Institute, March 22, 2001.

never its tool. If the church does not recapture its prophetic zeal, it will become an irrelevant social club without moral or spiritual authority."[11]

But cannot religious organizations simply refuse government funding if it begins to harm their ministries? Yes, that is possible, but not likely. Government money may be irresistible to churches on meager budgets. "Charitable choice" is a temptation of biblical proportions. Once the money is taken, religious organizations can develop a dependency, not unlike an addiction to a drug. As conservative Christian commentator Timothy Lamer pointed out,

> Federal funding is a narcotic. Once addicted, recipients find it hard to live without.... Once Christian charities get used to collecting the subsidy, they will develop programs and goals premised on receiving government aid. The threat of losing such aid will be genuinely terrifying. They will surely fight such cuts and thus become what conservatives detest—recipients of federal grants lobbying for "more." Are Christian conservatives prepared for the sight of Christian charities lobbying to their place at the federal trough?[12]

Fifth, "charitable choice" authorizes discrimination in employment. Under Title VII of the Civil Rights Act of 1964, churches and some other religious organizations are granted an exemption to discriminate on the basis of religion in their hiring and firing practices. This exemption, when it applies to privately funded enterprises, appropriately protects the church's autonomy and its ability to discharge its mission. For example, the Catholic Church must be free to exercise its religion by hiring only Catholics as priests. Courts have interpreted this exemption to apply not only to clergy, but also to all the religious organization's employees, including support staff, and not only to religious affiliation, but also to religious beliefs and practices.

"Charitable choice" explicitly allows religious organizations to retain their Title VII exemption, even in a program substantially funded by government money. Allowing religious organizations to discriminate in the

[11] Martin Luther King, Jr., "Strength to Love," 1963, Atlanta GA.

[12] Timothy Lamer, "I Gave at Church," in *The Weekly Standard*, January 15, 2001, 13–14.

private sector is a welcomed accommodation of religion, but to subsidize religious discrimination with tax dollars is an unconscionable advancement of religion that simultaneously turns back the clock on civil rights in this country.

Sixth, "charitable choice" encourages unhealthful rivalry and competition among religious groups. We enjoy religious peace in this country despite our dizzying diversity for the most part because government has stayed out of religion.

I have heard your colleague, Representative Chet Edwards (D-TX), say on several occasions that if he maliciously wanted to destroy religion in America, he could think of no better way than to put a pot of money out there and let all the churches fight over it. I agree. "Charitable choice" is a recipe for religious conflict.

"Charitable choice" also drags religion into the ugly governmental appropriations process—the underbelly of democracy. Government does not have the money to fund every religious group in this country. It will have to pick and choose. All too often the majority faith in a particular area will prevail. But regardless of who wins, the process will not be pretty.

These six examples are just a few of the problems with "charitable choice." Simply put, "charitable choice" is the wrong way to do right. Thankfully there are right ways to do right.

Doing Right the Right Way
In dealing with church-state disputes, I always try to find a workable, practical solution even while acknowledging constitutional tension. Common sense often suggests the best way to proceed. There is a better way. Government and religion may cooperate in the provision of social services in many ways that are good for government, religion, taxpayers, and the people served.

To help people of faith evaluate the many permissible ways to cooperate with government and avoid ill-advised financial partnerships between government and pervasively religious organizations, the Baptist Joint Committee, along with the Interfaith Alliance Foundation, has published a document titled *Keeping the Faith: The Promise of Cooperation, the Perils of Government Funding: A Guide for Houses of Worship*.[13] The guide first

---

[13] Please see BJC web site, www.bjconline.org/resources/pubs/pub_keeping-thefaith.pdf, for the full text of *Keeping the Faith*.

advises houses of worship to define the vision of their enterprise and then to determine whether government funding or other forms of cooperation will promote or detract from that vision. *Keeping the Faith* offers the following basic advice.

There are many ways for government and religion to cooperate in the provision of social services while protecting the quality of tax-funded services and the autonomy and integrity of religious organizations. First, houses of worship may continue to pay for social service ministries the old-fashioned way: with tithes, offerings, and funds from other private sources. Government may and should encourage increased private giving. Tax deductions and other incentives to foster corporate, foundation, and individual giving are absolutely proper. The idea of encouraging corporate matching funds for employees' gifts to religious organizations is a good one.

Increasing private funding for charities may also be achieved through expanding deductibility rules for charitable gifts for the 70 million Americans—two-thirds of all taxpayers—who do not currently itemize deductions. This is one of President Bush's faith-based proposals with which there is room for widespread consensus and a positive impact on the nonprofit sector. According to some estimates, the provision found in Title I of the Community Solutions Act (HR 7) would increase annual charitable giving by more than $14.6 billion—a growth of 11 percent over 2000 giving levels—and encourage more than 11 million non-itemizing taxpayers to become new givers.[14]

Government priorities may also encourage the private sector to fund the social service ministries of pervasively religious organizations. Last month, the Robert Wood Johnson Foundation announced plans to provide $100 million grants to 3,000 religious programs for the disabled and elderly.[15] Last week, participants in a conference titled "Faith-based Demonstration for High-risk Youth" reported that private foundations seem to be more generous with their funding of religious organizations since the launch of President Bush's "faith-based initiatives."[16]

---

[14] "Incentives for Nonitemizers to Give More: An Analysis," PriceWaterhouse-Coopers, January 2001.

[15] "$100 Million Pledged for 'Faith-Based' Aid," *Washington Post*, March 28, 2001.

[16] Brian DeBose, "Private Sector Follows Bush, Funds Faith-Based Programs," *Washington Times*, April 19, 2001.

Second, houses of worship may spin off religiously affiliated organizations to accept tax funds and provide social service ministries—out of religious motivations, to be sure, but without integrating religion into the government-funded programs. This option was available even before "charitable choice" was passed in 1996, and President Bush's faith-based initiative may inspire more religious organizations to explore this option. This way of delivering social services is exemplified by the good work of Catholic Charities, Lutheran Social Services, and United Jewish Communities. Religiously affiliated organizations can continue to minister to the needs of people out of religious motivation and even make available some privately funded, separately offered religious activities so long as they do not proselytize, require religious worship, or discriminate on the basis of religion in hiring or service providing. In this vein, Sharon Daly, who leads Catholic Charities, has said, "We help others because we are Catholic, not because we want them to be."[17]

This option also has another benefit. It sets up a firewall against government regulation of and entanglement with the pervasively religious organization. As long as this is done through a separate organization, the regulation should not seep through the corporate distinction and infect that church or house of worship. The institution-wide application of some regulation mandated by the Civil Rights Restoration Act makes this protection even more critical.

It has been suggested by some that the process of setting up a separate religiously affiliated organization is too cumbersome for some houses of worship, particularly for those that are small in size and resources. This suggestion ignores two important realities. First, many churches have successfully established separate religiously affiliated organizations and have operated within safeguards for decades. Second, setting up a 501(c)(3) affiliate should be no more onerous than complying with governmental regulation in the first place. If the real concern in easing regulatory burdens, then the government, specifically the Internal Revenue Service, could provide technical assistance to religious and other community providers wanting to utilize this option.

Third, government should lift onerous restrictions on houses of worship that unreasonably interfere with their ministries. Congress and state legislatures should make sure that religion, including the provision of social

---

[17] Rogers, "The Wrong Way to Do Right," 78.

services by religious organizations, is properly accommodated. Congress has already taken the lead by passing the Religious Land Use and Institutionalized Persons Act,[18] which protects religious organizations from burdensome zoning laws absent a compelling governmental interest. States should continue to pass state Religious Freedom Acts and localities should adopt zoning classifications that respect the autonomy of churches to run their social services with minimal restrictions.

Fourth, government and religious organizations—even pervasively religious ones—may carefully cooperate in creative, non-financial ways. Houses of worship can expand their influence in this area by partnering with other private organizations that have ties with the government. Government may also support the work of pervasively religious organizations without the use of taxpayer money. For example, government may tout the good work that religious organizations do, make referrals when appropriate, share information, and invite religious providers to serve on government task forces.

These illustrations are just some of the ways in which we are able to forge a win-win situation. They demonstrate that social services can be delivered by religious organizations, the autonomy of pervasively religious organizations can be protected from governmental regulation, and the constitutional values that promote religious liberty, such as separation of church and state, can be preserved.

Implementation of "Charitable Choice"
Although "charitable choice" is now law in four different federal statutes, few pervasively religious organizations have elected to apply for government funds for their social service ministries. There are several reasons for this gap between legislation and implementation.

First, according to reports, only a handful of states have aggressively implemented "charitable choice" since 1996.[19] Most states have not instituted local regulations to assist pervasively religious organizations in applying for "charitable choice" grants.

Not surprisingly, Texas, the state that has most aggressively implemented "charitable choice," has also drawn the most litigation. Two of

---

[18] Public Law 106-274 (2000).
[19] "Charitable Choice Compliance: A National Report Card," Center for Public Justice, September 28, 2000; Laura Meckler, "Charitable Choice Rarely Utilized," Associated Press, March 19, 2001.

the five pending cases involving government funding of pervasively religious organizations are in Texas.[20]

Second, the Clinton Administration did not promulgate rules and regulations to implement "charitable choice." In fact, acknowledging the constitutional problems, the Department of Justice interpreted "charitable choice" to exclude pervasively religious entities from qualifying for receipt of government funds. In his signing statement for the Children's Health Act of 2000, President Clinton noted,

> The Department of Justice advises, however, that this provision would be unconstitutional to the extent that it were construed to permit governmental funding of organizations that do not or cannot separate their religious activities from their substance abuse treatment and prevention activities that are supported by SAMHSA aid. Accordingly, I construe the Act as forbidding the funding of such organizations and as permitting Federal, State and Local governments involved in disbursing SAMHSA funds to take into account the structure and operations of a religious organization in determining whether such an organization is constitutionally and statutorily eligible to receive funding.[21]

Third, and most instructively, churches and other pervasively religious organizations are hesitant to enter into contractual, financial relationships with the government. The state of Wisconsin received an "A" on Center for Public Justice's report card on compliance with "charitable choice," with the following explanation: "Gov. Thompson (R) made faith-based subcontracts a key performance indicator for W-2 (welfare) contractors in 1998." However, Thompson, now Secretary for Health and Human Services, recently noted that they only awarded government funds to one religious organization: "We opened it up and we didn't have as many applications as we thought there would be. We didn't pursue it any more. We made it available."[22]

---

[20] *American Jewish Congress and Texas Civil Rights Project v. Bost* (W.D. TX) 00-A-CA-528-SS; *Lara v. Tarrant County* (Texas Supreme Court).

[21] President William J. Clinton, statement of the president, October 17, 2000, signing of HR 4365, the "Children's Health Act of 2000."

[22] Meckler, "Charitable Choice Rarely Utilized."

The situation in Wisconsin is not an anomaly. Churches and other pervasively religious organizations understand the dangers of government funding of their social service ministries. Thousands of houses of worship are providing social services across the country, but they are doing it in the right ways—using private funds for their pervasively religious ministries or spinning off separate religiously affiliated organizations to accept government funds.

Conclusion

The Baptist Joint Committee and other religious groups oppose "charitable choice" not because we want to discourage the delivery of faith-based social services. On the contrary, we oppose it precisely because of our religious conviction and our desire to maintain maximum religious freedom in this country.

We all want to do right—to help those in need. Let's do it in the right ways.

Bad Things Happen when
Church and State Mix[1]

Two recent columns in major national publications have reinforced truths that the Baptist Joint Committee has long articulated. We have often said that, when church and state get mixed up together, one of two things always happens—and both are bad. At worst, consciences are violated initially and persecution results ultimately. At best (if it can be called "best"), state-controlled religion—even in the hands of a benevolent government—waters down religion and strips it of its vitality.

In an op-ed piece titled "A Theocracy Won't Forgive Our Trespasses" published on November 18, 2004, in the *Atlanta Journal-Constitution*, Jay Bookman highlights the first of these consequences. Bookman observes, "We used to understand that government and religion function best when they function independently, when the only link between them is the indirect link of human beings acting out their private faiths through public service. We used to understand that if religion takes a direct role in government, government must inevitably take a direct role in religion, and that the long-standing wall between them was built for the protection for both institutions."

He then continues, "There is no case in recorded human history...in which religion and government have been intertwined without eventually compromising basic human freedoms. Inevitably...that relationship gets out of control and people get hurt." Examples abound. A quick survey of history—the Crusades, the Spanish Inquisition, religious wars in seventeenth-century Europe, the jailing of Baptist preachers in colonial Virginia—and a survey of contemporary events—the September 11 tragedy, the atrocities of the Taliban, and repressive theocracies around the world—provide overwhelming evidence of what happens when religious zeal is combined with coercive power.

But that's not the whole story. Something else sometimes happens. Even where persecution is held in check, religion itself can be the casualty.

---

[1] *Report from the Capital* 59/10 (December 2004): 3.

This is the focus of Eduardo Porter's November 21, 2004, op-ed in the *New York Times*, titled "Give Them Some of That Free-Market Religion." Porter observes that America is an anomaly among progressive twenty-first-century industrialized democracies, such as in Western Europe. All of these countries have grown inexorably more secular. Although these nations may not engage in religious persecution, they have all experienced a marked diminution in religious devotion. If, in Porter's words, religion and modernity don't mix, then how do you explain the fact that America—the wealthiest and perhaps most modern of them all—is, by and large, fervently religious?

The answer he offers is a variation on the theme of supply-side economics. America's religious landscape is vibrant precisely because there are so many groups vying for the allegiance of Americans. That is to say, "Americans are more churchgoing and pious than Germans or Canadians because the United States has the most open religious market, with dozens of religious denominations competing vigorously to offer their flavor of salvation, becoming extremely responsive to the needs of their parishes." And, quoting Baylor University scholar Rodney Stark, Porter writes, "Wherever you've got a state church, you have empty churches." How true.

Porter rightly concludes that this free-market model depends for its effectiveness on a full-bodied understanding of the separation of church and state. To the degree that government participates in the creation of a religious monopoly, the competitive forces that have caused religion to thrive are undercut.

As soon as government starts to meddle in religion (for or against) or take sides in matters of religion (favoring one over others), religious liberty is threatened at that very point. And, in the end, even the religion that government seeks to help is actually hurt and its vitality is vitiated.

John Leland, the Baptist preacher in colonial Virginia, was prophetic when he exclaimed more than 200 years ago that "the fondness of magistrates to foster Christianity has caused it more harm than all the persecutions ever did."[2]

Elder Leland had it right. The American experiment in religious liberty demonstrates that the best thing government can do for religion is simply to leave it alone.

---

[2] Cf. Green, ed. *The Writings of the Late Elder John Leland*, 278.

Vouchers:
The Constitutional Issues[1]

Should tax dollars be spent for religious education? Is aid to parochial schools constitutional or even desirable? Does such aid open the door for government regulation? These are some of the fundamental issues we must address as we consider one of society's most important tasks—the education of its children. People come at this issue with different and sometimes mixed motives. Many are troubled by a perceived failure of the public school system; some want to receive taxpayer assistance for their own schools; others have a veiled agenda to "privatize" all education; still others are looking for election-year issues. For many, religious education funded by the government is the answer. They say, "I want to send my kids to parochial school, and I choose you, fellow taxpayers, to foot the bill."

I believe these schemes are unconstitutional, bad public policy, and contrary to my Baptist heritage. Other than that, I guess they are OK. Today I have been asked to focus on the constitutional issues.

Any analysis of public aid to parochial institutions must begin with the First Amendment's establishment clause. The establishment clause prohibits government from aiding one religion in particular or all religions in general. Government must be neutral toward religion, neither advancing nor inhibiting it, but turning it loose to allow people of faith to practice their religion as they see fit. The Supreme Court has adopted the metaphor—initially coined by Roger Williams and later popularized by Thomas Jefferson—of a "wall of separation" between church and state. Both the civil state and religious institutions are better off when neither tries to dominate, do the work of, or give a helping hand to the other.

Under the establishment clause, the Supreme Court has struck down most forms of financial aid to parochial schools at the elementary and secondary levels. While some non-financial aid has been upheld, these exceptional cases have involved benefits given to the *students* and available to all regardless of whether they attend public or private schools, and they

---

[1] Lecture delivered at Cornell University School of Law, April 24, 1998.

often target handicapped students. These include bus transportation, secular textbook loans, remedial educational services, and interpreters for the hearing impaired. Such aid benefits mainly the students and inures to the advantage of the religious institution only tangentially.

The decisions prohibiting aid are based on the fact that elementary and secondary parochial schools are typically "pervasively sectarian" institutions. Every aspect of parochial education includes religious training and indoctrination of some kind. Thus, it is impossible to isolate and fund the secular activities of parochial schools. Accordingly, the Court has consistently struck down aid programs that benefit these religious schools or help fund the instructional process. Examples include construction and repair grants for parochial schools, tuition reimbursements for parents, salary supplements for parochial school teachers, and instructional equipment and materials that can be diverted for religious uses.

Although the Supreme Court has not ruled on vouchers per se, an important case is *Committee for Public Education and Religious Liberty v. Nyquist* (1973).[2] It involved a New York law providing tuition reimbursement grants and tuition tax credits to parents of children attending private schools. The Supreme Court held that grants and tax benefits had the unlawful effect of advancing religion, because the aid unavoidably would be used to fund sectarian activities, even though the financial benefit flowed through the parents. Consequently, these benefits amounted to an unconstitutional subsidy of the schools' religious mission.

Mueller v. Allen (1983),[3] often referred to by voucher advocates for support, is inapposite. *Mueller* involved a Minnesota law that granted tax deductions for tuition, textbooks, and transportation expenses for students of both public and private schools. Since the public schools already provided these services, the economic benefits were enjoyed almost exclusively by parents of students who attended private schools. The Court focused on the law's facial neutrality (it purported to benefit the parents of all school children) and on the fact that only an "attenuated financial benefit" flowed to the parochial school and upheld (5-4) the deductions. The Court distinguished the passive nature of the deduction from the tuition reimbursement and the "thinly disguised 'tax benefits'" in *Nyquist*, which the

---

[2] *Committee for Public Education and Religious Liberty v. Nyquist*, 413 US 756 (1973).

[3] *Mueller v. Allen*, 463 US 388 (1983).

Court held "actually amount[ed] to tuition grants to parents of children attending private schools." Significantly, the Court reaffirmed in this decision that "the direct transmission of assistance from the State to [religious] schools themselves" would be unconstitutional. The Court's approval of tax deductions does not authorize a substantial financial benefit going to the school in the form of vouchers.

In *Witters v. Washington Department of Services for the Blind* (1986),[4] the Court upheld a program of educational assistance for handicapped *college* students. The Court ruled that a recipient's use of state funds for tuition to prepare for ministry did not violate the establishment clause. In separate concurring opinions, five of the nine justices based their decisions on the *Mueller* principle of facial neutrality. *Witters*, however, does not authorize public assistance at the elementary and secondary levels. The Court consistently distinguished college assistance from those aiding elementary and secondary schools on the basis that most religious colleges are not pervasively sectarian. Additionally, since public primary and secondary education is free, almost all of the government aid would go to parochial schools. This is not the case at the college level, where much of the aid will be used to defray tuition and other costs charged by even state-supported colleges and universities.

In *Zobrest v. Catalina Foothills School Dist.* (1993),[5] the Court upheld providing a state-paid sign language interpreter for a deaf student attending a parochial school. But *Zobrest*, too, offers no support for the constitutionality of a comprehensive voucher program. As in *Witters*, the Court classified the program as one providing limited disability assistance, not as providing financial support for students attending parochial schools (more like lending the students hearing aids). And, as in *Mueller*, the Court found that the discrete nature of the service provided no more than "an attenuated benefit" to the parochial school. Accordingly, the program was distinguishable for vouchers in that "no funds traceable to the government [would] ever find their way into sectarian schools' coffers."

In *Rosenberger v. Rector and Visitors of the University of Virginia* (1995),[6] the Supreme Court ruled that a religious student magazine was entitled to a subsidy from the student activity fee to defray printing costs. While some

---

[4] *Witters v. Washington Department of Services for the Blind*, 474 US 481 (1986).
[5] *Zobrest v. Catalina Foothills School District*, 509 US 1 (1993).
[6] *Rosenberger v. Rector and Visitors of the University of Virginia*, 515 US 819 (1995).

touted the decision as a breakthrough for vouchers, the facts do not support their assertion. The Court was badly split (5-4), and the decision was limited to the unique facts of the case. The Court made a distinction between funding from student activity fees and general tax funds. In addition, the Court ruled that the student organizations, unlike parochial schools, were not a pervasively sectarian institution. Finally, the money in *Rosenberger* was to be paid directly to service providers (printers), while under voucher schemes, it would be paid directly to religious schools. For these reasons, and many others, the *Rosenberger* decision does not justify the use of government funds to support sectarian institutions through vouchers or otherwise.

Finally, the Supreme Court's recent decision in *Agostini v. Felton* (1997),[7] does not argue for the constitutionality of vouchers. In a 5 to 4 vote, the Court overruled *Aguilar v. Felton*,[8] which it had decided in 1985. In so doing, it held that secular, supplementary, and remedial educational assistance under Title I could be provided on parochial school campuses in much the same way that it had authorized in *Zobrest*. This rather limited decision did not abandon the excessive entanglement principle embodied in the establishment clause jurisprudence, and it quite properly refused to overrule settled law that prohibited the use of public funds to finance religious enterprises. It reached the commonsense conclusion that there is no constitutional significance to allowing public school teachers to teach remedial subjects across the street in a trailer but prohibiting it in a parochial school classroom, and that the expenses associated in doing so inured to the significant detriment of everybody—whether in public, private, or parochial schools.

Thus, in a typical voucher plan, the unique combination of (1) actual public expenditure (unlike passive tax deductions in *Mueller* and SAF in *Rosenberger*), (2) the direct and substantial economic benefit to parochial schools (unlike the discrete aid in *Agostini* and *Zobrest*), and (3) involvement of elementary and secondary schools (unlike colleges in *Witters*) makes voucher schemes constitutionally flawed. This is all the more the case in states with robust establishment clauses with express prohibitions—"no money from public treasury—directly or indirectly—to aid any church." Trying to alter the character of these public funds by passing educational

---

[7] *Agostini v. Felton*, 521 US 203 (1997).
[8] *Aguilar v. Felton*, 473 US 402 (1985).

vouchers through parents' pockets does not change the fact that significant tax dollars will eventually be paid directly to parochial schools and that 85 percent of all such funds will go into the coffers of a church school. This will have the effect of advancing religion and thereby violate the establishment clause of the First Amendment.

By way of conclusion, I offer a word or two from my faith tradition on this issue. Baptists have always spoken out on behalf of religious liberty and have staunchly defended church-state separation as the political mechanism for protecting that liberty. This commitment to religious liberty has led many Baptists to oppose aid to religion in general and aid to parochial schools in particular.

Virginia's Statute for Religious Freedom, passed largely as a result of the efforts of Baptists, declared that it is both "sinful and tyrannical" for government to compel people to pay taxes for the propagation of religious opinions with which they disagree.

Public funding would also open the door for invasive government regulation of and unwholesome entanglement with religion. Ron Trowbridge called it a "devil's deal" in a recent issue of *National Review*.[9] This is what a fellow Baptist pastor from Virginia meant when he asked government not to give us any "pats on the back." For all too often a friendly pat by Uncle Sam turns into a "hostile shove" from Big Brother.

Moreover, when religion bellies up the public trough, it becomes lazy and dependent. How can religion raise a prophetic fist against government when it has its other hand opened for a handout? It can't. This is what my hellfire-preaching colonial Baptist ancestor John Leland had in mind when he said, "The fondness of magistrates to foster Christianity has done it more harm than all the persecution ever did. Persecution is like a lion. It tears the saints to death, but it keeps Christianity pure. State-established religion, though, is like a bear. It hugs the saints, but it corrupts Christianity."[10]

Finally, government funding would engender unhealthful rivalry among religions and denominations. The same divisions that have encouraged civil war in other countries would at least result in very uncivil competition in our own.

Authentic religion must be wholly uncoerced. Religion should depend for its support on the persuasive power of the truth it proclaims and not on

[9] Ronald Trowbridge, "Devil's Deal," *National Review* September 15, 1997.
[10] Cf. Green, ed., *The Writings of the Late Elder John Leland*, 278.

the coercive power of the state. Utilizing the things of Caesar to finance the things of God is adverse to true religion and violates the spirit of freedom upon which it is based. The same principle applies to religious education.

Public financial aid to parochial schools—in the form of vouchers or otherwise—earns a failing grade. These programs are unconstitutional and violate the historic Baptist—and, I believe, American—understanding about the proper relationship between church and state.

Testimony on Church Burnings[1]

Thank you, Mr. Chairman and members of the caucus, for the opportunity to testify before this distinguished body on a matter as important as the proper governmental response to the recent burnings of churches in the South.

I grieve over the senseless loss of property that was devoted to God's work in our country. But my heart aches more over the indignity heaped upon worshipping congregations and the spirit of hatred and intolerance that had no doubt motivated the burnings of church buildings.

I come today to talk about the proper role of government in addressing this problem. In short, I think that government should focus on prevention and enforcement. An expansion of federal investigative and law enforcement authority may be warranted here. But, since I am not an expert on law enforcement, I leave it to others to advise you in that respect. What I want to focus on today is the extent to which the government should be involved in providing funds for, or facilitating the funding of, efforts to reconstruct the buildings that have been destroyed by fire. Although government has a role to play here too, it should be secondary and supportive.

Money to help churches rebuild should come though the private sector. Many churches and denominations are already rallying to support this effort. I know that the National Council of Churches began work immediately on this issue and is in the process of raising more than $2 million for reconstruction. Recently, the Southern Baptist Convention, at its annual convention in New Orleans, was able to raise about $300,000 in pledges just from those in attendance. The American Baptist Churches in the USA and the Cooperative Baptist Fellowship are also engaged in this effort, along with the Baptist Joint Committee. I understand that the National Association of Evangelicals and the National Black Evangelical Association have asked their affiliate, World Relief, to start a fund to assist churches in rebuilding. The Christian Coalition has recently pledged $1 million to support the effort. It is not just the Christian community that is

---

[1] Testimony before the Congressional Black Caucus of the United States House of Representatives, June 20, 1996.

helping. My office had a call earlier this week from a friend who works for Soka-Gakkai International-USA, a Buddhist organization, to ask how his organization could participate with the Baptist Joint Committee in this effort. Finally, I understand that Habitat for Humanity, an organization that has historically constructed houses for the homeless, will be diving headlong into the area of rebuilding churches.

Sympathy for this cause cuts across the theological and ideological spectrum. This is exactly what people of faith should be doing—pulling together and pooling resources to help those among us who have suffered at the hands of hate and intolerance. We talk a lot about ecumenism. Now we have the opportunity to put our money where our mouths have always been. Government simply should not let churches and religious organizations off the hook by arrogating to itself the role of trying to rebuild these churches.

This is not to say that the government should be uninvolved. Certainly it should be. There is much that government properly can do to facilitate this effort in a way that acknowledges the private sector's primary role and does not violate the separation of church and state.

First, I would think it appropriate for victim churches to be allowed to seek aid from the Crime Victims' Fund under 42 USC §§10601 and 10602. I understand this would not involve any public taxpayer dollars, but would be funded though fines collected from persons convicted of offenses against the United States, penalty assessments, proceeds of forfeited appearance bond, and other money to be paid from other non-public sources.

Second, I endorse the proposal of the administration and the Senate permitting HUD to guarantee loans by private lending institutions. I applaud the president's call for such efforts in his recent Greeleyville, South Carolina, speech. I am somewhat concerned about the prospect of the government foreclosing on a church after default, but I think the likelihood of default on the part of the churches is rather slim.

Of course, these avenues of relief should not be directed solely to churches. Rather, they should be made available to all similarly situated organizations that suffer property damage because of their race, color, ethnicity, or religious affiliation.

There is a limit, however, to what the government can and should do. The establishment clause in the First Amendment simply does not allow government to provide outright grants or comparable financial support to religious organizations. Some have said that, because this tragedy is so severe, we need not assiduously enforce the constitutional separation of church and state. I submit, however, that it is especially important to stand on constitutional principal when tragic events conspire to tug at our heartstrings to do otherwise. It would set a dangerous precedent for the next occasion when circumstances might not be as compelling.

Simply put, the First Amendment does not allow the use of taxpayer dollars to build churches; it does not allow taxpayer dollars to *rebuild* churches either. The Supreme Court jurisprudence on this point is clear. Taxpayer money cannot be used to assist "pervasively sectarian" religious institutions—which churches clearly are—even for an ostensibly secular purpose like providing funds for brick and mortar. See *Brown v. Kendrick*, 487 US 589 (1988) (Court upheld federal funding of church-affiliated counseling centers promoting chastity, but ruled that pervasively sectarian organizations would not be allowed to participate); *Rosenberger v. Rector and Visitors of the University of Virginia*, 515 US 819 (1995) (Court upheld the use of student activities fees to fund a religious publication printed and distributed by college students, but rejected the notion that it would approve any tax dollars to be used to fund a publication by a pervasively sectarian religious organization); *Tilton v. Richardson*, 403 US 672 (1971) (Court upheld constitutionality of federal construction grants for non-sectarian purposes at a church-related college that was not pervasively sectarian); *Hunt v. McNair*, 413 US 734 (1973) (Court upheld constitutionality of state revenue bonds for a church-related college that was not pervasively sectarian).

Some have suggested that grants may be given to help churches rebuild property that "provides essential services of a governmental nature." I do not think grants are permissible even in this context. Again, the law is clear that thoroughly sectarian organizations cannot receive government funds even if the religious use is mixed with secular use. Indeed, the Supreme Court, in *Tilton v. Richardson*, struck down a mixed-use plan, even though the religious use would not begin for twenty years.

Moreover, I am not sure what "essential services of governmental nature" means, but I suspect it has to with things such as church-related schools, community careers, homeless shelters, soup kitchens, and the like. One is opening up a can of worms when one tries to fund these kinds of activities that operate out of a building that is also used for religious purposes. It is unacceptably entangling for the government to get into the business of deciding what activity is sacred and what is secular, what percentage of the building is used for one over the other, and what is a "governmental" service versus what is a religious one.

It does not make any sense to give churches these kinds of grants. The constitutional difficulties are apparent, and the payoff is slight. The proper avenues for governmental involvement—victims' funds and guaranteed loans—taken together with what I trust will be a generous outpouring of money from the religious community, will be more than sufficient to rebuild churches.

It is important for us to do good, but we must never do good at the expense of compromising constitutional principles that, after all, have stood for more than 200 years to ensure the religious liberty we seek to uphold here.

Churches Can Help Students without Crossing First Amendment Lines[1]

Recently the attorney general of Virginia, Mark L. Earley, called a "faith summit" with more than 300 religious leaders from across the state to encourage them to become "mentors" to students in the public schools. According to a *Washington Post* report, this meeting was preceded by four regional gatherings where law enforcement officers, lawyers, business groups, and other nonreligious organizations were also solicited to participate.

This kind of school-based Big Brothers program is springing up around the country, and it takes a variety of forms. It can involve, for example, on-campus counseling programs in the wake of a school tragedy; ongoing mentoring programs, such as a "lunch buddy," in which the volunteer has a meal with the student once a month; tutoring programs—usually after school and at a church—as safe havens for latch-key kids; on-campus listening posts with chaplains, in which students are allowed to vent problems; and anti-drug speeches by clergy during school assemblies.

Do these partnerships raise church-state concerns? Yes, but they are not insurmountable. Both the schools and the religious community have a vital stake in the moral and academic development of our children. With proper planning and careful supervision, these partnerships can benefit students and at the same time comply with constitutional requirements for church-state separation. Here are several principles to follow in running these partnerships:

• Participation in the program should be strictly voluntary. Students should not be rewarded for joining in or penalized for not participating.

• Along the same lines, these programs should never involve captive audiences, such as classroom-based programs. This would clearly rule out presentations and distribution of Bibles by Gideons in classrooms.

---

[1] *Report from the Capital* 54/8 (April 20, 1999): 3.

• Schools must remain neutral toward religion. Volunteers should be informed that contact with students must not be used as occasions for proselytizing or recruiting for church membership.

• Nonreligious counterparts should be encouraged to participate. For example, secular counselors should accompany clergy in grief counseling in the aftermath of a crisis such as the shooting last year in Jonesboro, Arkansas.

• If off-campus religious buildings are used for a school-related purpose—such as "safe house" for latch-key kids in dangerous neighborhoods—the school should confirm the safety of the surroundings, and religious worship and instruction should not be permitted.

• Clergy who speak at assemblies must not be permitted to preach a sermon or, with a wink and a nod, invite students to an evening pizza party as a prelude to preaching.

• All volunteers should receive training in the program they are participating in and be made sensitive to potential church-state problems.

There are a lot of good reasons to encourage these cooperative efforts, and they should be done without violating the consciences of students and parents or seeking to force-feed religious convictions. We must remain ever vigilant, but the mere possibility of abuse is no justification for scuttling an otherwise helpful program from the start.

Foes of Bible-in-School Guidelines
Make Strange Bedfellows[1]

The Bible is the most important book in the world. Some think it contains the actual words of God. Others believe it was written by people who were uniquely inspired by the Holy Spirit. Most everyone at least concedes that it is a work of fine literature worthy of being read and understood.

Biblical literacy, therefore, is part of being an educated American, whatever one's religious affiliation or commitment. That's why it's so important that the Bible—and other sacred literature as well—be included in the public school curriculum. No, it should not be read devotionally in the classroom as in a worship service or Sunday school. The Supreme Court correctly so ruled in 1963.[2] But the Bible should not be ignored either. In that same decision, Justice Tom Clark said, "It might well be said that one's education is not complete without a study of comparative religion or the history of religion. ...It certainly may be said that the Bible is worthy of study for its literary and historic qualities."[3] The Court went on to conclude that the objective study of the Bible is both constitutionally protected and desirable.

It is important that we help our public school teachers do it right. Many of us, including the Baptist Joint Committee, have endorsed a helpful statement called "The Bible and Public Schools: A First Amendment Guide."[4] The guide explodes the wrong-headed assumption that public schools should be either "sacred" or "religion-free." It endorses a third model, "one in which the public schools neither inculcate nor inhibit religion, but become places where religion and religious conviction are treated with fairness and respect."

The guide then discusses, among other things, how the Bible fits in the curriculum: teaching about the Bible, the Bible as literature, the Bible in literature, teacher selection and training, the Bible and history, and the Bible

---

[1] *Report from the Capital* 54/24 (December 7, 1999): 3.
[2] *Abington v. Schempp*, 374 US 203, 225 (1963).
[3] Ibid.
[4] See *Report from the Capital* 54/23 (November 23, 1999): 4.

and world religions. It also affirms the rights of students to study the Bible devotionally in Bible clubs, to distribute religious literature, and to talk about their faith and the Bible with their peers.

Isn't this approach positive, proactive, pro-education, and indeed, pro-religion? Of course it is. That's why I was surprised to read that the Southern Baptist Convention's Ethics & Religious Liberty Commission has criticized much of it publicly. Why? Baptist Press quotes Richard Land as saying that the fact that People for the American Way and other "very liberal" groups endorsed the guide "should make us very cautious."[5] (Never mind that the National Bible Association, the National Association of Evangelicals, the Christian Legal Society, and the Christian Educators Association International enthusiastically support it.) He also objected that it is "extremely difficult, probably impossible" to teach the Bible objectively and fairly and opposes "a role for the public school to start teaching about religion and about the Bible." (Yes, teaching about religion in general and the Bible in particular is challenging. But it is too important not to try.)

So the Ethics & Religious Liberty Commission wants to keep the Bible out of the public school classroom and disassociate itself from "liberal" groups like People for the American Way. But, irony of ironies, the only other group I'm aware of who has publicly criticized the guide is the American Atheist Association! Using similar words in a press release, Ellen Johnson, president of the association, said it would be "difficult if not impossible" to teach about the Bible in an objective and balanced way.[6]

As head of an agency often criticized for consorting with supposed liberals, it is hard to resist the temptation to ask the real "liberals" to please stand up.

---

[5] Daniel Guido, Baptist Press article, "Land Says Bible Teaching Guidelines 'Mixed Blessing,'" November 22, 1999.
[6] www.atheists.org/flash.line/school3.htm.

A High School Civics Lesson and Test[1]

We can and must teach about religion in our public schools! After striking down school-sponsored devotional exercises, Justice Tom Clark reminded us that "one's education is not complete without a study of comparative religion or the history of religion and its relationship to the advancement of civilization.... Nothing we have said here indicates that such a study of the Bible or of religion, when presented objectively as part of a secular program of education, may not be effected consistently with the First Amendment."[2]

We must also teach about *religious liberty*. I came across a good example of how to do this the other day. My daughter, Layton, is a sophomore at George Mason High School in Falls Church, Virginia. She has a wonderful government class. The class is studying about the adoption and ratification of the Constitution, including the Bill of Rights. The class focused on the twin pillars of religious liberty: the religion clauses in the First Amendment. It is not the superficial stuff they are learning. Rather, they are plumbing the depths of the proper relationship between church and state.

For example, the teacher posed the following questions to the class in a test and asked whether what is being done is constitutional. How many of them can you answer?

1. A congresswoman is asked to officiate at the grand opening of a holiday store in her district by plugging in the lights behind the Nativity scene.

2. A group of First Evangelists has applied for federal money to set up a place for the homeless. They will teach their religion very quietly as they help people find places to live.

3. The city council wants to place both a Christmas tree and a menorah (candles used during Hanukkah) in the entrance hall of the city council building.

4. One of the beliefs of the "New Mind" religion is that its members should kill anyone who disagrees with them.

---

[1] *Report from the Capital* 52/22 (November 18, 1997): 3–4.
[2] *Abington Township School District v. Schempp*, 374 US 203, 225 (1963).

5. A Protestant school has applied for federal money to buy textbooks to teach science.

6. A member of the religious group "The Right Path" tries to convince her friend that her religion is the best faith to follow.

7. A leader of a religious group forbids its followers to leave the religious community.

For short answers to these questions, keep reading:

1. This would most likely be upheld as constitutional. The Nativity scene is generally regarded as a religious symbol. But, in the hypothetical case, it is apparently being displayed by a merchant on private property, rather than by the government on public property.

2. It is unconstitutional for a pervasively sectarian religious organization to receive federal money; it's also unconstitutional for a religiously affiliated organization to receive federal money if the money is used to pay for the teaching of religion. The fact that the religious instruction is being done "very quietly" does not matter.

3. This is probably constitutional. For better or worse, the Supreme Court has held that a Christmas tree and menorah are sufficiently secular symbols that do not offend the establishment clause.

4. Even under the strict test embodied in the Religious Freedom Restoration Act and the traditional understanding of the free exercise clause, government will always have a compelling interest in protecting the life of innocent persons. This is certainly true under the more attenuated standard in place after the demise of RFRA.

5. The Supreme Court has held that the government may *lend* secular textbooks to religious schools without violating the establishment clause. Whether the school can receive an outright grant of public money to buy textbooks is a closer question.

6. The free exercise and free speech clauses protect proselytizing. However, there are some situations (e.g., public schools and the workplace) when proselytizing can be controlled if it becomes disruptive.

7. While reprehensible, this does not violate the separation of church and state. The First Amendment only protects against state action, not private conduct.

How did you do? Pretty heady questions for tenth graders and for most adults, too! If the religion clauses were taught like this in every school, we would have fewer misunderstandings about the proper relationship between church and state, and religious liberty would be more secure in our country than it is today.

Gullibility Travels[1]

Despite the wise admonition of one of the Niebuhr brothers that "we cannot claim any knowledge of the furniture in heaven or the temperature of hell," eschatology—the study of last things—has been an all-consuming passion for some Christians. In 1988, Edgar Whisenant (with World Bible Society) published a book titled *Eighty-Eight Reasons Why the Rapture Will Occur in '88*. He predicted it would happen during the Jewish holiday of Rosh Hashanah. (I was particularly glad he was wrong, because he had pinpointed my birthday—September 13.) During the early weeks of September preachers all over the country announced Whisenant's prophecy from the pulpit, and thousands of Christians started preparing from Christ's imminent return. Of course, to their chagrin, the prediction misfired along with the slew of previous millennial prognostications.

This apocalyptic fervor continues to rage. Last summer, it was reported by someone in the press that a deep space probe had penetrated the outer reaches of our solar system and had sent back astonishing pictures of a shining city, which some accepted as convincing evidence of the existence of heaven. The pictures allegedly revealed "a beautiful city of crystal buildings and lush gardens—teeming with human beings!"

Recently, I guess in order to render some eschatological balance, one Finnish newspaper reported that a group of Soviet scientists had managed to drill 9 miles into the earth's crust and, through sensitive microphone, heard the sounds of human screaming in an environment that exceeded 2,000 degrees Fahrenheit. Hell had been discovered too! I wonder how many readers of these two articles believed their findings without any further thought? Probably quite a few.

This almost amusing naiveté—this bent to accept as gospel the word of someone perceived to have greater knowledge, expertise, or authority—finds expression in the secular realm as well. For example, did you know Madalyn Murray O'Hair has been granted a hearing before the FCC on her petition number RM-2493, which seeks to ban all religious broadcasting from the airwaves? In response to a ubiquitous circulating petition urging Christian

---

[1] *Report from the Capital* 45/5 (May 1990): 11.

folk to do something, the FCC by latest count has received in excess of 21 million letters and postcards protesting O'Hair's effort to strip the broadcasting media of its religious programming.

Trouble is, there was never such a request by Madalyn Murray O'Hair. Petition 2493 was filed not by Ms. O'Hair, but by two California broadcasters asking not that the FCC ban religious broadcasting, but that the commission investigate the operating practices of noncommercial educational radio and television stations, including religious broadcasters. The petition only sought a freeze on licensure of new stations pending completion of the investigation. The FCC unanimously denied the petition on August 1, 1975!

Fortunately, some people have the good judgment to check out the petition before signing it. In fact, we at the Baptist Joint Committee get at least one or two calls every week. By and large, though, the letters of protest keep coming to the FCC unabated. A spokesperson from the FCC recently declared, "No matter how many times we stamp it out, it keeps popping up again. It shifts from one part of the country to another, from one time to another and from one denomination to another."[2] (If any one ever doubted the resurrection, he or she doesn't know about the irrepressible 2493!)

No one know for sure who keeps churning this issue and sending out the protest petition for otherwise well-meaning, if somewhat gullible, Christians to sign. The point is, this is a good example of how we tend to let others do our thinking for us and accept their word without investigating the matter further to see if it is legitimate and worthy of our support.

We Christians need to wise up. I am not talking about an exaggerated emphasis on head religion over heart religion, nor am I extolling the virtues of reason at the expense of revelation, nor am I urging the elevation of rationalism to the detriment of genuine piety. What I am saying is that each individual Christian needs to develop and nurture a certain measure of intellectual dubiety and spiritual discernment to evaluate the events and issues that impact his or her daily life in this modern world.

In his autobiography, *The Struggle to Be Free*, one of my mentors, Wayne Oates, writes of his struggle to be free from "pack thinking," sometimes called "bandwagon thinking."[3] To break the bond of the

---

[2] Michael Hirsley, "Rumor That Wouldn't Die," *Washington Post*, December 17, 1985.

[3] Wayne Oates, *The Struggle to Be Free: My Story and Your Story* (Philadelphia: Westminster Press, 1983) 47.

insidious shackle, we must take responsibility for thinking for ourselves. It means not being a "wet-finger" Christian—going along with the prevailing winds of the majority. It means, according to Oates, "not being a yea-sayer, a pawn of propaganda, a worshiper of…the idols of the marketplace."[4]

We Baptists must reaffirm or "free thinking" tradition. We need to understand and embrace again the bedrock of our denominational existence—"soul freedom." This requires that we make up our own minds about our religious beliefs and our spiritual destiny. It suggests that we are competent to read the Bible for ourselves and, through the guidance of the Holy Spirit, make good decisions about religious commitment, theological beliefs, and ethical behavior. It argues for the repudiation of any ecclesiastical potentate who, through self-arrogation, seeks to make decisions about the future of our churches, expecting individual Baptists to fall in behind in cultic fashion.

It means, in the final analysis, that we listen to one voice and one voice alone—to the voice of Jesus Christ, as revealed in Holy Scripture and illuminated by the Holy Spirit. He is our sole source of authority—not autocratic pastors, not denominational politicos, not self-righteous civil religionists in public office.

Appropriately, this is the theme of Religious Liberty Day emphasis that comes up in Baptist life in June. It is titled "Walking in Christ, Living by Faith." The focal verse of Scripture is Colossians 2:6: "As therefore you received Christ Jesus the Lord, so love in Him…" (RSV).

This should always be our watchword. We think, we act, and we do for ourselves—exercising our God-given freedom. We reject all claims of worldly demigods on our conscience, relying only on our faith in Christ and being guided solely by our understanding of His leadership in our lives. This is the biblical way and the Baptist way.

---

[4] Ibid.

My Address to the ACLU
on Religious Liberty Issues[1]

I was happy to be asked to address the plenary session of the 2006 Nationwide Staff Conference of the ACLU in Park City, Utah, earlier this month. The Baptist Joint Committee and the ACLU have worked closely with each other over the years. Of course, we partner only on church-state issues, not on the many other First Amendment and civic rights issues that the ACLU addresses. Even with that more limited cooperation, we do not always see eye to eye.

I was asked to give the assembled ACLU staffers—national offices and state affiliates—my thoughts on how the ACLU could more effectively address religion and religious liberty issues. The following is a summary of my remarks.

Let me outline briefly four ideas that suggest how we should speak about religion and religious liberty in a way that honors our religious heritage, is faithful to our constitutional tradition, and communicates effectively to policy makers, the media, and the public. Mission and message must go together.

First, do not stereotype those whom you consider to be your enemies (or those who consider *you* to be *their* enemies). We make a mistake if we lump everybody together as the "religious right" or as "fundamentalist." These are not monolithic categories; those who fall within those general descriptions are not all the same. They differ on policy issues, in views about church and state, and in temperament. Some who are conservative theologically may be liberal politically, such as Ron Sider and Jim Wallis. And don't lump all Baptists together either. There's a world of difference, theologically and politically, between Tony Campolo, Jimmy Carter, and Bill Moyers on the one hand, and Jerry Falwell, Roy Moore, and Pat Robertson on the other. Finally, some political conservatives, because of their distrust of government and belief in the doctrine of original sin, are strong advocates for church-state separation.

---

[1] *Report from the Capital* 61/5 (May 2006): 3.

Second, continue to fight hard to defend the establishment clause, but be equally assiduous about promoting free exercise values. The religion clauses must be given equal dignity. We need a robust enforcement of both of these clauses. If one camps too hard on one to the neglect of the other, the protections for religious liberty immediately tilt like a pinball machine. The ACLU has been at the forefront of some far-reaching religious liberty legislation in the past several decades, including the Religious Freedom Restoration Act. I urge you to continue that effort with regard to state religious freedom acts and the Workplace Religious Freedom Act, for example, currently pending in Congress. I know you have countervailing civil rights concerns, but I hope these can be mediated to allow you to endorse this much-needed free exercise legislation.

Third, as you continue to defend the First Amendment, understand that not every brush with publicly expressed religion or civil religion amounts to a full-blown establishment clause violation. It does not serve the ACLU's cause well to make a constitutional mountain out of a civil religion molehill.

In a country with religious roots as deeply planted as ours, it should surprise no one that references to the deity will be reflected in our public rituals and civic ceremonies, our patriotic songs, slogans, and mottos. Why would we expect to have a public square shorn of religious conversation and debate? As Justice William O. Douglas reminded us, Americans are a "religious people."[2] It seems to me these relatively benign expressions of religion do little harm but serve to remind us of our religious heritage and tradition. These are examples of what James Madison, the father of our Constitution, considered *de minimis* concerns and what he called the "unessentials."[3] Some arguable violations are simply not worth fighting over. So, while some of us may have theological concerns about excessive civil religion—where it can turn into an idolatry of nationalism and serve actually to trivialize religion—most expressions of civil religion do not amount to constitutional violations.

Finally, find ways to work with folks on the other side of the religion/culture divide. Again, there's good precedent here. In addition to RFRA and other efforts to pass free exercise legislation, I would point to the

---

[2] *Zorach v. Clauson*, 343 US 306, 313 (1952).
[3] Letter to Edward Livingston, July 10, 1822; see Robert S. Alley, ed., *James Madison on Religious Liberty* (Buffalo NY: Prometheus Books, 1985) 78.

variety of consensus statements on religion in the public schools that have been so helpful in the past decade or two. Much good will and trust was built up and developed among folks on diametrically opposed sides of issues and the culture debate generally. I fear that we are using up more of that capital nowadays than we are replacing. We should look for areas of common ground and work together on that sacred soil of civic cooperation for the public good.

I hope the BJC and the ACLU will continue to be partners in the all-important task of ensuring religious liberty for all—as we have for many decades—and model how religious and secular groups can cooperate in common enterprises for the commonweal.

Testimony on Proposed
Constitutional Amendment[1]

Thank you, Mr. Chairman and members of the Committee, for the opportunity to testify before this distinguished body on a matter so important as religious liberty.

The first sixteen words of the First Amendment read, "Congress shall make no law respecting an establishment of religion, or prohibiting the free exercise thereof." The Baptist Joint Committee believes that these two religion clauses require the government to be neutral toward religion—setting people of faith free to practice their religion as they see fit, not as government sees fit. Government should accommodate religion without advancing it; protect religion without privileging it; and lift burdens on religious liberty without extending religion a benefit. In short, government may, and sometimes must, get out of the way, but it can never get behind and push.

Both of these clauses ensure our religious liberty; both require the separation of church and state as the means of accomplishing that goal.

Some say that the separation of church and state is hostile to religion or anti-religious. I say they are wrong. As a minister, I know that separation of church and state is good, not bad, for religion; and as an attorney, I understand that the separation of church and state is good for government too. When we tie the church and the state together, the church tends to use civil power to enforce its brand of religion and the state palms off the name of God to support its stripe of politics. But when we separate the two, religion tends to flourish, and the state is relieved of the daunting task of making decisions about religion—something it does poorly.

We Baptists have long resisted incursions on religious liberty and have traditionally supported the separation of church and state. Many of my forebears were exiled, ostracized, horsewhipped, and thrown in jail when the dominant religious sentiment became infused with governmental power.

---

[1] Testimony before the Committee on the Judiciary of the United States Senate, October 25, 1995.

Spawned by a deep belief in the inviolability of conscience and forged by the sting of persecution, "a free church in a free state" has long been our slogan. In fact, it was Baptist preacher Roger Williams, 160 years before Thomas Jefferson, who first talked about the "hedge or wall of separation between the garden of the church and wilderness of the world."[2]

Baptists were instrumental in urging the founders to protect our God-given religious freedom. Along with many religious minorities—Quakers, Presbyterians, and others—Baptists applauded the new Constitution that, in Article VI, prohibited the federal government from requiring any religious test for public office. But the memory of persecution lingered, so Baptists—particularly in Virginia—insisted upon a full Bill of Rights with an explicit guarantee of religious freedom. James Madison heard their cry and, along with others, included religious liberty as our "first freedom" among the panoply of preferred protection in the Bill of Rights. Over the ensuing two centuries, the religion clauses in the First Amendment have afforded Baptists and all Americans the freedom to practice their religion to a degree envied by the rest of the world.

This is why we say "no" to those who want to fiddle with the First Amendment by adding a school prayer or "religious equality" amendment to the Constitution. Such an amendment is both unnecessary and foolish.

We should never try to amend the Constitution, particularly the First Amendment, unless there is a compelling need for it. There is none here. Indeed, just last week in his written testimony before this committee, Professor McConnell stated, "By any realist standard of comparison, religious liberty in the United States is in excellent shape.... Americans are free to practice their faith, for the most part, without fear or hindrance, with a diversity and freedom that does not exist elsewhere in the world."[3] The First Amendment and an array of supporting laws, such as the Religious Freedom Restoration Act and the Equal Access Act, currently provide vigorous protection for our religious freedom. These laws make clear that prayer has not been kicked out of the public schools, and religion has not been banished from the public square.

---

[2] In Edwin S. Gaustad, *Liberty of Conscience: Roger Williams in America* (Grand Rapids MI: William B. Eerdmans, 1991).

[3] Testimony of Michael W. McConnell to the Subcommittee of the Constitution of the Committee on the Judiciary, June 8, 1995, http://judiciary.house.gov/legacy/2108.htm.

Under current law, students may pray silently at school at any time—even orally and collectively, as long as they are not disruptive. The First Amendment also protects activities such as the annual "See You at the Pole" day, in which students gather before or after school, join hands around the flagpole, and pray out loud. Truly neutral moments of silence provide another opportunity for prayer at school. Furthermore, the Equal Access Act allows student religious clubs to meet on school property to pray or read their Bibles. In fact, a court recently ruled that not only may students in a San Diego school hold Bible club meetings on campus before and after school, but they may also meet on campus during lunch.[4] Only school-sponsored and school-organized prayer are ruled out by the Constitution, and properly so.

Citizens' rights to express their religion in public places are also well protected by current law. Our law permits citizens to speak of their religious convictions in public settings such as town hall meetings, and religious leaders like Billy Graham and the Pope to hold rallies in public parks. Indeed, this past term, the United States Supreme Court, in *Rosenberger v. Rector and Visitors of the University of Virginia*[5] and *Capitol Square v. Pinette*,[6] ruled that citizens' religious speech generally must be given access as nonreligious speech. See also *Lamb's Chapel v. Center Moriches Union Free School District* (1993)[7]; *Widmar v. Vincent* (1981)[8]; *Board v. Mergens* (1990).[9] Only state-funded and state-sponsored religious messages and displays have been ruled out by the Constitution, and properly so.

Well, fine, some say, the rights are there, but sometimes these rights are not understood or respected. The answer is not to pass more laws with which to comply, but to educate society about the laws that are already on the books and enforce them. As part of this effort, the Baptist Joint Committee joined a number of different religious and civil liberties groups, including the Christian Legal Society and the National Association of Evangelicals, in drafting *Religion in the Public Schools: A Joint Statement of*

---

[4] *Ceniceros v. Board* (1995).

[5] *Rosenberger v. Rector and Visitors of the University of Virginia*, 515 US 819 (1995).

[6] *Capitol Square Review Board v. Pinette*, 515 US 753 (1995).

[7] *Lamb's Chapel v. Center Moriches Union Free School District*, 508 US 384 (1993).

[8] *Widmar v. Vincent*, 454 US 263 (1981).

[9] *Board of Education of Westside Community Schools v. Mergens*, 496 US 226 (1990).

Current Law.[10] By setting forth the law of church and state in a clear and concise fashion, this statement is helping parents, teachers, and students to understand their rights and responsibilities.

This educational effort recently was reinforced by the bully pulpit of the presidency. In September 1995, the Clinton administration mailed to every school district in the country a copy of the president's guidelines on religion in the public schools, which, the president acknowledged, were based largely on this statement. These guidelines describe the many ways in which students may express their religion at school, emphasizing that schools are not, as the president said in a speech last July, "religion-free zones."

Not only is a religious equality amendment unnecessary, but it would also violate a basic rule of legislating—"do no harm." Such an amendment would foolishly permit government to coerce, control, and compromise religion.

Although proponents of a constitutional amendment argue that the measure will protect only voluntary prayer and other voluntary religious expressions, the draft amendments that have been circulated go much further. For example, the language in some proposals would allow the teacher to lead the class in prayer or select a student to lead the class in prayer. These situations raise a host of troubling questions: Whose prayer will be prayed? Which faith group gets more days for their prayer? Who will assign the prayer opportunities—a teacher or administrator who may or may not share our faith or any faith at all? What will we do with the kids who object to hearing another faith group's prayer? These questions remind us why we have insisted that the government keep its hands off religion; our religion is simply too precious and too personal to entrust to the state.

The draft amendments would permit not only government-sponsored religious expression, but also government-funded religious activities. Every proposal would allow, if not require, government to fund religion just as it funds secular activities.

What is wrong with the government funding religion? Plenty!

First, it would violate the religious liberty of citizens whose taxes are used to pay for the advancement of someone else's religion. This is exactly what Thomas Jefferson had in mind when he said that "to compel a man to

---

[10]   www.bjconline.org/resources/pubs/pub_relinpubschools.htm (April 1995 pamphlet).

furnish contributions of money for the propagation of opinions which he disbelieves and abhors, is sinful and tyrannical."[11]

Second, it would open the door for invasive governmental regulation of and unwholesome entanglement with religion. This is what a fellow Baptist pastor from Virginia meant when he asked government not to give us any "pats on the back." For all too often a friendly pat on the back by Uncle Sam turns into "hostile shoves" by Big Brother.

Third, when religion bellies up to the public trough, it becomes lazy and dependent. How can religion raise a prophetic fist against government when it has its other hand opened for a handout? It can't. This is what my hellfire-preaching colonial Baptist ancestor John Leland had in mind when he said, "The fondness of the magistrates to foster Christianity has done it more harm than all the persecution ever did. Persecution is like a lion. It tears the saints to death, but it keeps Christianity pure. State-sponsored religion, though, is like a bear. It hugs the saints, but it corrupts Christianity."[12]

Finally, government funding would engender unhealthful rivalry among religions and denominations. At a recent hearing in the House on this issue, Representative Jose Serrano said that the passage of an amendment would bring about another "civil war." Overstatement? Think Bosnia. The same divisions that have encouraged civil war in other countries would at least result in very uncivil competition in our own.

When government takes sides in matters of religion—favoring one denomination over another or religion over irreligion—only mischief results. This is particularly the case when government puts its money where its mouth is.

I hasten to add that religiously affiliated organizations may receive governmental aid if it is not used to advance religion. For example, a church-related college can receive a federal grant to construct a science building, but not to erect a chapel. Religious social service agencies, such as Catholic Charities and Lutheran Social Ministries, routinely receive public money to feed the hungry, nurse the infirm, care for the elderly, and relocate refugees; but they do not proselytize, discriminate, or teach religion. The proposed amendments do not respect these time-honored

---

[11] Thomas Jefferson, A Bill for Establishing Freedom (1779).
[12] Cf. Green, ed., *The Writings of the Late Elder John Leland*, 278.

distinctions. Public funds could go to a pervasively sectarian organization to propagate its religious mission.

The religious equality amendment must be defeated because it goes too far. In another sense, it is also flawed because it doesn't go far enough! We don't want religious "equality"; we want governmental neutrality. Sometimes equality is not enough, despite its seductive egalitarian ring. While equality makes sense when applied to truly private religious speech, in other contexts government must treat religion *differently* to be neutral. Everyone on this committee believes religion should be treated better, not equally, when government lifts burdens on the free exercise of religion. The need to exempt religion from onerous regulation is what the Religious Freedom Restoration Act was all about—passing the Senate by a 96-3 vote. There are dozens of other examples: General Motors pays taxes, while churches don't; Holiday Inn has to comply with the public accommodation provisions of the Americans with Disabilities Act, while churches don't; McDonalds can't discriminate on the basis of religion, while churches can.

By the same token, sometimes neutrality justifies different treatment on the establishment clause side, such as when government denies religion benefits in order to avoid promoting religion. Examples abound here too: public aid to parochial schools and grants to pervasively sectarian religious organization under the Adolescent Family Life Act.[13]

No people of faith who argue for "equality" really want to give up their right to be treated differently when it suits them. But they can't have it both ways. Just as neutrality sometimes requires better treatment, sometimes it mandates the withholding of benefits. This kind of governmental neutrality results in greater religious freedom than would be engendered by formal religious equality.

As a Baptist and an American, I long for spiritual and moral revival in our nation. The absence of spiritual roots and the presence of moral decline cry out for a return to prayer and vigorous evangelism. This work must be done by churches, families, and individual citizens. Schools must do better in teaching core civic values, and government must allow religious conviction to take its rightful place in the public forum. However, attempts by government to inculcate religion in the schools or to promote religion in the public square are both wrong and counterproductive.

---

[13] *Bowen v. Kendrick*, 487 US 589 (1988).

The best government can do is get out of religion's way; the worst it can do is to get behind and push. The present constitutional language requires the former; the proposed amendments would allow the latter. Persons of faith who treasure religious liberty don't need or want an amendment.

Accommodations:
Walking that Fine Line[1]

Recently the *New York Times* published an above-the-fold, front-page series on legal accommodation of religion and religious practice.[2] You can read all of the articles on the *New York Times* website.[3] But before you wade in, let me provide a primer on when government may, and sometimes must, accommodate the exercise of religion by exempting it from otherwise applicable laws.

The First Amendment's two religion clauses (no establishment and free exercise) require government neutrality toward religion. That often requires government to treat religion differently from secular activities—sometimes imposing constraints to ensure against the establishment of religion (i.e., no state-sponsored prayers in the public schools, no financial aid for teaching religion) but sometimes involving concessions to lift burdens on the exercise of religion (i.e., tax exemption; exemption for Native Americans' use of peyote). Religious exemptions generally fall into one of three categories: (1) mandatory, (2) permissible, and (3) impermissible exemptions.

Accommodations may be required when government has placed a substantial burden on the exercise of religion. These are usually dispensed by the courts where the burden violates the free exercise clause or overarching religious liberty statutes such as the Religious Freedom Restoration Act. Government can avoid this obligation only if it can show that it has a compelling governmental interest. Examples of these mandatory exemptions are demonstrated in Supreme Court cases involving excusal of Amish children from compulsory education laws, giving Seventh-day Adventists unemployment compensation benefits even though they refuse to work on the Sabbath, permitting religious organizations to make internal theological and ecclesiastical decisions without governmental second guessing (church autonomy doctrine), and affording the right to

---

[1] *Report from the Capital* 61/9 (October 2006): 3.
[2] Diana B. Henriques, "In God's Name," 7-part series, October 9, 2006–May 13, 2007, *New York Times.*
[3] www.NYTimes.com/ref/business/churchstate.html.

discriminate in the hiring and firing of clergy (ministerial exemption). Where government regulation would violate one's free-exercise rights, the courts—and sometimes legislatures—generally must provide an exemption to remove that burden.

Other cases involve situations where accommodations may not be required, but, for policy reasons, legislatures may decide to exempt religion anyway. These accommodations will lift some governmental impediment to religious practice, even though it may not be substantial enough to trigger constitutional rights. Examples of this kind of accommodation are seen throughout federal and state law. They include tax exemption generally and various other tax breaks such as the ministerial housing allowance, an exemption from annual reporting requirements for churches, and special protection against governmental audits. Another example involves an exemption in the Civil Rights Act of 1964 to allow religious organizations to discriminate on the basis of religion in hiring, even with respect to non-ministerial personnel. Religious organizations are often exempted from the nettlesome land-use regulations and zoning laws that would impede their ability to discharge their ministry and community service. Finally, the Supreme Court has ruled that states may provide financial aid for ministerial students in college or seminary, even though states are not constitutionally required to make such aid available.

Sometimes an accommodation is neither required nor permitted. These involve ones that actually advance religion rather than accommodating it; promote religion rather than protecting it; provide a palpable benefit rather than lifting a burden. They often violate the establishment clause. For example, a Connecticut law that required employers to grant leave to workers upon request for religious observance went too far and violated the establishment clause in large measure because that law prejudiced the employer and burdened the rights of other employees who were not seeking accommodation. The Court also has struck down attempts on the part of states to exempt religious periodicals from sales tax because they were deemed an indirect subsidy and elevated religious speech to a higher level than comparable secular speech.

Accommodations—those required and permitted—are necessary fully to ensure religious liberty. They are nothing new. Exemptions for oath-taking, military conscription, and compulsory tithes existed even in colonial times. But, as *The New York Times* series pointed out, today there are hundreds of accommodations in federal law alone. Many of these are necessary and well taken; some may go too far and will not withstand scrutiny when tested.

We should take away two lessons from this summary: first, this plethora of religious exemptions belies often-heard cries of a "war on Christianity" or any widespread persecution of religion in this country. These charges are bogus, and our willingness to accommodate religion in our laws confirms that understanding. Second, it's important that exemptions not be pressed too far. The old expression that "pigs get fat but hogs get slaughtered" is apt here. Establishment clause concerns and the rights of third parties must be respected. Attempts on the part of some to overreach may well prompt a political backlash that will create an atmosphere in which even needed and reasonable accommodations may not be available. In that event, the loser would be religious liberty.

"See You at the Pole"
Gatherings Provide Chance for Prayer[1]

As I write this column, millions of students all over America, indeed throughout the world, are attending "See You at the Pole" prayer meetings in public as well as private schools. First begun by Texas Baptists, but now garnering participation by students of many denominational traditions, "See You at the Pole" has spread like wildfire through the past ten years.

It is important to highlight this program because it provides an example of how students can properly engage in religious exercises, even in the public schools.

The football game prayer over the public address system struck down in *Santa Fe vs. Doe* demonstrates the wrong way to do it.[2] That prayer was saturated with state sponsorship. But, as the Supreme Court itself pointed out, "nothing in the Constitution as interpreted by this Court prohibits any public school student from voluntarily praying at any time, before, during, or after the school day." "See You at the Pole" prayer meetings—along with Bible clubs and prayer before meals and tests, silently throughout the day, and during neutral moments of silence—provide ample opportunity for students to communicate with God while at school.

It is important, however, to understand some areas of concern and possible pitfalls. First, public school teachers and administrators should not participate. As recognized in Religion in the Public Schools: A Joint Statement of Current Law, "School officials acting in an official capacity, may neither discourage nor encourage participation in [See You at the Pole]."[3] This means that the school officials should not give those wishing to pray at the pole any special advantage or treat them more favorably than any student speakers. By the same token, they should not discourage or put unreasonable impediments in the way of this religious practice. In short,

---

[1] *Report from the Capital* 55/19 (September 26, 2000): 3.
[2] *Santa Fe Independent School District v. Doe*, 530 US 290 (2000).
[3] April 1995 pamphlet, bjconline.org.

school officials should remain neutral and allow students to run the program.

Second, parents should not join in the prayer circle. These are to be student-initiated, student-run prayer gatherings. Attempts on the part of parents to participate directly can be problematic, and many schools ask parents to stay away. However, this doesn't mean parents can't be involved. For example, in my home church, Columbia Baptist Church in Falls Church, Virginia, parents of school-aged children meet at the church the hour following the meeting on campus and pray together for their children, other students, and the school.

Third, students should strive to model their piety through their behavior. Administrators and other students will be watching. Participating students must respect the rights of others to disagree with them and not participate. Others should not be put down for failing to join the group or aggressively proselytized or rudely hectored.

Moreover, student leaders should inform the school administration about their plans for the prayer meeting and accept reasonable time, place, and manner limitations on their meeting. School officials are not allowed to prohibit the meeting, but they can impose reasonable guidelines. For example, if the flagpole is near a bus lane and 200 students want to crowd around the pole to pray, the school would be justified in moving the prayer meeting from the flagpole to a safer area of campus.

Finally, students should avoid being lulled into a civil religion trap. Joining hands in a circle facing the quintessential symbol of our country, the American flag, makes this a real risk. Yes, we are told in scriptures to pray for our leaders. Students should understand that they are not praying to Caesar, but to God.

In sum, there are so many ways to do religion in the public schools right. "See You at the Pole," when properly done, is one of the best. We don't need, and should not want, the government's help in our religious activities. Let the students pray, but let the government keep out of it.

Testimony on Free Exercise Legislation[1]

Thank you, Mr. Chairman and members of the subcommittee, for this opportunity to speak to you about the need to pass the Religious Liberty Protection Act of 1999 (RLPA)—HR 1691. I am J. Brent Walker, general counsel of the Baptist Joint Committee on Public Affairs (BJC). I am an ordained Baptist minister. I also serve as an adjunct professor of law at the Georgetown University Law Center, where I teach an advanced seminar in church-state law. I speak today, however, only on behalf of the BJC.

The BJC serves fourteen Baptist bodies, focusing exclusively on public policy issues concerning religious liberty and its political corollary, the separation of church and state. For more than sixty years, the BJC has adopted a well-balanced, sensibly centrist approach to church-state issues. We take seriously both religion clauses in the First Amendment—no establishment and free exercise—as essential guarantors of God-given religious liberty.

Accordingly, we have stood against attempts to return school-sponsored prayers to the public schools and to provide public money for vouchers for parochial education. For example, we opposed the so-called "Religious Freedom Amendment" to the constitution in the 105th Congress. On the other hand, we support the Equal Access Act of 1984 and have defended it from constitutional attack as we applauded its effectiveness in ensuring voluntary, student-initiated religious exercise in the public schools. Significantly for our purposes today, the BJC—under the leadership of my predecessor, Oliver Thomas, and now mine—has had the privilege of coordinating the seventy-five-member Coalition for the Free Exercise of Religion for nearly a decade. This diverse coalition—from People for the American Way and the National Council of Churches to the Christian Legal Society and the National Association of Evangelicals—led the charge to support the passage of the Religious Freedom Restoration Act in 1993

---

[1] Testimony before the Subcommittee on the Constitution of the Committee on the Judiciary, United State House of Representatives, in support of HR 1691, May 12, 1999.

(RFRA), defended its constitutionality in the courts, and over the past two years has urged passage of RLPA.

This button I wear today—"Religious Freedom for All"—was worn by hundreds on the Hill the day the Senate passed RFRA. It bears witness to our common commitment to providing increased protection for religious liberty without advancing any particular sectarian interest. It highlights the fundamental proposition that if anyone's religious liberty is left unprotected, everyone's rights—religious and civil—are threatened.

So, in 1993, the coalition said "no" to those who wanted exemptions from RFRA for claims and defenses concerning abortion, public education, prisons, historical land marking, and land use. We said "yes" to a bill that would provide wall-to-wall protection for religious liberty without dictating a specific outcome in any particular case. Restoring the "compelling state interest" standard testified to the importance of the free exercise clause in the panoply of constitutional rights, and the government should be put on a short leash whenever it tries to run roughshod over the dictates of conscience.

The same salutary principles motivate the BJC's support for RLPA. We applaud your attempt to provide legislative protection consistent with the US Supreme Court's decision in *City of Boerne v. Flores* (1997),[2] which struck down parts of RFRA as unconstitutional. We also applaud your courage exhibited in restoring the commerce clause provision in the bill, and we urge you to stand fast in that commitment.

Some critics claim that RLPA is not needed to protect religious freedom. They are wrong. True, in America we do not have the clear and obvious persecution of religion that plague many foreign countries. Fortunately, some states enjoy increased protection for religious freedom, either as a matter of state constitutional interpretation or due to the passage of state religious freedom restoration acts.[3] It is also true that some courts are using the few tools available to them under the US Supreme Court's

---

[2] *City of Boerne v. Flores*, 521 US 507 (1997).

[3] The following states have interpreted their state constitution to provide strict scrutiny for religious liberty claims: Massachusetts, Minnesota, Wisconsin, Kansas, Oregon, Vermont, and Michigan. The following states have passed legislation: Rhode Island, Connecticut, Florida, and Illinois. Alabama adopted a state RFRA as a new constitutional amendment.

decision *Employment Division v. Smith* (1990),[4] including finding hybrid rights and lurking discrimination against religion.

However, we need a national commitment to preserve and protect our "first freedom"—religious liberty—across the board. This patchwork of protection has not eliminated violations of free exercise. This was dramatically portrayed at this subcommittee's hearings in the 105th Congress. A parade of witnesses detailed instances of governmental suppression of and insensitivity to religion and religious freedom. There was only a small slice of incidents across the country where governmental officials violate religious freedom and the rights of conscience.

As we call upon all nations around the world to respect human rights and religious liberty and to take seriously the teachings of the Universal Declaration of Human Rights, we must demonstrate our resolve as Americans to do the same for everyone in this country. Our words will not be taken seriously unless they are backed up with action that matches our rhetoric.

In addressing the charge that RLPA is not needed, I am reminded of a lesson from our nation's early history. When the Constitution was being debated in Congress, many of our nation's founders, including James Madison of all people, thought there was no need for a Bill of Rights or any specific protection for religious freedom. After all, state churches had been disestablished throughout almost all of the colonies, and religious liberty protection was included in nearly every state constitution. The federal government was to be a government of delegated powers. Since no powers respecting religion would be given to it, there was no need to limit the federal government from exercising a power it did not have in the first place. However, Baptists, Presbyterians, and other people of faith wisely disagreed. They knew from painful persecutions what havoc even well-meaning governments could wreak. Thus they demanded a Bill of Rights, including specific protection for religious freedom. Aren't we glad our spiritual forebears prevailed? Had they not been able to negotiate a Bill of Rights in 1789, I doubt that political conditions would ever again have been congenial to its adoption. Thus, this bill is needed to signal a clear and constant federal commitment to ensuring protection for religious liberty.

Some say RLPA will not effectively protect religious liberty, and that restoring the compelling interest test to the law is only window dressing.

---

[4] *Employment Division v. Smith*, 494 US 872 (1990).

They say that the courts will apply it lackadaisically and unevenly. While this Congress should not and cannot tell the courts how to apply the compelling interest test, recent history suggests that having the standard in place does make a difference. After the Court's decision in *Employment Division v. Smith*, the BJC began tracking cases decided under the new, attenuated standard put forth in that case. Of hundreds of religious liberty cases decided from 1990 to 1993, the religious claimant prevailed in only a handful of them, and then usually because of the presence of a more protective state constitutional protection. However, from 1993 to 1997, the time during which RFRA saw its most widespread application, religious claimants did much better. Indeed, the religious claimant either prevailed or obtained a favorable result in approximately one-third of the cases reviewed during this time. Also, just because the compelling interest test has not always been applied vigorously or correctly is no excuse not to restore it where possible.

Moreover, those of us who advise constituents and clients who have run-ins with government know about the prophylactic effect of a strong statute. When there is strong protection for religious freedom, many cases, as they should be, are resolved without litigation and are never seen by those who like to keep score by counting court decisions.

Some people have claimed that increased protection for religious liberty through RLPA threatens other rights and constitutional values. These are the folks who are members of what I think Doug Laycock has referred to as the "religious liberty, but..." crowd. They claim to be for religious liberty in principle but are willing to compromise it away in one specific application after another. For example, "Yes, I'm for religious liberty, but not if it will compromise historical preservation, and not if it means letting prisoners worship like the rest of us." Unfortunately, folks who make these qualifications do not think religious freedom is that important. To them, it is not the first freedom; it stands behind their own parochial interest.

In the current political milieu, those who lack this sense of the preeminence of religious liberty come from both ends of the ideological spectrum. Some of the strongest criticism of RLPA has come from the Far Right, including the Home School Legal Defense Association. This is ironic, because Mike Farris, the association's president, helped draft RFRA! They do not object to RLPA in principle, but oppose Congress exercising its commerce clause powers in enforcing RLPA's protections. Their disdain for the commerce clause is greater than their devotion to religious liberty. In no way will protection under the commerce clause hurt home-schooling families. But it will certainly help others, such as religious organizations that engage in or affect commerce. We must use every tool available to protect religious liberty.

Then there are opponents on the left. Some in the civil rights community—particularly many who advance gay and lesbian rights—have argued that RLPA may prejudice those rights. They seek an exemption so that, in cases where religious liberty and civil rights are seen to conflict, their claims will always prevail over the religious claim. This is simply wrong.

There should be no carve-outs to religious liberty, even for good causes such as nondiscrimination. RLPA is formulated in such a way that courts will balance these two fundamental principles—religious freedom and civil rights—and that is the way it should be. If a court finds a compelling interest in enforcing nondiscrimination, including on the basis of sexual orientation, that claim will prevail; where the interest cannot be shown, the religious liberty claim will prevail. Thus, as with other parts of society, the gay and lesbian community will win and lose some cases under RLPA. However, it would be unwise, and maybe unconstitutional, for Congress to judge ahead of time these deep-seated and delicate issues that rage in national debate.

No, there should be no carve-outs to religious liberty, even for good causes such as federalism and civil rights. Those who object to RLPA for parochial reasons should temper those concerns by enjoying the happy circumstances of increased protection for religious liberty for *themselves* as much as for society in general.

In conclusion, I urge members from both sides of the aisle to rise above this political maelstrom and to do the right thing by our nation's first freedom, which the wise architects of our republic gave us more than 200 years ago. Many of us at this table opposed last year what we thought were misguided, if well-meaning, attempts to restore religious freedom by amending the Constitution. We do not need to amend the Constitution. Our founders—yes, even Mr. Madison—got it right the first time. What we need is for the Supreme Court to begin once again to interpret the free exercise clause in a way that is consistent with their intention and that provides full-blown protection for religious liberty. In the meantime, however, it is incumbent upon Congress to stand in the gap. I urge you to do so by passing RLPA.

Church and State on Campus:
A View from the Wall[1]

Introduction

Two hundred and eight years ago the wise architects of our republic embarked on a bold construction project of erecting a wall of separation between church and state as the means of ensuring religious liberty. They did this mainly through twin pillars in the First Amendment in the Bill of Rights—commonly called the "religion clauses." The first sixteen words provide that "Congress shall make no law respecting an establishment of religion, or prohibiting the free exercise thereof"—the very "first freedom" listed in the panoply of constitutional rights.

These two clauses require government to be *neutral* toward religion, neither advancing nor inhibiting it, but turning it loose to flourish or flounder on its own. Government must accommodate religion without advancing it; protect religion without privileging it; lift burdens on free exercise without extending religions an impermissible benefit. Both clauses also require what has been metaphorically called a "wall of separation between church and state." Originally coined by Roger Williams and made famous by Thomas Jefferson, it has become a shorthand expression for a constitutional reality that the US Supreme Court has employed more than fifty times in the last century and a quarter.

The first clause, known as the establishment clause, prevents government from advancing, promoting, or helping religion. The seminal modern-day expression of this concept came from a former Baptist Sunday school teacher from Alabama, Supreme Court Justice Hugo Black, who wrote in 1947, "The 'establishment of religion' clause of the First Amendment means at least this: neither the state nor the federal government can set up a church. Neither can it pass laws which aid one religion, aid all religions, or prefer one religion over another. In the words of Jefferson, the

---

[1] Lecture delivered at Grinnell College, Grinnell IA, November 5, 1997.

clause against the establishment of religion by law was intended to erect a 'wall of separation' between church and state."[2]

Over the next few years, culminating in a 1971 decision in *Lemon v. Kurtzman* (1971),[3] the Court fashioned a three-part test to be used in deciding the constitutionality of government action challenged under the establishment clause. In order to be upheld, the law or government action under this test must (1) have a secular purpose (moment of silence, religious "motivation"), (2) have a primary effect that neither advances nor inhibits religion (teaching about religion), and (3) not foster excessive governmental entanglement with religion (oversight, monitoring). In recent years the *Lemon* test has been criticized by the religious/political right for allegedly encouraging hostility to religion, not neutrality. Five members of the Court have questioned it, but it has not been overruled or changed.

The second religion clause, the free exercise clause, is intended to prevent government inhibiting, burdening, or hurting the free exercise of religion. By necessity, sometimes government can regulate religious practice, but this should be the exception, not the rule. The courts historically have subjected such regulation to searching judicial scrutiny.

In 1963 the Supreme Court adopted a test for evaluating free exercise claims called the "compelling interest" test.[4] Under that test, before government will be permitted to burden religion, it must show a compelling state interest (an interest of the highest order, such as health and safety) and that it has chosen the least restrictive means of achieving that interest. In holding government to this high standard, the courts in effect "stacked the deck" against government when it tries to fiddle with the rights of conscience.

All this changed in 1990. The Supreme Court did away with the compelling interest test and established a watered-down "reasonableness" test for most free exercise cases under which government will almost always win (*Employment Division v. Smith*, peyote case).[5]

In 1993, Congress passed and President Clinton signed the Religious Freedom Restoration Act (RFRA) that restored the compelling interest test to the law across the board as it stood before 1990. It did by statute what the Court refused to rule was provided by the free exercise clause itself.

---

[2] *Everson v. Board of Education*, 330 US 1, 15-16 (1947).
[3] *Lemon v. Kurtzman*, 403 US 602 (1971).
[4] *Sherbert v. Verner*, 374 US 398 (1963).
[5] *Employment Division v. Smith*, 494 US 872 (1990).

Unfortunately, this summer in *City of Boerne v. Flores*,[6] the Court struck down as unconstitutional RFRA as it applies to state and local government.

Supreme Court Decisions

I want to spend a few minutes sketching out several cases decided by the Supreme Court that deal with religious liberty and church-state relations on the college campus. They have tended to focus on establishment clause issues rather than free exercise. And, of course, because the First Amendment applied only to limit the power of the government and state actors, these issues almost always come up in state universities rather than private colleges like Grinnell. I would hope, though, that the same fundamental principles of toleration and respect for pluralism that underpin the religion clauses would also cause private parties to treat each other no worse.

As with most establishment clause cases, these nucleate around either funding issues or religious expression issues. When government gives public funds to a religious college or endorses a religious message, it runs the risk of violating the establishment clause.

Funding. The Supreme Court has advanced the general rule that any public funds given (directly or indirectly) to a *pervasively sectarian* organization, including a college, violates the establishment clause. For example, in *Habel v. Industrial Development Authority of Lynchburg*, a state court recently disqualified Liberty University from receiving public funding because it was found to be so pervasively sectarian.[7] To date, the Supreme Court has never found an institution of higher education (as opposed to primary and secondary parochial schools) to be "pervasively sectarian" and, thus, ineligible for these types of aid. But, if the organization is only *religiously affiliated*, the appropriation is constitutional, as long as it is not used for religious purposes. Colleges are almost always religiously affiliated instead of pervasively sectarian.

Thus, the Supreme Court in *Tilton v. Richardson* (1971),[8] upheld a federal grant for construction of buildings at four Catholic colleges and universities in Connecticut. The Court required that the funds not go

---

[6] *City of Boerne v. Flores*, 521 US 507 (1997).
[7] *Habel v. Industrial Development Authority of Lynchburg*, 400 S.E. 2d 516 (1991).
[8] *Tilton v. Richardson*, 403 US 672 (1971).

toward the support and maintenance of buildings or facilities that could be used for religious worship or instruction (i.e., a chapel).

Then, in *Hunt v. McNair* (1972),[9] involving a South Carolina revenue bond issue for a Baptist college, the Supreme Court recognized that government aid to private education violates the establishment clause "when it flows to an institution in which religion is so pervasive that a substantial portion of its functions are subsumed in the religious mission."[10] But the Court concluded that the Baptist college, as the college in *Tilton*, was not pervasively sectarian and upheld the program. The college was governed by a religious organization, but there were (1) no religious qualifications for faculty membership or student admission, (2) no showing on the record that the school placed any special emphasis on sectarian education, and (3) no inhibiting on the exercise of academic freedom.

Finally, in *Roemer v. Maryland Public Work Board* (1976),[11] the Court reviewed the extension of categorical grant money to religiously affiliated colleges. The grants were restricted by the prohibition against the use of money "for sectarian purposes." Again, the Court upheld the state aid program for most of the same reasons on which it relied in earlier cases.

The Supreme Court has decided one case involving aid to a *student*. In *Witters v. Washington Department of Student Services for the Blind* (1986),[12] the Supreme Court upheld a program of educational assistance for handicapped students. The Court ruled that the blind students' use of state funds for tuition at a Bible college to prepare for ministry did not violate the establishment clause. The Court was influenced by the fact that the "link between the state and the school was a highly attenuated one," and the aid was given to the *student* who exercised a meaningful private choice about how to spend it.[13] Interestingly, the Supreme Court sent the case back to the state court to examine the case under the Washington state constitution, and the Washington Supreme Court ruled that such assistance would violate the state constitution.

Expression. Moving over to the religious expression side, the landmark religious speech case in the Supreme Court dealing with colleges is *Widmar*

---

[9] *Hunt v. McNair*, 413 US 734 (1972).
[10] Ibid., 743.
[11] *Roemer v. Maryland Public Work Board*, 426 US 735 (1976).
[12] *Witters v. Washington Department of Student Services for the Blind*, 474 US 481 (1986).
[13] Ibid., 752.

v. Vincent (1981).[14] The Supreme Court held that a state university that allowed secular extracurricular student groups to use classrooms could not deny access to religious student groups. Since the university was a limited public forum—a place set aside for members of the student body to express and exchange views—the university's rule distinguishing between secular and religious groups constituted discrimination against religious speech based on content and was, therefore, impermissible unless justified by some compelling interest by the university.

The university has argued that it had a compelling interest in not aiding or endorsing religion. But the Court found that the granting of access to religious clubs did not have that effect. Accordingly, the Court struck down the university's rule against using school premises for religious clubs. (As you know, this rule of constitutional interpretation at the university level has been extended by statute, the Equal Access Act of 1983, to allow religious groups to meet at public secondary schools—the middle schools and high schools—before and after school.)

Both Funding and Expression. The final Supreme Court case I want to discuss involves both funding and expression. In *Rosenberger v. Rector and Visitors of the University of Virginia* (1995),[15] the Supreme Court ruled that an evangelical student magazine was entitled to a subsidy from the student activity fee (SAF) to defray printing costs. The university (and BJC) had argued that such payments by the university of SAF money violated the establishment clause. This was particularly so, we argued, because the club was thoroughly religious and the publication was proselytizing in nature.

The Court disagreed and ruled (5-4) that the establishment clause concerns were not sufficiently compelling to trump the free speech rights of the students, but the majority's ruling was narrow and limited. The Court made a distinction between funding from the SAF and general taxpayer dollars. In addition, it held that the student organization, through thoroughly religious, was not a "religious organization." Finally, the Court found significant that the money in *Rosenberger* would be paid directly to service providers (printers) rather than to the religious club itself.

Free Exercise. The only free exercise case the Supreme Court has decided dealing with colleges and universities is *Bob Jones University v.*

---

[14] *Widmar v. Vincent*, 454 US 263 (1981).
[15] *Rosenberger v. Rector and Visitors of the University of Virginia*, 515 US 819 (1995).

United States (1983).[16] Bob Jones University had a policy that denied admission to applicants engaged in interracial marriage or known to advocate interracial marriage or dating. Because of this admission policy, the IRS revoked its tax-exempt status. Bob Jones asserted that its view of scripture required that policy, and, therefore, the government was violating its free exercise rights. The Supreme Court ruled that the right of tax exemption depends on meeting certain standards of charity, and the organization must serve a public purpose and not be contrary to established public policy. Thus, the Court held that the government had an overriding interest in eradicating racial discrimination that substantially outweighed whatever burden might have been placed on Bob Jones's exercise of their religious belief. Accordingly, the university lost its tax-exempt status.

Contemporary Issues

Having sketched the general constitutional lay of the land as well as significant Supreme Court decisions on the topic, let me move to four or five contemporary issues that we need to examine to flesh out the topic more fully.

Aftermath of Rosenberger.[17] Universities across the land have been struggling in the wake of *Rosenberger* to decide how to administer their SAF program in a way that respects the Court's teaching and without violating other constitutional rights or creating additional problems. Again, the Court, in *Rosenberger*, held that providing financial support from the student activities fund to a thoroughly religious organization to publish an evangelical magazine does not violate the establishment clause, at least when the payment is made to a third-party provider.

Other establishment clause issues remain open, however. For example, *direct* financial support to a religious student organization would arguably violate the establishment clause, particularly if paid for by taxpayer dollars instead of SAF funds. Certainly, giving greater support for religious clubs than others or giving support specifically earmarked for religious worship or instruction would run the risk of creating an establishment clause problem.

A number of free speech and free association issues are created as well. Even if the university does not discriminate in its *recognition* of groups and in granting *access to facilities*, it may well have to make choices in the allocation

---

[16] *Bob Jones University v. United States*, 461 US 574 (1983).
[17] *Rosenberger v. Rector and Visitors of the University of Virginia*.

of limited *funds*. How you do that without violating the speech rights of students remains open and fuzzy. Moreover, taking student activity fees from student A to pay for the club activities of student B who is engaged in an enterprise that student A finds offensive has been alleged to violate student A's free association rights.

Graduation Prayer. Another establishment clause issue currently in the news involves graduation prayer. The Supreme Court last month declined to review a decision of the Seventh Circuit Court of Appeals, in *Tanford v. Brand*, dealing with graduation prayers at Indiana University.[18]

In 1992, the Supreme Court, in *Lee v. Weisman* (1992),[19] dealt with graduation prayers at the middle and high school levels. In that case, a principal invited a Jewish rabbi to give an invocation and benediction before and after the graduation ceremony, and then gave the rabbi detailed guidelines to follow in how to fashion his prayer. The Supreme Court struck down that practice by noting the coercive effect it had on those in attendance, particularly students, and rejected the argument that attendance was in any sense voluntary. Justice Kennedy, for the five-member majority vote, wrote, "The Constitution forbids the state to extract religious conformity from a student as a price of attending his or her own high school graduation. This is the calculus the Constitution demands."[20]

But, in the Indiana University case, *Tanford*, the circuit court ruled differently. It held that the nonsectarian invocation and benediction was permissible, because in a real and meaningful sense, those in attendance were voluntarily present. Unlike in *Lee*, there was no compulsory education law at work, and about a third of the graduates had skipped the ceremony anyway. There was also a comparable afternoon ceremony where no prayer was involved. The court went on to hold that the nondenominational prayer had the legitimate secular purpose of solemnizing a public occasion rather than approving religious beliefs. The Court ruled that the instructions the university gave to the clergy—to offer a unifying and uplifting prayer—were less entangling than the more detailed instructions given to the Jewish rabbi in *Lee*.

I personally think the Supreme Court in *Lee* was absolutely correct. Clergy-led prayer—even student-led prayer in the context of a high school

---

[18] *Tanford v. Brand*, 104 F. 3d 982 (7th Cir. 1997).
[19] *Lee v. Weisman*, 505 US 577 (1992).
[20] Ibid., 596.

graduation ceremony—violates the establishment clause. Although I think it depreciates prayer to have it spoken in a secular public ceremony, the graduation prayer at the university level, as done at IU, is probably constitutional. Again, there is something of a different standard between colleges and universities on the one hand, and high schools and middle schools on the other hand. As the Court said in *Widmar v. Vincent*, "university students...are less impressionable than younger students and should be able to appreciate that the University's policy is one of neutrality of religion." Additionally, the courts always have more assiduously policed the perimeter of church and state at the elementary and secondary level.

In a word, graduation prayer at the high school level is more like classroom prayer (which is prohibited), whereas graduation prayer at the college level is more like prayer before a legislative body (which the Court has upheld).

Student Free Exercise Accommodation. Having talked about a couple of establishment clause issues, I now want to move to free exercise. There is a whole range of situations dealing with the right of student clubs to discriminate in terms of whom they allow to lead as officers. The leading case in this area, again, deals with high schools. In *Hsu v. Roslyn Union Free School District*,[21] the Supreme Court last year let stand a decision of the Second Circuit Court of Appeals dealing with a school district's attempt to prohibit a Christian Bible club from discriminating on the basis of religion in the election of officers. The lower court ruled that district-wide nondiscrimination policy applied to all extracurricular clubs, and the school district had a compelling interest in preventing religious discrimination. The appellate court held that the president, vice-president, and music coordinator are essential to the expressive content of the club's meetings and preservation of its purpose and identity. Therefore the court ruled that the club could discriminate on the basis of religion. As for other leadership positions—secretary and activities coordinator—whose duties are not "unambiguously religious," the club could not discriminate.

These disputes are happening on the college level, and I understand you had a similar one here that gave rise to this symposium. It has also bee an issue at Georgia Tech. Georgia Tech is balking at allowing on-campus meetings of a student chapter of a national campus ministry called reJoyce in Jesus (RIJ). The club is requiring that a student be a Christian to vote or to

---

[21] *Hsu v. Roslyn Union Free School District*, 85 F.3d 839 (2d Cir. 1996).

be a candidate for a group leader. If non-Christian students were allowed to vote, the argument goes, they could elect a leader who would divert the mission and ministry of the club, if not change it altogether. It comes down to whether the members have the right to define their message and establish leadership qualifications. Similar issues are afoot at California State University at Monterey Bay, where the university relented and recognized the campus chapter of InterVarsity Christian Fellowship, and there are half a dozen chapters of Christian Legal Society in dispute with attempts to discriminate on the basis of religion in membership or officers or both.

I think the clubs should win these cases. The university may have an interest in eliminating discrimination (religion/sexual orientation) in hiring and admission, but not where applied to the internal operation of a student religious organization whose belief and practice would be burdened by enforcing such rules of nondiscrimination.

Another issue that is quite prevalent in the student free exercise context is dormitory living arrangements. For example, in *Rader v. Johnston* (1996),[22] a freshman at a state university in Nebraska applied to live off campus in a Christian housing facility. This ran headlong into the university's rule generally requiring on-campus residency for all freshmen. The student was able to show he was being discriminated against because the university granted exemptions to the rule for secular reasons: (1) if the student is nineteen or older; (2) if the student is married; or (3) if the student lives with his or her parents and is commuting. The university also granted exemptions for various reasons under the rubric of "significant and truly exceptional circumstances." Exemptions were generously given, especially if you knew a regent or trustee member. Thus the court ruled the student's free exercise rights were effectively diminished because he was being treated in a discriminatory fashion. This is the right result. There is simply no reason (other than a failure to take religious claims seriously) for refusing to accommodate the religious liberty claim.

Along the same lines, I'm sure you read about the Orthodox Jewish freshmen at Yale who object to living in the on-campus residence facilities because the environment is secular, offensive, and violates their free exercise rights. They are seeking permission to live off campus. A lawsuit in this case has just been filed. Since Yale is a private institution rather than a public institution, the claim is a bit trickier, again because the free exercise clause

---

[22] *Rader v. Johnston*, 924 F. Supp. 1540 (D. NE 1996).

and the Religious Freedom Restoration Act protect only against state action. However, Nat Lewin, a premier religious liberty attorney, put together a creative complaint effectively arguing that Yale is a state actor and alleging violations of the federal Fair Housing Act, federal anti-trust laws, breach of contract, etc. We will have to wait and see how the issue will resolve.

Faculty Free Exercise/Accommodation. The rights of free exercise of *faculty members* at state universities are sometimes circumscribed by the establishment clause. This limitation is clearer in the primary and secondary levels, but it still applies at the college level as well.

For example, in *Bishop v. Aronov* (1991),[23] a professor at the University of Alabama who taught exercise physiology occasionally referred to his religious beliefs during instruction time. The university prohibited the professor from making such statements (i.e., "I believe God came to earth in the form of Jesus Christ and he has something to tell us about life that is critical to success and happiness."). The professor sued, claiming the university unconstitutionally restricted his speech, academic freedom, and free exercise. The court of appeals ruled in favor of the university. Importantly, the court did note that if a student had asked the professor's religious views, he might have answered the question.[24] Moreover, because this does amount to a limitation on speech and academic freedom, the court ruled that the prohibition needed to be narrowly tailored. Accordingly, the professor could conduct meetings of students after hours, as long as it was clear that the meetings were neither required for course credit nor sanctioned by the university.[25] With these qualifications and limitations, I agree with the court's opinion. The Supreme Court declined to review the case.

Another aspect of faculty free exercise is the other side of the coin. That is, to what extent a religiously affiliated college can discriminate on the basis of religion in hiring and retaining faculty members.

Title VII of the Civil Rights Act of 1964 prohibits discrimination in hiring even in private enterprises, including colleges and universities, if they affect interstate commerce. However, section 702(a) provides that Title VII does not apply to a "religious...educational institution...with respect to the employment of individuals of a particular religion to perform work

---

[23] *Bishop v. Aronov*, 926 F.2d. 1066 (11th Cir. 1991).
[24] Ibid., 1076.
[25] Ibid., 1078.

connected to the carrying on by such [institution]...of its activities."[26] Then, another section says, "if a school, college, university, or other educational institution or institution of learning is, in whole or substantial part, owned, supported, controlled, or managed by a particular religion or religious corporation, association or society...," it may discriminate on the basis of religion.[27]

The Eleventh Circuit Court of Appeals recently ruled, in *Killinger v. Samford University* (1997),[28] that these two exemptions in the Civil Rights Act allowed Samford, a Baptist college in Alabama, to remove a professor from the divinity school because of disagreements with the dean over theological views. The Eleventh Circuit interpreted the provisions of Title VII broadly and ruled in favor of the university. The court held that Samford was exempt, even though it could fairly be characterized only as *religiously affiliated* rather than pervasively sectarian. It is still a "religious educational institution." The court also ruled that Samford could take advantage of the second exemption in Title VII. That is, Samford qualifies as an educational institution that is in "substantial part" supported by a religious association, even though the Alabama Baptist Convention no longer appoints trustees to its board and only 7 percent of its budget comes from the convention.

Thus, this case is typical of a trend in the courts to interpret expansively the exemptions for discrimination on the basis of religion for church-affiliated colleges, and the Supreme Court has held that these exemptions, as applied to religious organizations, do not violate the establishment clause.[29]

Institutional Autonomy. Let me conclude with a third genre of issues. Alongside the cases flowing from the establishment and free exercise clauses, there is a long history of jurisprudence called the "church autonomy" or "ecclesiastical issues" doctrine. Basically, this says that the courts will defer to religious organizations to make their own decisions about matters of doctrine, governance, polity, and administration. You often see these cases in the context of employment disputes within religious organizations and property ownership issues surrounding church schisms.

---

[26] Civil Rights Act of 1964, title VII, sec. 702(a), 42 USC § 2000e-1(a).

[27] Ibid., 42 USC § 2000(e).

[28] *Killinger v. Samford University*, 113 F.3d 196 (11th Cir. 1997).

[29] See *Bishop v. Amos*, 483 US 327 (1987).

This doctrine can apply to religious colleges and universities. *Sisam v. Bethel College and Seminary*,[30] involving a Baptist college in St. Paul, Minnesota, is a recent example of this. Bethel has a prohibition on the possession and use of pornographic material, and it holds itself out as a Christian college. In that case, a former student claimed that the college violated its contract with her and other Bethel students because of certain sexual content of films and literature they were obliged to study in class. These included viewing the film version of the novel *The Tin Drum*, which contains several scenes in which child characters engage in sexual activity. The former student also objected to films such as *Like Water for Chocolate* and *Do the Right Thing*.

The court ruled for the college, holding that the claim is an "attack on the general quality of the educational experience Bethel College provided to its students, rather than a claim that Bethel failed to provide specifically promised educational services, such as the delivery of a promised number of hours of instruction." But the court could easily have dismissed the case on the grounds that to decide the case would require it to determine whether Bethel had strayed from the Christian path and, in so doing, invade the constitutional guarantees of institutional autonomy.

In *State of North Carolina v. Pendleton* (1994),[31] a case involving Campbell University, a Baptist-related college in North Carolina, a campus police officer arrested a student for driving while under the influence. The student was convicted but, on appeal, the court dismissed the charges against the student, finding that the delegation of police powers to a private, church-owned institution under North Carolina law violated the separation of church and state. The law is clear that a governmental unit cannot delegate important discretionary governmental power to a religious institution. The court held that Campbell was a "religious institution" because the school's secular purpose and religious mission were "inextricably intertwined."

Conclusion

It is only in the last fifty years that we have seen the twin pillars of the religion clauses applied to the states. The judicial pendulum is swinging from a Supreme Court cautious about the intersection of church and state to

---

[30] *Sisam v. Bethel College and Seminary.*
[31] *State of North Carolina v. Pendleton*, 339 N.C. 379, 451 S.E.2d 274 (1994).

one willing to allow a yield rather than a stop sign. Many questions have yet
to be decided. The sixteen words in the religion clauses remain a fertile field
for exploration and discovery. Perhaps many of you here today recently had
your first exposure to challenges based on religious belief and how that
intersects with a governing authority's nondiscrimination policy. Thus,
conflicts over freedom of religious consciousness and exercise are not
limited to state colleges and universities. These other issues of establishment
and free exercise will continue to impact upon you in your walk through life.
I urge you to practice not merely tolerance but respect for others' religious
beliefs and to stop, look, and listen when you begin to cross into the
fascinating intersection of church and state.

Two Sides of the Same Coin[1]

Matthew 22:15-22; Galatians 5:1, 13-14

You know the story don't you? It started out as a clever plot to trap Jesus, hatched by the most unlikely of allies: Pharisees and Herodians. The Pharisees were religious purists, Jewish patriots who despised Roman rule. The Herodians supported the descendants of Herod and were in league with the Romans. These groups feared Jesus more than they respected God; they despised Jesus more than they hated each other. So they got together to ask Jesus a question that was bound to get him in trouble. With probably a touch of sarcasm in their voices, they said, "Teacher, we know that you are sincere, and teach the way of God, and don't care what people think of you. Tell us what you think—is it lawful to pay a poll tax to Caesar?" It must have happened sometime in April.

They had him! The Jewish people despised the tax. If Jesus said yes, his credibility would be ruined. If he said no, the Romans would charge him with treason. "Either way, we win and Jesus loses."

But Jesus saw through their trick, and he would not be trapped. Nor would he avoid the issue. It had to be addressed. In a day when the state was sacred, Jesus dropped a bombshell that silenced his critics. "Yes," he said, "you do have an obligation to support the government. But the authority of the state has its limits because there is also a duty to God's kingdom, which claims a higher citizenship. So, pay your tax to Caesar—it belongs to him. His picture is on it. But render to God the things that are God's—obedience, service, praise, honor—the things that are due in God's kingdom."

Part of our difficulty here is that Jesus didn't give us specific instructions. He didn't tell us exactly what belonged to whom. He didn't say, for example, how many taxes to pay to Caesar. Remember the Ray Stevens song titled "If 10 Percent Is Good Enough for Jesus, It Ought to Be Enough for Uncle Sam"? Jesus did not say that, and we don't know if Jesus would

---

[1] Unpublished sermon.

support a cut in capital gains tax or repeal the estate tax, as someone in a Sunday school class of mine once tried to argue with a straight face.

But the general principle is clear that we are citizens of two realms—the country in which we live and the kingdom of God. Although the two realms only sometimes clash, they often require us to make difficult choices about to whom to "render."

Jesus used a coin—a denarius—for an object lesson, and this quarter continues to serve us well today. As we think about (1) our allegiance to these two kingdoms, (2) the proper relationship between church and state, and (3) the connection between rights and responsibility, we are confronted by both sides of that coin. The coin always has two sides. We can't simply flip the coin and hope for the best. Faithful discipleship and responsible citizenship require us to grapple with the tension between the two.

Patriotism versus Piety. The first tension is between patriotism and piety. We have always struggled with this. In fact, the coin I'm using for this object lesson bears the religious inscription "In God We Trust" on one side and our secular motto, *E Pluribus Unum*, on the other. Since 1954, our patriotic pledge to Caesar has included the pietistic affirmation "under God."

This dualism has always challenged us, but perhaps never as much as during the past five years. A healthy sense of patriotism is good, natural, and even biblical. In Romans 13, the Apostle Paul tells us to respect civil leaders and governmental structures because they are put in place by God for our protection. Paul relished his Roman citizenship. We should celebrate the goodness of America and thank God for our freedom.

But the same Paul who tells us to respect government authorities also warns us to discriminate when listening to the "rulers of this age" (1 Corinthians 2:6). After all, Romans 13 was the favorite proof text for the German Church during the Nazi reign. And we should always read Romans 13 alongside Revelation 13 and 17 where the state is called a blasphemous beast and a great harlot. As Tony Campolo has said, the USA may be the best Babylon on the face of the earth, but it is still Babylon![2]

In times of national crisis and war, we often see a rise in a "civil religion"—a merger of piety and patriotism—where love of country becomes a secular religion and Jesus is relegated to a deputy secretary of defense. Nor should it surprise us, in a country as religious as ours, that

---

[2] Speech, Religious Liberty Council luncheon, Charlotte NC, June 27, 2003.

references to God will pervade our patriotic songs, our national motto, our civic ceremonies, and public rituals. In its most benign form, civil religion is a unifying balm that reminds us of our religious heritage. However, if we aren't careful, it can quickly morph into an idolatry of nationalism or serve to trivialize religion.

For example, in an attempt to express our patriotism, we often say or sing "God Bless America." When sung in a spirit of worship, "God Bless America" is a beautiful prayer for our country and its leaders—something we are told to do in Scriptures. But when we say "God Bless America" in a spirit of triumph—something of a rallying cry that assumes God is on our side—it is not a pious prayer but a patriotic gloat. It really does matter whether we are kneeling with hands folded or marching with fists raised! When we pray, "God, bless America," we should also pray, "God, bless the whole world: no exceptions." When we sing "God Bless America," we should also sing "Jesus loves the little children, all the children of the world. Red and yellow, black and white, they are precious in his sight. Jesus loves the little children of the world."

Piety and patriotism? They are both good things, but they are not the *same* thing. It is wrong to baptize our political agendas and policy aims in the sacred water of divine approval.

Church versus State. The second tension is the one between church and state on a more legal/constitutional level. Our wise founders gave us the First Amendment to protect our God-given religious liberty by prohibiting the government from entering the precincts of religion. The first sixteen words of the First Amendment provide that "Congress shall make no law respecting an establishment of religion, or prohibiting the free exercise thereof."

Working together, these two clauses—no establishment and free exercise—require government to be neutral toward religion, neither helping nor hurting religion, but turning it loose to allow people of faith to practice their religion as they see fit, not as government sees fit. Government must accommodate religion without advancing it; protect religion without privileging it; sometimes lift burdens on our religious liberty without extending religion a benefit.

Both of these clauses ensure our religious liberty; both require the separation of church and state. Full religious liberty is a goal; church-state separation is the political means of accomplishing that goal.

History teaches that government and religion are both better off when neither tries to do the job of the other. This is especially important in our religiously diverse culture. The plush pluralism that we see in twenty-first-century America demands a robust enforcement of the First Amendment. A separation of the institutions of government and religion promotes a free state and a healthy church.

As we survey history—the Crusades, the Spanish Inquisition, religious wars in seventeenth-century Europe, the jailing of Baptist preachers in colonial Virginia—and contemporary events—the September 11 tragedy, the atrocities of the Taliban, and repressive theocracies from east to west—we see the bad things that happen when religious zeal is combined with coercive power. We are alarmed and shocked by the sectarian violence in Iraq. Americans now should be even more insistent upon upholding the wall of separation our founders erected. As Sandra Day O'Connor wrote in her final church-state opinion before retiring, "Those who would renegotiate the boundaries between church and state must answer a difficult question: Why would we trade a system that has served us so well for one that has served others so poorly?"[3]

I'm afraid we're headed in the opposite direction. Many politicians, pundits, and even people in the pews call for the privileging of Christianity in our laws and long for the restoration of a time that never was.

Some of this is an understandable reaction to the anger and fear we have all shared over the past several years, but we need to be especially careful in times of national crisis and grief—days of heightened nationalism and war—not to forsake the time-honored constitutional principles that make America America. We must insist upon security and freedom. It's a both/and deal.

Rights versus Responsibility. The final tension is between rights and responsibility. Freedom is fundamental to what it means to be an American citizen and a Baptist Christian, but it is important to realize that our freedom is not unlimited. We are to avoid license as well as legalism, and put freedom to good use. After extolling the virtues of Christian freedom, Paul writes in the fifth chapter of Galatians, "Brothers and Sisters, do not use your freedom as an opportunity for self-indulgence, but through love, become slaves to one another. For the whole law is summed up in a single commandment, 'you shall love your neighbor as yourself'" (vv. 13-14).

---

[3] *McCreary County v. ACLU of Kentucky*, 545 US 844 (2005).

Our freedom can never be separated from—and must always be limited by—the responsibility that we have to one another. As Bill Moyers has aptly put it, "[Our Baptist beliefs]...do not make for lawless anarchy or the religion of Lone Rangers.... They aim for a community with moral integrity, the wholeness that flows from mutual obligation. Our religion is an adventure in freedom within the *boundaries of accountability*."[4] Part of what it means to love one's neighbor and to be accountable to one another is to take responsibility for each other's rights and to respect differing opinions—even those with which we disagree. In our diverse religious culture, we will never agree on religious dogma—not even in Baptist life. Nor should we water down our own beliefs to achieve some politically correct (or patriotically correct) superficial consensus. The vague relativism of a lowest-common-denominator religion makes people who take their religion seriously a little queasy. But we can agree to take responsibility for ensuring that everyone has the right to his or her opinion and religious belief. My rights are no stronger than your willingness to stand up for them; your rights are no more secure than my courage to defend them.

Martin Niemoeller, a German Evangelical Lutheran pastor, was imprisoned for eight years by the Nazi regime. He spoke of the days in the early 1930s when Hitler was coming to power: "First they came for the communists, but we were not communists, so we said nothing. Then they came for the trade unionists, but we were not trade unionists, so we said nothing. They then came for the Jews, but we were not Jews, so we said nothing. They then came for the mentally deficient, but we were not mentally deficient, so we said nothing. Then they came for me, and there was no one left to say anything."[5] Pastor Niemoeller's haunting words remind us that liberal protestants, conservative evangelicals, progressive and fundamentalist Baptist and Catholics of every stripe must be as concerned about the religious liberty of the Muslim, the Mormon, the Jew, the Jain, the Rastafarian, the Zoroastrian, the Buddhist, the Baha'i, the Hindu, the Hare Krishna, the Christian Scientist, and the Scientologist as they are for their own.

We've made some strides here in recent years. Many have stepped forward to defend the rights of American Muslims. However, others stupidly

---

[4] Speech, First Baptist Church of the City of Washington, DC, January 19, 1993, reproduced in *Report from the Capital* 48/2 (February 1993): 5.

[5] Leo Stein, *Hitler Came for Niemoeller: The Nazi War against Religion* (1942; repr., Gretna LA: Pelican Pub., 2003).

indict all Muslims for the crimes of a few radical Islamists, forgetting that most Muslims embrace the Qur'an's prohibition on any "compulsion in religion." "Religious liberty for me but not for thee" often characterizes how we treat others. A recent survey shows that nearly half of those polled think church-state separation either goes too far or is unnecessary, and nearly 20 percent are okay with an officially established church. Their own, of course! Forty percent endorse greater surveillance of Islamic mosques.

I worry about how we will treat Muslims and others of Arab decent on our soil as we continue to wage war in Iraq and fight terrorism. I worry about other religious minorities in a culture all too quick to submit rights of conscience to majority vote. We must respect, defend, and stand up for the "least among us"—even those, particularly those, with whom we disagree.

The two sides of that coin continue to confront and challenge us—piety/patriotism, church/state, rights/responsibility. The tension will not go away! Faithful discipleship as followers of Jesus Christ and responsible citizenship in the United States of America require that we pay attention to both sides as we seek to render unto Caesar the things that are Caesar's and unto God the things that are God's.

May the Holy Spirit guide us as we go, and may God forgive and be gracious unto us if we don't quite get it right.

SCOTUS

(Supreme Court of the United States)

Congress shall make no law respecting an establishment of religion, or prohibiting the free exercise thereof

Turf Wars[1]

It was the most important and popular piece of religious liberty legislation since the First Amendment was ratified more than 200 years ago.

It was suggested by the broadest coalition of religious groups ever assembled in the United States: Jews and Muslims, Buddhists and Baptists, Christian Scientists and Scientologists, Latter-day Saints and Seventh-day Adventists, and nearly every stripe of mainline and evangelical denomination.

It was sponsored by unlikely allies: Senators Orrin Hatch (R-UT), Ted Kennedy (D-MA), Representatives Charles Schumer (D-NY) and Christopher Cox (R-CA), along with 532 members of Congress. Only three voted no, probably because the act applied to prisoners.

It was signed by a Baptist president and touted as one of the Clinton administration's most important first-term accomplishments.

It was applauded by most of the academic community, hailed by the Left and the Right, and welcomed by all religious minorities who had felt the brunt of persecution and intolerance. Only a handful of people thought this landmark legislation—the Religious Freedom Restoration Act of 1993 (RFRA)—was poor policy and/or unconstitutional. That is the good news. The bad news is that six of them sit on the United States Supreme Court.

What Happened?
The First Amendment forbids government from prohibiting the free exercise of religion. As a practical matter, however, government must restrict religion under certain circumstances, an act that should be the exception, not the rule. Accordingly, the Supreme Court for many years required government to show a compelling interest (i.e., health and safety) before it would be allowed to burden the exercise of religion, and then only if it had selected the least restrictive means of advancing that interest. Stringent, if not absolute, protection for the "first freedom" was the order of the day.

---

[1] *Liberty* 92/6, November/December 1997, pp. 6–9.

In 1990 this changed. In *Employment Division v. Smith* (1990),[2] the Court deprived the free exercise clause of any meaningful protections. Writing that robust protection for religious freedom is a "luxury" we can no longer afford, a five-justice majority did away with the compelling interest test in most cases. If religion is singled out for discriminatory treatment, then strict judicial scrutiny would still apply. But where protection is needed most—to ensure that neutral laws do not indirectly burden the practice of religion—there would be no bar to governmental interference with religion. The Court concluded that it was the province of the legislative branch, not the judiciary, to extend to religious practice an exception from neutral, generally applicable laws.

The outcry was swift and widespread. Fifty-four law professors and a score of religious groups petitioned the Court to reconsider its decision. Denied! The sixty-eight-member Coalition for the Free Exercise of Religion quickly formed to urge Congress to take the Court up on its offer—to exempt religious practice from burdensome governmental interference. This is precisely what Congress sought to do in passing RFRA: create statutory protection for religious freedom in the wake of the Court's refusal to recognize any meaningful constitutional rights. Rather than legislating piecemeal, Congress chose to protect everyone's religious freedom in one fell swoop and once again require government—federal, state, and local—to have a compelling state interest before substantially burdening religious practice.

Thus, RFRA was a "mile wide and an inch deep," as legal scholar Doug Laycock has said. It applied across the board to all persons of faith, but instead of creating outright exemptions, it only tilted the playing field in religion's direction by requiring government to have a good reason before fiddling with our first freedom.

The salutary effect of RFRA was dramatic. During the three and a half years between *Smith* and the passage of RFRA, persons of faith rarely prevailed in a free exercise claim against government. Only a few cases were won under the more protective provisions in state constitutions.[3] But during

---

[2] *Employment Division v. Smith*, 494 US 872 (1990).

[3] E.g., *Cooper v. French*, 460 N.W.2d 2 (MN 1990); *First Covenant Church v. City of Seattle*, 840 P. 2d 174 (1992); *Minnesota v. Hershberger*, 462 N.W.2d 393 (MN 1990); *Society of Jesus v. Boston Landmarks Common*, 409 Mass. 38, 564 N.E.2d 571 (1990).

the three and a half years following RFRA's passage, the tables turned and the free exercise claimant prevailed much more often.

For example, when the city government in Washington, DC, tried to use its zoning laws to prevent a Presbyterian church from feeding the homeless, the court ruled for the church.[4] A California court barred the state from trying to force a Jehovah's Witness employee to take a loyalty oath, and thereby protected the right of conscience.[5] When a bankruptcy court ordered a church to turn over a tithe given by the debtor years before in good faith, the court stopped the state-sponsored raid on the collection plate.[6] The court ruled in each of these cases that under RFRA the government had failed to prove an interest sufficiently compelling to trump the free exercise of religion.

In these and numerous other cases, RFRA's constitutionality was challenged. The arguments usually asserted were that in passing RFRA, Congress breached the separation of powers doctrine, interfered with states' rights, and violated the First Amendment's prohibition on establishing religion.

Arguments marshaled and presented in RFRA's defense included the following:

1. Congress was not attempting to overrule a Supreme Court decision or tell the Court how to interpret the Constitution; it was simply protecting a fundamental right by statute after the Court declined to recognize such a right under the Constitution.

2. Congress was not seeking to trample on the sovereign rights of the states; it was only trying to require the states under the Fourteenth Amendment to the Constitution to honor the rights enjoyed by its people as American citizens.

3. Congress did not improperly advance religion in passing RFRA; it was only accommodating religion by shielding it from unwarranted governmental interference.

---

[4] *Western Presbyterian Church v. Board of Zoning Adjustments*, 862 F. Supp. 538 (D. DC 1994).

[5] *Bessard v. California Community Colleges*, 867 F. Supp. 1454 (E.D. CA 1994).

[6] In re Young, 82 F.3d 1407 (8th Cir. 1996), vacated and remanded, 65 US L.W. 3860 (June 27, 1997).

In response to these arguments, every appellate court—including four federal courts of appeal—upheld RFRA's constitutionality.[7] This included the New Orleans-based Fifth Circuit Court of Appeals' decision in *City of Boerne v. Flores*.[8] Because of the importance of this issue, the US Supreme Court agreed to review *Flores*. In an opinion written by Justice Kennedy, the Court declared RFRA unconstitutional. A majority of six justices ruled that Congress violated principles of federalism by requiring the states to comply with RFRA. The Court reasoned that section 5 of the Fourteenth Amendment did not give Congress substantive powers to say what the Constitution means; and though Congress has *remedial* power under that section to "enforce" other constitutional rights, RFRA transgressed that limited role. The Court wrote, "While the line between measures that remedy or prevents unconstitutional actions and measures that make a substantive change in governing law is not easy to discern, and Congress must have wide latitude in determining where it lies, the distinction exists and must be observed."[9]

Stressing that there must be "a congruence and proportionality between the injury to be prevented or remedied and the means adapted to that end," the Court concluded that RFRA lacked that connection and therefore was unconstitutional. Specifically, the Court faulted Congress for failing to amass a sufficient record of religious discrimination (as opposed to indirect burdens) to justify its sweeping legislative response.

One can critique the Court's opinion on a variety of scores.

1. Although Congress cannot tell the Court how to interpret the Constitution, it should have the right to protect, by legislation, the basic liberties of US citizens and to make sure the states do not encroach on these liberties.

2. Even if Congress has no authority to define substantive constitutional rights, RFRA should survive scrutiny as "remedial" to the

---

[7] *Mockaitis v. Harcleroad*, 104 F.3d 1522 (9th Cir. 1997); *Sasnett v. Sullivan*, 91 F.3d 1018 (7th Cir. 1996), vacated, 65 US L.W. 3850 (1997); *EEOC v. Catholic University*, 83 F.3d 455 (DC Cir. 1996); *Flores v. City of Boerne*, 73 F.3d 1352 (5th Cir. 1996); *State v. Miller*, 538 N.W.2d 573 (WI App. 1995), aff'd other grounds 549 N.W.2d 235 (WI 1996); *South Jersey Catholic School Teachers Association v. St. Teresa Elementary School*, 675 A.2d 1155, 1167 (NJ Super. App. Div.), cert. granted on other grounds 683 A.2d 1162 (NJ 1996).

[8] *City of Boerne v. Flores*, 65 US LW 4612 (1997).

[9] Ibid., 4615.

extent it seeks to enforce the *Smith* case's prohibition on discrimination against religion.[10]

3. The Court's insistence on "proportionality and congruence" between the ends and means is a novel principle of law and smacks of judicial activism.

4. The Court's statement that RFRA's "least restrictive means" requirement was not used in pre-*Smith* jurisprudence is simply wrong.

5. The Court's observation that RFRA's legislative record is devoid of examples of "religious bigotry...[or] persecution...in the past 40 years" ignores the fact that religious discrimination often lurks behind facially neutral laws.

6. The Court's opinion is ambiguous about whether RFRA continues to apply to the federal government, and it gives Congress almost no guidance about the scope of its Fourteenth Amendment powers.

What to Do About What Happened
Though the criticism of the *Flores* opinion could continue,[11] the academic faultfinding must give way to practical solutions. The Court clearly has the right to interpret the Constitution and strike down laws that it judges to be unconstitutional,[12] but religious freedom is too sacred a right to be left on the floor of the Supreme Court chambers. As Senator Edward Kennedy has said, "This decision cannot be the final word."

Here are some suggestions on how we can protect religious freedom while respecting (although disagreeing with) the Court's decision. Indeed, the Coalition for the Free Exercise of Religion has decided to urge these steps to that end. First, Congress should adopt immediately a joint resolution stating its conviction that religious liberty is not a "luxury," but a fundamental right, and resolving to find ways to protect religious liberty beyond that afforded in *Smith*. The *Flores* decision can be read to say that RFRA still applies to the federal government even though it has been struck down *vis-à-vis* the states. Congress should remove any doubt by unequivocally reaffirming in the resolution its intention to apply RFRA to federal agencies.

---

[10] *Employment Division v. Smith*, 494 US 872 (1990).
[11] *City of Boerne v. Flores*, 521 US 507 (1997).
[12] *Marbury v. Madison*, 5 US (1 Cranch) 137 (1803).

Second, Congress should adopt a RFRA-like statute under other congressional powers set forth in article I of the Constitution, including its spending power and its power to regulate interstate commerce. Congress's spending powers have been used before as a jurisdictional predicate for other similar legislation. Title VI of the Civil Rights Act of 1964,[13] which prohibited programs receiving federal funds from discriminating on the basis of race, as well as the Equal Access Act of 1984,[14] which authorized religious clubs in the public schools, are based on this power. Governmental units administering federally funded programs would have to agree to protect the religious freedom of the programs' beneficiaries.

While Congress's spending power would tend to protect individuals, the rights of religious organizations could be protected under the Commerce Clause. Most churches affect interstate commerce to some extent. Although the Court has cut back on Congress's commerce powers, scholars are confident that such an exercise of power could be sustained. Models for the exercise of this power can be found in the Privacy Protection Act of 1980[15] and Title II of the 1964 Civil Rights Act,[16] dealing with public accommodations.

The drawback to tying RFRA to Congress's spending and commerce powers is, of course, that it would afford less than comprehensive coverage. Nevertheless, this federal legislative remedy would be an important part of a more comprehensive solution.

Third, there is nothing in the Court's opinion to suggest that the states could not choose to bind themselves to heightened protection for religion. Accordingly, we must encourage the adoption of "little RFRAs" at the state level. Some states already have greater protection as a matter of state constitutional interpretation. These include Maine, Massachusetts, Minnesota, Washington, Montana, Kansas, and probably California. Others—such as Connecticut and Rhode Island—already have little RFRAs. Others—Florida, Michigan, Ohio, and New York—have legislation pending. The states should use RFRA as a model act and resist political pressures to carve out exemptions or reduce the level of judicial scrutiny from compelling state interest.

---

[13] 42 USC sec. 2000d (1994).
[14] 20 USC sec. 4071 (1994).
[15] 42 USC sec. 2000aa (1994).
[16] 42 USC sec. 2000a (1994).

Fourth, we must urge the Court at the appropriate time to overrule *Smith*. This gets to the heart of the matter. Once the *Smith* problem is fixed and strict scrutiny is restored as a constitutional right, there is little or no need for legislation. The three *Flores* dissenters—Justices O'Connor, Souter, and Breyer—suggested this avenue of relief. The trouble is that only three wanted to do it, and five are needed. Thus, this is a long-term strategy and must await a retirement or two, or a conversion of one or more members of the majority.[17]

Additional alternatives have been offered that, while they may have some merit, do not enjoy widespread support. For example, some have suggested tying RFRA to Congress's treaty powers to enact legislation to implement the International Covenant on Civil and Political Rights. But by all accounts this may be a political non-starter, particularly on the political right.

Others have called for specific, targeted legislation addressed to some of the more problematic areas of government activity such as zoning, landmarking, and prison administration. However, these would afford only a limited scope of protection and would draw political fire from affected interest groups.

Finally, a few have advocated a constitutional amendment that is narrowly focused on the protection of free exercise. The drawbacks to a constitutional amendment are obvious. It probably would not pass without harmful changes either in the form of specific exemptions or in proposals like Representative Ernest Istook's "Religious Liberty Amendment," which would obliterate the First Amendment's establishment clause. In any event, it would take years to be ratified by the states, leaving religious freedom unprotected in the meantime. A constitutional amendment is a remedy of last resort; it should not be pursued unless all else has failed.

The Court's decisions in *Smith* and *Flores*, taken together, are tragic. They leave in their wake precious little protection for religious freedom. But that is not the end of the story. Robust religious freedom must and will be restored. Not only is religious freedom not a "luxury"; it is a fundamental God-given right that we cannot live without. Persons of faith will lay aside their theological and political differences to seek something that transcends their disagreements—religious liberty for all.

---

[17] Although Justice Ginsburg voted with the majority on the constitutional issue, I am hopeful that she would reverse *Smith* on a straight up-and-down vote.

On the Confirmation
of David Souter[1]

Events swirling around Washington, DC, lately have been dizzying—from the S&L crisis, to the Middle East conflict, to threatened furloughs and Gramm-Rudman sequestration, to the student takeover at the University of the District of Columbia. But cutting through all of this morass and capturing the imagination and curiosity of the public was that terribly laconic, somewhat reclusive, Pat Paulsen-look-alike Supreme Court nominee, David Souter. As court watchers scrambled to follow the tracks laid down by the jurist over his twenty-five-year legal career, the paucity of information only added to the shroud of mystery around him and piqued the public's interest more.

Judge Souter's record on church-state relations is as meager as that in any other area of law. Although he had been a trial court judge and a state supreme court justice for a number of years, only two cases illustrate a church-state philosophy. In both, he was attorney general for the state of New Hampshire, not a judge trying to decide a dispute objectively. So the church-state community waited with baited breath to hear what Judge Souter would say to the Senate Judiciary Committee on church-state issues.

Historically, Supreme Court nominees have been loathe to commit themselves ahead of time to positions on specific questions of law, especially ones that have a chance of being decided by the Court in upcoming terms. Not only would such an advance ruling be jurisprudentially premature, it would politically unwise—as Judge Bork found out three years ago.[2] Nevertheless, Supreme Court nominees can be expected to expound on their basic judicial philosophy, demonstrate requisite expertise in constitutional law, and show appropriate judicial temperament.

Despite Judge Souter's desire to keep most of his answers general, he became as specific about the church-state questions as any. First, with

---

[1] *Report from the Capital* 45/10 (November/December 1990): 6.

[2] Federal Circuit Court Judge Robert Bork was nominated by President Reagan to serve on the US Supreme Court. After an acrimonious debate, Judge Bork's nomination was not confirmed by the US Senate.

respect to the no establishment clause, he was asked by Senator Leahy about his defense of New Hampshire Governor Thomson's executive order requiring that the state flag be flown at half-mast on Good Friday "to memorialize the death of Christ on the Cross...."[3] Souter answered that he was only representing his client—the governor—and conceded that if he were judging the case today, rather than advocating one side, he probably would declare the action unconstitutional.

Moreover, Senator Specter asked Judge Souter whether, on a continuum, he would align himself with Mr. Jefferson's wall of separation or with Justice Rehnquist's "non-preferentialism" (i.e., allowing some governmental aid to all religion as long as it does not show preference). Souter responded that, while he had some problems with the *Lemon* test (i.e., a three-pronged test the court uses to decide establishment clause cases),[4] he nevertheless had no reason to reexamine the basic presuppositions embodied in the Jeffersonian metaphor or in *Everson v. Board of Education* (1947),[5] which incorporated it.

On the free exercise side of the First Amendment, Judge Souter's only tracks again are found in the New Hampshire statehouse rather than in any courtroom. As attorney general he had approved the prosecution of a Jehovah's Witness who, objecting to the motto "Live Free or Die," obliterated those words from his license plate. The Jehovah's Witness felt strongly that such words were inconsistent with his religious faith. New Hampshire's brief in the US Supreme Court claimed that the Jehovah's Witness's conduct was "whimsy or bizarre behavior" that fell short of First Amendment protection.[6] Again, Judge Souter claimed only to have been representing his client but conceded that the state did not have a "compelling interest" in requiring the exhibition of the motto on the license plate.

Judge Souter further testified that he favored "strict scrutiny" for fundamental rights, including free exercise of religion. He was aware of *Employment Division v. Smith* (1990), which overturned the compelling state interest doctrine in free exercise jurisprudence.[7] Souter seemed to be more

---

[3] Ruth Marcus and Joe Pichinallo, "Souter's Life in the Law Detached Intellect over Idealogy," *Washington Post*, September 13, 1990, A1.

[4] Decided in *Lemon v. Kurtzman*, 403 US 602 (1971).

[5] *Everson v. Board of Education*, 330 US 1 (1947).

[6] *Wooley v. Maynard*, 430 US 705 (1977).

[7] *Employment Division v. Smith*, 494 US 872 (1990).

comfortable with Justice O'Connor's concurring opinion, which found against Native Americans' right to use peyote in religious worship but upheld the all-important compelling state interest doctrine.

On balance, Souter's answers appear to be "right" in church-state issues. Of course, none of his testimony can be taken as a firm commitment, but assuming, as we must, that he is proceeding in good faith, he appears to be headed in the right direction for the lovers of religious liberty.

This is extremely important. Recent decisions of the Court indicate that there are at least four justices who are ready either to abandon or water down the Court's historic establishment clause jurisprudence. For example, Justice Rehnquist wants to abandon Jefferson's "wall" metaphor entirely and would interpret the establishment clause only to forbid a "national religion" or preference among religious sects or denominations.[8] Justices Kennedy, White, and Scalia would limit establishment clause protection of governmental coercion directly benefiting religion to a degree that in fact establishes a state religion or tends to do so.[9] Even Justice O'Connor would revise the *Lemon* criteria to incorporate an arguably less stringent "endorsement" test.[10]

Moreover, as we saw last term, five justices have already demonstrated their willingness and ability to violate the free exercise clause without remorse. Justice Scalia has written, and Justices Rehnquist, White, Kennedy, and Stevens concur, that complete religious liberty is a "luxury" we can ill afford as a society and that any society adopting full-bodied religious liberty in the historic Baptist sense would be "courting anarchy."[11]

Thus, Judge Souter's position on First Amendment issues becomes critically important as this new, conservative-leaning, philosophically statist Court moves into the 1990s. We cannot expect Judge Souter to fill William Brennan's strong leadership role in church-state cases, at least not immediately. However, one hopes that Judge Souter's voting record will be as good as Brennan's and that in time he will be able to steer the Court in a direction that will restore our "first liberty" to the constitutional preeminence that it deserves.

---

[8] See *Wallace v. Jaffree*, 472 US 38 (1985).
[9] *Allegheny County v. Greater Pittsburgh ACLU*, 492 US 573 (1989).
[10] See *Lynch v. Donnelly*, 465 US 668 (1984).
[11] See *Employment Division v. Smith* 494 US 872 (1990).

On the Confirmation
of Clarence Thomas[1]

The Senate Judiciary Committee has just finished reviewing President George Bush's second nominee for the Supreme Court. Although the confirmation of David Souter last year gave the conservatives on the Court a working majority on most issues, the confirmation proceedings of Clarence Thomas are still vitally important. If he serves until the age at which his predecessor retired, Judge Thomas's tenure on the court will have spanned ten presidential terms! Thus, Judge Thomas, if confirmed, will powerfully influence the country's jurisprudence decades into the twenty-first century.

Judge Thomas has a mixed and scant record on religious liberty and church-state separation. As a judge he decided no church-state cases. As director of Equal Employment Opportunity Commission, Thomas signed a policy advisory requiring religious institutions to give equal benefits to employees who do not adhere to the institution's religious tenets and another ruling that companies who use "new age" motivational programs cannot force employees to attend if it violates their religious beliefs. As a public speaker, Judge Thomas told the Heritage Foundation in 1985, "My mother says that when they took God out of the schools, the schools went to hell. She may be right."[2] Finally, as a husband, Judge Thomas might be less tolerant of minority religion, some have speculated, because of Mrs. Thomas's involvement in the Cult Awareness Network—a clearinghouse and advocacy group fighting cults. It was against this backdrop of a spotty record on church-state relations that Judge Thomas was called upon by the committee to give his views.

With respect to the no establishment clause, Sen. Paul Simon asked Judge Thomas whether he agreed with the *Lemon* test that requires government to be neutral toward religion.[3] Judge Thomas responded that he had no "personal disagreement" with the test but understood that it had

---

[1] *Report from the Capital* 46/9 (October 1991): 7.
[2] Nancy Gibbs, "America's Holy War," *Time*, December 9, 1991.
[3] Decided in *Lemon v. Kurtzman*, 403 US 602 (1971).

been difficult for the Court to apply. He also endorsed the wall of separation as an "appropriate metaphor" and opined that it was good to "keep government out of our religions and...separation between our religious lives and the government."[4]

This is important testimony. The Court will soon hear *Lee v. Weisman*.[5] The administration is asking the court to adopt, in place of the *Lemon* test, a so-called "coercion" test allowing considerably more governmental involvement in and promotion of religion. If we take Judge Thomas at his word, his description of the Jeffersonian wall as an "appropriate metaphor" suggests that he might not side with the four justices who argued for some species of the coercion test (Rehnquist, Kennedy, Scalia, and White) but would tend to vote with the more separationist wing of the Court and possibly adopt Justice Sandra Day O'Connor's "endorsement" test.

A note of caution, however: not everyone who says he believes in church-state separation really means it. Even Jerry Falwell and other members of the religious right have given lip service to church-state separation, but they take a one-sided view of this doctrine. They believe government should not hamper religion but argue that it is appropriate for government to aid religion. Judge Thomas's testimony here was too incomplete to know for certain whether he understands that true separation cuts both ways.

On the free exercise clause, Sen. Strom Thurmond asked Judge Thomas what he thought about *Employment Division v. Smith* (the so-called peyote decision that did away with the compelling state interest doctrine in free exercise cases).[6] Judge Thomas acknowledged that the majority opinion by Justice Scalia was an "important departure from prior approaches," but he would not say he disagreed with the decision. Judge Thomas later told Chairman Joseph Biden that he did not want to take an "absolutist" position but said that the proper approach would be the one that "maximizes [free exercise] protection."

Here, too, Judge Thomas's responses appear to go in the right direction. If he sticks by what he said, there is some hope that he will not join the statist, conservative wing of the Court that routinely defers to the

---

[4] Senate Confirmation Hearings, September 11, 1991.
[5] *Lee v. Weisman*, 505 US 577 (1992).
[6] *Employment Division v. Smith*, 494 US 872 (1990).

political branches of government at the expense of individual liberties. But, amid charges of "vanishing views," "confirmation conversion," and "unartful dodging"—and in light of evasive answers on civil rights, abortion, and employment opportunity—no one can be sure where Judge Thomas will wind up on any specific issue.

Judge Thomas's tendency to embrace natural law is also a confusing factor. Natural law is that school of jurisprudence that recognizes fixed principles of right and wrong that lie behind and transcend government's attempt to express moral precepts in constitutions and statutes. Some think these principles emanate from religious sources, others from secular moral truths. Although natural law thinking can lead to abuses (e.g., defense of slavery, exclusion of women from the legal profession, upholding economic rights over social legislation), it can provide a bulwark for liberty (e.g., religious liberty is a God-given right). One would hope that Judge Thomas's affinity for natural law would help him resist the tendency of the present Court to read the constitutional text narrowly and inhospitably. For example, if one believes that religious liberty results not from an act of toleration by the state, but as a gift from God, he would be hard pressed to join the majority in the *Smith* case. This is natural law working at its best.

But Judge Thomas waffled even on his natural law testimony. Instead of embracing natural law to the extent that it preserves individual freedom and rejecting it to the extent that it is abused for a contrary purpose, Judge Thomas disassociated himself from it altogether as a guide for constitutional decision-making. Instead, he testified that natural law was important only as a political theory that lies behind our constitutional wisdom. In summary, Thomas's natural law testimony sheds little light on how he will decide cases including church-state issues.

Finally, there is some thinking that, because of Judge Thomas's African American heritage, humble origins, and experience with discrimination, he will bring some measure of counter-majoritarian thinking to the court and that, because of his youth, he is likely to grow and develop in office. There may be some merit to these contentions. Again, it is difficult to tell. It's a long way from Pin Point, Georgia, to the lofty heights of the Supreme Court bench. And, even if Judge Thomas matures into a full-fledged libertarian, we will only be even. After all, it is Thurgood Marshall—a staunch defender of the Bill of Rights—whom he is replacing.

At the writing of this column, the hearings have just been completed, and although the Senate has not yet voted, many observers think that Judge

Thomas will become Justice Thomas. While his answers on church-state relations tended to be right, one would have hoped for a less tentative endorsement of government neutrality and a more forceful commitment to free exercise. Only time will tell whether his inchoate answers ripen into good judicial decisions.

Religious Equality's Level Playing Field Levels Religion, Harms Liberty[1]

I am often asked what I consider the biggest threats to religious liberty as we enter the twenty-first century. My reply is always the same: religious equality and majoritarian religion. Say what? As a democracy, don't we decide the major issues of our day by majority vote? And what could possibly be wrong with "religious equality"? Shouldn't religious people have the same rights as everybody else?

The answer to both of these questions is yes, but it is a bit tricky. We elect our leaders and decide public policy issues by majority vote, but the Bill of Rights—including the first sixteen words protecting religious liberty—operates just the opposite. It is, in Justice O'Connor's words, "counter-majoritarian," protecting against the tyranny of the majority.[2]

This majoritarian attitude is directly related to the insidious notion of "religious equality." Yes, all religions should be treated equally, one with another. And, yes, in a forum for speech by private citizens (e.g., Bible clubs in public schools, churches renting space in public buildings, etc.), religious speech should be treated the same as secular speech. However, when government treats religion the same as secular pursuits, religious liberty is threatened. Religious liberty is best secured when government treats religion differently.

Deferring to the will of the majority and treating religion the same as secular activities is precisely the mentality that informed the Supreme Court's disastrous opinion in *Employment Division v. Smith*—holding that as long as a law is facially neutral and generally applicable, religion should get no special exemption.[3] Thus, religion has the right only to be treated no worse than secular enterprises, but no right to be treated any better.

There are numerous ways in which religion is and should be given special consideration to lift burdens on the exercise of religion. First Baptist

---

[1] *Report from the Capital* 55/8 (April 18, 2000): 3.
[2] *Employment Division v. Smith*, 494 US 872, 903 (1990).
[3] Ibid.

Church is allowed to hire a Baptist music director instead of a Buddhist; McDonald's down the street cannot discriminate on the basis of religion. Calvary Baptist Church is exempt from being forced to install ramps and elevators under the Americans with Disabilities Act; the Holiday Inn around the corner, however, must comply. Lobbyists on K Street are obliged to register under the lobbying disclosure laws; religious lobbies on Capitol Hill are exempt. The United Way has to file Form 990 with the IRS disclosing a variety of data about its operation; religious nonprofits are exempt from this burdensome requirement.

Religion should be treated differently under the First Amendment's establishment clause as well. Public school teachers can voice the Pledge of Allegiance, recite the Gettysburg Address, and say a lot of other things in the class, but they may not lead in prayer or preside over religious exercises. Government may fund many things, including the public schools, but it may not fund parochial schools or other forms of religious speech. Government may hang a picture of the president in public buildings or of George Washington in schools, but it ordinarily may not display a religious symbol or a portrait of Jesus. These limitations on religion operate to ensure government neutrality and promote religious liberty for all, especially for the minority.

But the trend in our country and among several Supreme Court justices is in the other direction: to defer to the majority, without giving religion any special protection under the free exercise clause and no limitations under the establishment clause.

Don't be taken in by plaintive calls for "majority rule" and the seductive rhetoric about "religious equality." The majority in a democracy can sometimes be as tyrannical as a dictator in a totalitarian regime, especially with regard to religion, and the notion of religious equality really demeans religion and vitiates religious freedom. If you level the playing field for religion, don't be surprised when religion gets "leveled."

Religion is special and different. Religious liberty is best preserved by treating it as such.

Justice Powell Kept Low Profile
but Made Big Impact on Court[1]

Last week Lewis F. Powell Jr., retired justice of the Supreme Court, died at
the age of ninety. He was one of those low-profile justices that members of
the general public most likely would not recognize on the street. If asked to
name the nine justices of his day, most probably would have left him out,
but he made an indelible mark on the court and American constitutional
law.

Justice Powell was special in several ways. He was one of the few post-
World War II nominees to come from private practice rather than from the
bench, government, or academia. He was also older than most justices when
he ascended the bench. When nominated in 1972 to replace Hugo Black,
Powell already had completed a forty-year career as a prominent attorney
(including a stint as president of the ABA) and, at sixty-four, was close to the
age when many retire. He was a lifelong Democrat who was nominated by a
Republican president, Richard Nixon. He was uncharacteristically humble
and self-effacing. Because of his advanced age and lack of judicial experience,
he had serious misgivings about going on the Court. In fact, he turned
Nixon down when he was first asked to serve.

Justice Powell will be remembered primarily as a swing voter—a
majority maker and breaker—much the same role Justice Sandra Day
O'Connor plays today. He occupied the pragmatic, sensible center of the
court during his fifteen years of service. Regardless of whether one agreed
with how he voted, one could be assured that it was a principled decision in
which he sought to interpret and apply the law with care and integrity.

This centrist voting pattern can be seen in his church-state
jurisprudence. For example, Justice Powell wrote the majority opinion in
Committee for Public Education and Religious Liberty v. Nyquist (1973).[2] In this
seminal establishment clause case, the Court declared unconstitutional a

---

[1] *Report from the Capital* 53/17 (September 1, 1998): 3.
[2] *Committee for Public Education and Religious Liberty v. Nyquist*, 413 US 756
(1973).

New York law that provided financial assistance to parochial elementary and secondary schools, including direct aid, tuition reimbursement, and tuition tax credits. But in *Widmar v. Vincent* (1981), Powell wrote a landmark opinion, recognizing college students' right to use state university facilities to meet for religious worship and discussion and opined that such use did not violate the establishment clause.[3] This decision set the tone for passage of the Equal Access Act of 1984 in which Congress extended the same rights to students in secondary schools. In sum, Justice Powell delicately and faithfully applied the *Lemon* test[4] in establishment clause cases in a way that resulted in benevolent governmental neutrality, rather than hostility, to religion.

Justice Powell's free exercise jurisprudence was less laudable. Although he properly appreciated the need to keep government from advancing religion, Justice Powell was less assiduous in requiring government to accommodate the exercise of religion. For example, he joined a plurality opinion, along with Chief Justice Burger and then-justice Rehnquist in *Bowen v. Roy* (1986),[5] denying a Native American's religiously based objection to using a Social Security number. This decision foreshadowed the decimation of the free exercise clause four years later in *Employment Division v. Smith* (1990),[6] when the plurality became a Court majority. Moreover, Justice Powell voted with the majority in *Goldman v. Weinberger* (1986),[7] which upheld the right of the Air Force to forbid an Orthodox Jewish rabbi to war his yarmulke when in uniform.

But, on balance, Justice Powell's tenure on the Court was a positive one. We will continue to long for intelligent, practical, and commonsense jurists like Justice Powell who decide cases based on an honest interpretation of the Constitution as an organic document protecting the freedom of all Americans. This Virginia gentleman stood squarely in the tradition of earlier Virginians—Jefferson, Madison, and Mason—who crafted the Constitution he so faithfully sought to interpret.

---

[3] *Widmar v. Vincent*, 454 US 263 (1981).
[4] Decided in *Lemon v. Kurtzman*, 403 US 602 (1971).
[5] *Bowen v. Roy*, 476 US 693 (1986).
[6] *Employment Division v. Smith*, 494 US 872 (1990).
[7] *Goldman v. Weinberger*, 475 US 503 (1986).

New Court Test Hinders
Free Exercise Claims[1]

Last year the Supreme Court dropped a constitutional bombshell that nearly destroyed the First Amendment's free exercise clause. The case, *Employment Division v. Smith*, should have been fairly routine.[2] Two members of the Native American Church claimed they had a free exercise right to use peyote as a sacrament in their religious worship. Most constitutional scholars expected the court to apply established precedent and simply decide whether the state of Oregon had demonstrated a "compelling interest" in restricting the Native Americans' religious practice.

The compelling state interest doctrine requires that any attempt by government to burden an individual's religious liberty will be closely scrutinized by the courts. The courts will allow such governmental action only if the state demonstrates that it was advancing an interest of the very highest order and that it had chosen the least restrictive means of doing so.

Few court watchers were surprised when the Court ruled that the Native Americans did not have the right to ingest peyote as a sacrament, but they stood in slack-jawed amazement when Justice Antonin Scalia, writing for a 5-4 majority, all but overturned the compelling state interest doctrine itself and substituted a less stringent "reasonableness" test under which the government will almost always win. Justice Scalia wrote that our pluralistic society cannot tolerate strict judicial scrutiny of every alleged violation of religious liberty because to do so would court "anarchy." He even called this liberty-protecting doctrine a "luxury" that we can no longer afford.

Hoping to communicate forcefully the gravity of the Court's erroneous decision, some eighteen religious and civil liberties groups and fifty-five constitutional scholars joined in a petition for rehearing. The court summarily denied the petition.

In the ten months since *Smith* was decided, our worst fears about its consequences have been realized. It has directly impacted some fifteen state

---

[1] *Report from the Capital* 46/3 (March 1991): 3.
[2] *Employment Division v. Smith*, 494 US 872 (1990).

and federal court decisions that have already been reported in the law books. (One can only speculate on the number of additional such cases pending in the trial courts across the country.) The precedential tentacles of the *Smith* decision extend far beyond peyote and the Native American Church. They have reached to cases involving religious objections to traffic ordinances, mandatory autopsies, burdensome zoning laws, restrictions on prisoners, and historical landmarking regulations. *Smith* has affected not only minority sects—such as the Amish, Hmongs, and Quakers—but mainline Episcopalians, Orthodox Jews, Roman Catholics, and Baptists as well.

Under the less stringent reasonableness standard called for by *Smith*, free exercise claimants have won only three of the fifteen cases, and in two of those cases the state court did an "end run" around *Smith* and based on its decision on its own state constitution. Additionally, several of the lower federal courts that were required to follow *Smith* did so reluctantly and made their displeasure clear in their written opinions.

What is the answer to this most unfortunate situation? First, we can continue to take free exercise cases to the Supreme Court and argue that *Smith* should be overruled or at least limited in its application. However, even a cursory reading of the *Smith* decision reveals that the majority knew exactly what it was doing. Also, it was mainly the younger justices who led the way. Thus, there is little reason to think that the court will reverse itself anytime soon.

Second, we can continue to bring cases through the state court systems and ask the state supreme courts to rule in favor of free exercise under the state constitutions. As mentioned, this has already been done. This avenue is not entirely satisfactory, however, because not all states have more generous free exercise provisions in their constitutions.

The Baptist Joint Committee believes the best solution lies with Congress. In the waning months of the 101st congress, Reps. Stephen Solarz (D-NY), and Paul Henry (R-MI), introduced the Religious Freedom Restoration Act. This bill seeks to undo the damage done by *Smith*. It will not legalize peyote or advance anyone's particular religious belief or practice. Rather, it will turn the clock back and restore the compelling state interest test to all free exercise cases.

The bill has broad bipartisan support. To have Barney Frank and Newt Gingrich in the House and Joseph Biden and Orrin Hatch in the Senate all cosponsoring a bill is remarkable. A diverse coalition of religious and civil liberties groups have endorsed the bill. Who can imagine a more motley alliance than one that includes the American Civil Liberties Union and the National Association of Evangelicals, the American Jewish Committee and the American Muslim Council? The bill likely will be reintroduced and taken up by the new Congress shortly.

It is time for all lovers of liberty (especially our "first liberty"—the free exercise of religion) to rally behind this legislative initiative. Reestablishing the compelling state interest doctrine would not be to court anarchy. It is precisely *because* of the rich mix of religious practice in our country that we need strict judicial scrutiny of any attempt to limit or homogenize it. The robust religious liberty this doctrine promotes is not a luxury we can ill afford. It is a fundamental *right* we cannot afford to live without.

On the Confirmation
of Ruth Bader Ginsburg[1]

The confirmation of Ruth Bader Ginsburg as the 107th justice of the US Supreme Court was unusual in many ways. Judge Ginsburg, the first justice appointed by a Democrat in more than a quarter century, comes to the high bench with extraordinary qualifications and an unblemished reputation for fairness. The American Bar Association gave her its highest rating, and the Senate rendered her near-unanimous (96-3) approval. In wake of the circus atmosphere surrounding the Clarence Thomas hearings, her confirmation process was remarkable in its civility and understated elegance. Only a narrow slice of the Far Right raised a protest. Ginsburg will be only the second woman and sixth Jew to sit on the court.[2] She will be the first to have served on the law reviews of two prestigious law schools, Harvard and Columbia. In another twist of history, this champion of women's rights was turned down for a clerkship by the great Felix Frankfurter unabashedly because of her gender.

Based on her stellar record as an advocate (six cases argued before the Supreme Court), professor (Columbia, Rutgers), and jurist (thirteen years on the Federal Court of Appeals for the DC Circuit), we have every reason to think that Ruth Bader Ginsburg will serve with great distinction. But for all of her scholarly articles, speeches, and judicial opinions, Judge Ginsburg's track record on church-state issues is rather scant.

While serving on the DC Circuit, Judge Ginsburg wrote several opinions that demonstrated profound respect for religious freedom and church-state separation. In *Murray v. Buchanan,*[3] taxpayers challenged the practice of employing congressional chaplains. Judge Ginsburg joined a unanimous panel ruling that the challenged practice does not violate the establishment clause. She reasoned that the Supreme Court in *Marsh v. Chambers* (1983)—upholding legislative chaplains at the state level—settled

[1] *Report from the Capital* 48/8 (September 1993): 7.
[2] The first Jewish nominee, Judah Benjamin, declined an appointment in 1853 to run for the Senate.
[3] *Murray v. Buchanan*, 720 F.2d 689 (DC Cir. 1983).

the issue.[4] To the same effect is *Kurtz v. Baker*, in which Ginsburg affirmed the dismissal of a suit brought by a humanist seeking to deliver a secular speech during time ordinarily reserved by Congress for opening prayer.[5]

In neither *Murray* nor *Kurtz* did Judge Ginsburg discuss the *Lemon* test.[6] Both cases were decided under *Marsh v. Chambers*, the only time the Supreme Court relied exclusively on historical practice rather than the three-prong *Lemon* test to decide an establishment clause issue. In applying *Marsh*, Judge Ginsburg was simply following clear and direct Supreme Court precedent.

In yet another establishment clause case, *Olsen v. Drug Enforcement Administration*, Ginsburg held that it was permissible to prohibit the Ethiopian Zion Coptic Church from using marijuana in its religious exercises even though a federal statue shielded Native Americans from prosecution for using peyote in their religious exercises.[7] She saw compelling reasons for the difference in treatment. Judge Ginsburg did not rely on or discuss the *Lemon* case in this decision either.

On the free exercise clause, she appears to favor heightened protection for religious liberty. In *Leahy v. District of Columbia*, Judge Ginsburg applied the compelling interest test.[8] An applicant for a driver's license alleged that requiring the use of Social Security numbers violated his free exercise rights. She ruled that the government had failed to show that using Social Security numbers was the least restrictive means of accomplishing a vital public purpose.

Along with her correct ruling in this case, Judge Ginsburg exhibited her sharp eye for the nuances of precedent. In *Bowen v. Roy* (1986),[9] the Supreme Court appeared to have adopted a "reasonableness test" for judging free exercise cases—the one it eventually adopted in *Employment Division v. Smith* (1990),[10] the Native American peyote case. The lower court in *Leahy* relied on *Bowen* in ruling for the government, but Judge Ginsburg astutely pointed out that the opinion in *Bowen* was really a plurality opinion

---

[4] *Marsh v. Chambers*, 463 US 783 (1983).

[5] *Kurtz v. Baker*, 829 F.2d 113, 1142 (DC Cir. 1987).

[6] Decided in *Lemon v. Kurtzman*, 403 US 602 (1971), the *Lemon* test is a three-pronged test the court uses to decide establishment clause cases.

[7] *Olsen v. Drug Enforcement Administration*, 878 F.2d 1458 (DC Cir. 1989).

[8] *Leahy v. District of Columbia*, 833 F.2d 1046, 1049 (DC Cir. 1987).

[9] *Bowen v. Roy*, 476 US 693 (1986).

[10] *Employment Division v. Smith*, 494 US 872 (1990).

(only three justices joined). Ginsburg continued to apply the traditional compelling interest test and ruled in favor of the claimant.

Finally, in *Goldman v. Secretary of Defense*, Judge Ginsburg urged the entire court of appeals panel to review the free exercise claim of an Air Force officer who, because of military policy, was unable to wear his yarmulke in uniform.[11] She criticized the government's "callous indifference" to the officer's religious beliefs and traditions.

In her two days of testimony, Ginsburg refused to be pinned down on finer points of church-state jurisprudence. She did not criticize *Lemon*, nor did she explicitly endorse the neutrality concept embodied in it. Ginsburg did say that she recognized *Lemon* to be the governing law on establishment clause issues and that she was not eager to do away with it until there was a reason to replace it with another test. She also was asked about the propriety of school choice proposals that would involve public funds being used to pay for private or parochial education. She refused to be specific on the question, but deferred judgment until a voucher plan was presented to the court for adjudication.

Further, in terms of free exercise, she was not asked specifically whether she agreed with *Employment Division v. Smith*. However, her testimony generally revealed sensitivity to the need for religious liberty and the propriety of religious accommodation on the part of the government. If I had to guess at this point, I would be surprised if she didn't follow the lead of Justices Sandra Day O'Connor and David Souter in criticizing the *Smith* decision and the attenuated protections for religious liberty that it spawned.

Despite these hopeful signs, one can never tell precisely how a judge is going to turn out. Justice Souter for example, gave good answers in his testimony and, despite some initial mixed signals, he exceeded our expectations on church-state cases. Justice Thomas, on the other hand said he was not out to overturn *Lemon*, but voted to do just that; he hinted that he believed in strict scrutiny for free exercise claims, but voted with Justice Antonin Scalia every time in free exercise cases.

Even if Justice Ginsburg turns out to be less than expected, she will be a far cry better than her predecessor, Justice Byron White. For all of Justice White's well-deserved reputation for even-handed justice and judicial pragmatism, he was awful on church-state issues. As someone quipped, "Justice White never saw a plan to spend public tax dollars for parochial

---

[11] *Goldman v. Secretary of Defense*, 739 F.2d 657 (DC Cir. 1984).

education that he didn't like." Of course, his vote was critical in the disastrous *Smith* case that denuded the free exercise clause of practically any meaning.

So we wait and see how Justice Ginsburg does. But everything that we know about her right now suggests she will do well.

City of Boerne v. Flores[1]

Alexander Hamilton once called the judiciary branch the "least dangerous" branch of government. He was wrong. The judiciary has turned out to be the most dangerous branch for those who value religious freedom.

The wise architects of our republic fashioned twin pillars—no establishment and free exercise—to uphold our God-given religious freedom. In recent years, the Supreme Court has interpreted these clauses in a way that weakens protections for religious freedom.

The Court continues to chip away at the mortar of the establishment clause. Yes, the Court invalidated clergy-led graduation prayers and special school districts for Orthodox Jews, but it has approved state-employed sign language interpreters and public school teachers providing remedial education on parochial school campuses.

More striking is the Court's demolition project on the pillar of free exercise. After the Court gutted the free exercise clause of any meaningful protection in *Employment Division v. Smith*,[2] Congress passed the Religious Freedom Restoration Act to restore the previously high level of protection to our free exercise of religion. But this summer, in *City of Boerne v. Flores*, the Court nullified RFRA as an unconstitutional exercise of congressional power.[3] For the time being, we are forced to rely on the good graces of legislatures, the benevolence of bureaucrats, and a patchwork of state constitutional provisions to protect our religious freedom. This is not the robust vision of religious freedom that our founders fought for and built into the First Amendment. The religious liberty of every American is now in peril.

What's going on? Why is the Court so ready to knock down constitutional protection for religious liberty? There are three reasons.

First is *majoritarianism*. Several on the Court believe that most public policy issues should be decided by the political branches of government—legislative and executive—not by the judicial branch. Majority

---

[1] *Report from the Capital* 52/14 (July 22, 1997): 3.
[2] *Employment Division v. Smith*, 494 US 872 (1990).
[3] *City of Boerne v. Flores*, 521 US 507 (1997).

vote should prevail most of the time. The courts will grant relief only in cases in which religion is targeted for discriminatory treatment. This is effectively what the Court said in *Smith*: "Don't come to the Court for exemptions from otherwise neutral laws. Go to the Congress."

The second factor is *federalism*. Just as the Court prefers political to judicial decisions, it emphasizes the importance of states' rights over federal power. This is the driving consideration behind the Court's decision in *Flores*. Just as the will of the majority is thought to be more important than the rights of the minority, so, too, are the sovereign rights of the state considered superior to federally protected freedom of conscience. Religious claimants will now seek relief, in the form of either little RFRAs or specific exemptions at the state level.

Finally, there is the matter of *judicial activism*. The Court's majority today decries the supposed activism of the Warren and Burger courts. However, this Court has been just as activist, proving the maxim that a judicial activist is simply defined as a justice with five votes. The Court was activist in its decision in *Smith* because neither party even asked the Court to change the law radically. It was activist in *Flores* when it strained to find constitutional justification to overrule a near unanimous act of Congress that was widely supported by the American people. The alleged liberal activism of former days has been replaced by activism on the right.

What is in store for the Court in the future? More of the same until a justice or two retires. The two justices thought to be closest to retirement are Chief Justice Rehnquist and Justice Stevens—a conservative and a liberal, respectively. Both Rehnquist and Stevens have an attenuated view of the free exercise clause. If they are replaced by free exercise-friendly justices, there would probably be sufficient votes to overturn the *Smith* case and restore a constitutional standard that protects religious liberty in a way that is consistent with the vision of our founders. In the meantime, beware of the "least dangerous" branch. The Court's slavish adherence to knee-jerk majority rule and its deference to states' rights have relegated what used to be our "first freedom" to the rear of the constitutional bus.

On the Death of Thurgood Marshall[1]

We have lost a true American hero. And I don't see anyone on the horizon who is worthy to stand in the breach. Thurgood Marshall was more than a courageous lawyer, an accomplished jurist, a champion of civil rights. He was an institution—at once an embodiment of the American dream and at times its severest critic—whose larger-than-life persona subsumed the causes and ideas he advocated.

His accomplishments are as improbable as they are legion. He was the great-grandson of a slave and the son of a waiter in a segregated Baltimore yacht club. He took his grandfather's name "Thorough Good" (shortened to Thurgood), but he was not thoroughly good as a child and adolescent. As punishment for cutting up (and worse) in school, Marshall recalled that he was sent to the basement and forced to memorize a paragraph of the Constitution for every misdeed. After a couple of years, he knew the document by heart. Appropriate punishment!

After working his way through college, he was barred from attending the then-segregated University of Maryland Law School. Thurgood didn't get mad; he got even. He went to the predominantly black Howard Law School in Washington and, upon graduating first in his class in 1933, promptly sued the University of Maryland to gain admission for another black student and to desegregate that institution.

He was head of the National Association for the Advancement of Colored People's Legal Defense and Education Fund for two decades. Marshall traversed the country trying (and winning) civil rights cases, often putting his life in jeopardy. In 1961, President John F. Kennedy appointed him to the US Circuit Court of Appeals for the 2nd Circuit (New York), and four years later President Lyndon B. Johnson made him solicitor general of the United States—the government's top lawyer before the Supreme Court.

Before and during his tenure as solicitor general, Marshall argued thirty-two cases before the Supreme Court, winning twenty-nine—a .906 batting average. His most famous case was the 1954 *Brown v. Board of*

[1] *Report from the Capital* 48/2 (February 1993): 7.

Education—overturning the separate-but-equal doctrine and desegregating our public schools.[2]

Marshall's most permanent legacy was left through his twenty-four years of service as the first black justice on the US Supreme Court. Justice Marshall always empathized with the disenfranchised, the minority, the downtrodden. His vote could be counted on to strike down a death penalty statute, to preserve the rights of the accused, to ensure equal protection under the law for everyone. Although Marshall often voted with the majority in the early years of his tenure, during the latter years, he usually found himself in the minority, along with his soul mate, Justice William Brennan. Indeed, he wrote more than 1,800 dissents during his years on the Court.

The readers of this column might ask, however, how Justice Marshall fared on church-state issues. Though raised an Episcopalian, he was not at all visibly pious. But his life and work were pregnant with a sense of prophetic justice and Christian charity. Consistent with his expansive understanding of the Bill of Rights, Justice Marshall was a staunch defender of the First Amendment's religion clauses—both no establishment and free exercise. But in surveying his decisions, I was surprised to find that Justice Marshall, while voting "right" on most church-state cases, did not write many of them. Nevertheless, it's fitting to listen to Justice Marshall's words again as he expounds on the importance of religious liberty and proper church-state relations.

In *Mueller v. Allen,* Justice Marshall dissented from a decision upholding a Minnesota law allowing taxpayers to deduct certain expenses incurred in providing education for their children. Justice Marshall reminded us, "Under our system the choice has been made that government is to be entirely excluded from the area of religious instruction.... The Constitution decrees that religion must be a private matter for the individual, the family, the institutions of private choice, and that while some involvement and entanglement are inevitable, lines must be drawn."[3]

In his concurring opinion in *Board of Education v. Mergens,* upholding the constitutionality of the Equal Access Act that permitted religious clubs in public schools, Justice Marshall demonstrated his dedication to free speech and free exercise: "We have long regarded free and open debate over

---

[2] *Brown v. Board of Education,* 347 US 483 (1954).
[3] *Mueller v. Allen,* 463 US 388 (1983).

matters of controversy as necessary to the functioning of our constitutional system. That the Constitution requires toleration of speech over its suppression is no less true in our Nation's schools." But, at the same time, Justice Marshall was sensitive to potential establishment clause violations:

> [T]he Constitution also demands that the State not take action that has the primary effect of advancing religion. The introduction of religious speech into the public schools reveals the tension between these two constitutional commitments, because the failure of a school to stand apart from religious speech can convey a message that the school endorses rather than merely tolerates that speech. Recognizing the potential dangers of school-endorsed religious practice, we have shown particular vigilance in monitoring compliance with the Establishment Clause in elementary and secondary schools.[4]

Finally, in a ringing dissent in *Trans World Airlines v. Hardison*, Justice Marshall defended the right of an employee to worship on Saturday and the need to accommodate that religious practice: "[A] society that truly values religious pluralism cannot compel adherents of minority religions to make the cruel choice between surrendering a religion or their job." Stating that a person should not be "forced to live on welfare as the price they must pay for worshipping their God," Justice Marshall concluded, "The ultimate tragedy is that...one of this Nation's pillars of strength—our hospitality to religious diversity—has been seriously eroded. All Americans will be a little poorer until today's decision is erased."[5]

Yes, we shall miss Justice Marshall, and we, too, are a little poorer as a result of his passing. He said he only wanted to be remembered as one who did the best he could with what he had.

Indeed, he did.

---

[4] *Board of Education v. Mergens*, 110 S.Ct. 2356 (1990).
[5] *Trans World Airlines v. Hardison*, 432 US 63 (1977).

Equal Access and *Mergens*[1]

Ever since the Supreme Court rendered its decisions striking down state-sponsored school prayer and devotional Bible reading,[2] many have accepted the great myth that God has been thrown out of the public schools. Some, including many school officials, have sought to purge every vestige of religion from the school system. Others, usually conservative Christians, bemoan religion's elimination and blame every social ill and cultural dysfunction that has arisen over the past thirty years on the demise of ceremonial civil religion in the public schools.

Both sides have it wrong! It is true that it is nowise the role of government to compose or encourage prayers. Teachers have no business leading children in devotional exercises. Ministers are conspicuously out of place preaching or proselytizing in the public schools. However, to assert that any civil authority has the power to throw almighty God out of the classroom is theological heresy, and to claim that this ouster has been accomplished is simply ludicrous.

The God of the universe (if not the puny god of civil religion) has a perfect attendance record. It has always been permissible for students to engage in "individual free exercise of religion" in school. No Supreme Court decision prevents students from reading Bibles silently during study hall, saying a personal blessing before lunch, praying for athletic safety and success, or even witnessing to their fellow students, assuming they do not disrupt the pedagogical process. It is only state-sponsored religious speech and exercise, not student-initiated religious practice, that the Supreme Court has condemned.

Similarly, although the state may not and should not provide religious indoctrination in school, it has been permissible—at least since the 1952 decision in *Zorach v. Clauson*[3]—to release students for voluntary religious instruction and devotion off campus at a church or synagogue.

---

[1] *Report from the Capital* 45/7 (July-August 1990): 5.

[2] *Engel v. Vitale*, 370 US 421 (1962); *Abington Township v. Schempp*, 374 US 203 (1963).

[3] *Zorach v. Clauson*, 343 US 306 (1952).

Finally, schools can and should teach students *about* religion and the role it has played in our history and culture. The opinion that outlawed state-sponsored devotional Bible reading expressly approved the study of religion. Writing for an eight-member majority, Justice Tom Clark opined,

> [I]t might well be said that one's education is not complete without a study of comparative religion or the history of religion and its relationship to the advancement of civilization. It certainly may be said that the Bible is worthy of study for its literary and historic qualities. Nothing that we have said here indicates that such study of the Bible or of religion, when presented objectively as part of a secular program of education, may not be affected consistently with the First Amendment.[4]

In addition to these always allowable (but in some cases rarely utilized) avenues of religious speech and exercise, students can do even more. In 1984, Congress passed the Equal Access Act. Supported and encouraged by the Baptist Joint Committee, this law was designed mainly to end discrimination against student religious groups. It permits students to engage in corporate religious exercises at school, along with private devotion and classroom study about religion. When a public secondary school allows "noncurriculum related" groups to meet (such as the chess club, Interact club, and the like), before or after school, it has to permit religious clubs to do the same. If the school allows only "curriculum related" groups (like the French Club or athletic teams), it need not allow religious clubs on campus. Meetings under the Equal Access Act have to be voluntary, student initiated, and student led, not sponsored by the school, and outside people cannot control or even regularly attend the group meetings. Within these parameters, the religious meetings need not be formal, academic, or objective; they rather may involve unabashedly sectarian Bible study, worship, and prayer.

Although many clubs successfully operated under this law since 1984, its constitutionality was always in some question. In June, in an 8-1 decision in *Westside Community Schools v. Mergens*, the Supreme Court upheld the Equal Access Act—at the express urging of the Baptist Joint Committee in a

---

[4] *Abington Township v. Schempp.*

"friend of the court" brief.[5] Equally important, the decision rendered an expansive interpretation of "noncurriculum related," thus tending to ensure the act's broad application.

This decision, authored by Justice O'Connor, also restored a proper balance between the separation of church and state and the constitutional guarantees of free speech and free exercise of religion. The Court recognized the critical distinction between state-encouraged religious speech and student-initiated religious exercise. The former is condemned by the no establishment clause, but the latter is not.

We at the Baptist Joint Committee believe that government should neither advance nor inhibit religion. The state should leave religion alone. It should maintain a posture of neutrality—allowing religious speech and free exercise to flourish or flounder without endorsing religion in general or any particular faith. This is especially important in our increasingly pluralistic public schools.

Equal access allows this to happen. By opening their ears to students' religious speech, and by treating such speech the same as political and philosophical dialogue, the schools are simply maintaining a posture of neutrality—neither promoting nor discouraging religion. In so doing, they allow the individual free exercise that has always been permissible to be expressed corporately, without running afoul of the no establishment clause of the First Amendment. This eliminates any artificial and discriminatory barrier to robust, full-bodied discourse. As a result, the schools, no less than the students, are beneficiaries of this law and supporting decision.

---

[5] *Westside Community Schools v. Mergens*, 496 US 226 (1990).

Justice O'Connor Leaves
a Legacy of Religious Protection[1]

The retirement of Justice Sandra Day O'Connor leaves a vacancy on the Supreme Court that could tip the balance of the Court's church-state jurisprudence.

As with other issues, Justice O'Connor was often the swing vote on cases calling for the interpretation of First Amendment's religion clauses. Over the past twenty-four years, she has exhibited a profound understanding of the importance of religious liberty and the necessity for keeping government out of religion. She was bent on upholding both no establishment and free exercise values and committed to ensuring robust religious speech in the public square. She typically rendered thoughtful, centrist opinions that were closely tailored to the facts of the case. In short, she was a very good justice.

I sometimes disagreed with the results of her decisions. For example, although she had written that "any use of public funds to promote religious doctrines violates the Establishment Clause,"[2] she upheld the constitutionality of a voucher program that included parochial schools.[3] Moreover, her refusal to condemn the government's building of a logging road through a sacred burial site—thereby having, even in her words, "devastating effects on traditional Indian religious practice"—was off base.[4]

But most of the time she was right. Concerning religious expression, she penned this now-classic formulation: "[T]here is a crucial difference between government speech endorsing religion, which the Establishment Clause forbids, and private speech endorsing religion, which the Free Speech and Free Exercise Clauses protect."[5] Accordingly, she upheld the constitutionality of the Equal Access Act, recognizing the right of public school students to organize and attend voluntary Bible clubs.

---

[1] *Report from the Capital* 60/7 (July–August 2005): 3.
[2] *Bowen v. Kendrick*, 487 US 589 (1988).
[3] *Zelman v. Simmons-Harris*, 536 US 639 (2002).
[4] *Lyng v. Northwest Indian CPA*, 485 US 439 (1988).
[5] *Board of Education of Westside Community Schools v. Mergens*, 496 US 226 (1990).

With regard to the free exercise of religion, she railed against the judicial activism that resulted in the elimination of any meaningful free exercise protection in the Native American peyote case. Quoting Justice Robert Jackson, she reminded us in that case that "[t]he very purpose of a Bill of Rights was to withdraw certain subjects from the vicissitudes of political controversy, to place them beyond the reach of majorities...and to establish them as legal principles to be applied by the courts. One's right to...freedom of worship...and other fundamental rights may not be submitted to vote; they depend on the outcome of no elections." She concluded that the traditional test, requiring government to demonstrate a compelling interest before burdening religious practice, best protects religious liberty in our pluralistic society.[6]

Her concurring opinion in the recent Kentucky Ten Commandments case is as fine a statement of the importance of religious liberty and church-state separation as I have seen from the Court. In three-and-a-half pages, she captured the pith of both our history and constitutional landscape as she condemned governmental endorsement of a religion. Her full opinion can be read on the BJC Web site.[7] Here is a sampling of her words:

At a time when we see around the world the violent consequences of the assumption of religious authority by government, Americans may count themselves fortunate: Our regard for constitutional boundaries has protected us from similar travails, while allowing private religious exercise to flourish.

Those who would renegotiate the boundaries between church and state must...answer a difficult question: Why would we trade a system that has served us so well for one that has served others so poorly?

Voluntary religious belief and expression may be as threatened when government takes the mantle of religion upon itself as when government directly interferes with private religious practices.

---

[6] *Employment Division v. Smith*, 494 US 872 (1990).
[7] www.bjcpa.org/resources/pubs/brief_t10c_mccrearyvaclu.pdf.

It is true that the Framers lived at a time when our national religious diversity was neither as robust nor as well recognized as it is now…. But they did know that line-drawing between religions is an enterprise that, once began, has no logical stopping point…. The Religion Clauses…protect adherents of all religions, as well as those who believe in no religion at all.[8]

The imminent debate about Justice O'Connor's successor will be as much about the continuation of religious liberty as we know it in this country as any other issue the Court will address. I pray the president and the Senate get it right.

---

[8] *McCreary County v. ACLU of Kentucky*, 545 US 844 (2005).

Independent Judiciary Under Attack[1]

It is emphatically the province and duty of the judicial department to say what the law is. —Chief Justice John Marshall, *Marbury v. Madison* (1803)[2]

Many people today—including many politicians—are ignoring Marshall's settled principle of our constitutional heritage. Along with the Bill of Rights, the separation of powers between the executive, legislative, and judicial branches and the checks and balances among them are fundamental to the preservation of freedom.

The legislative branch passes laws, the executive branch enforces the laws, and the judicial branch interprets them. Although the first two branches are thoroughly and properly political, our Founders sought to ensure an independent federal judiciary that would be free from direct political influences.

These long-settled principles are under a withering attack today. Hateful, inflammatory, and irresponsible words are leveled at the judiciary—even from the highest offices in the political branches. In 2004 the House of Representatives passed two bills to strip the federal courts of jurisdiction to hear certain constitutional issues simply because the House disagreed with how it thought the Court would decide them. These measures present enormous separation of powers issues and threaten judicial independence. The House passed the Pledge Protection Act to block federal lawsuits involving the Pledge of Allegiance, even cases involving actual coercion. It also passed the Marriage Protection Act to strip the federal courts of power to hear challenges to the federal Defense of Marriage Act. Other bills—to deprive the federal courts of jurisdiction to hear establishment clause cases involving the Ten Commandments and other government endorsements of religion—were also filed. We have every reason to think these efforts will intensify, particularly if the Supreme Court

---

[1] *Report from the Capital* 60/4 (April 2005): 3.
[2] *Marbury v. Madison*, 5 US (1 Cranch) 137 (1803).

strikes down the government-sponsored Ten Commandment displays in the two cases that are pending this term.[3]

The recent acts of violence against judges and their families in Chicago and Atlanta and the tragic Terri Schiavo case have provided an opportunity for demagogues to up the ante to a frightening level. Rep. Tom DeLay (R-TX), House majority leader, sought to bully the judges involved in the Schiavo case, declaring, "the time will come for the men responsible for this to answer for their behavior." He also leveled a not-so-veiled threat of reprisals when he said, "Congress for many years has shirked its responsibility to hold the judiciary accountable. No longer." Moreover, Sen. John Cornyn (R-TX), suggested on the floor of the Senate that there may be a link between recent acts of violence against judges and "raw political and ideological decisions" that judges have issued. As a former justice of the Texas Supreme Court, Sen. Cornyn should know better.

Finally, on April 7 and 8 a group called the Judeo-Christian Council for Constitutional Restoration sponsored a conference in Washington, DC, titled "Confronting the Judicial War on Faith." The promotional brochure shows a judge's gavel demolishing the second tablet of the Ten Commandments. It goes on to complain about "activist judges who are undermining democracy, devastating families and assaulting...morality."

Really? A war on faith? Undermining democracy? Devastating families? I don't think so. Judges are human beings who are trying to do their level best to uphold the Constitution, interpret the law, and mediate competing claims that come before them. Courts don't go fishing for cases to decide. They can act only when someone asks them to act. The raucous rhetoric surrounding this conference is simply outrageous.

The decisions courts make may be unpopular. In fact, the best they can ever hope to do is please about half the people. Since federal judges are often interpreting a "counter-majoritarian" Bill of Rights, they often raise the ire of a strong majority.

The decisions courts issue are sometimes wrong. They do not always get it right. I often disagree with the results in Supreme Court cases. I am not doing my job if I fail to critique Supreme Court decisions on the *issues*, but I do not dispute their right to make those decisions or the good faith of judges and justices 99 percent of the time.

---

[3] *Van Orden v. Perry*, 545 US 677 (2005); *McCreary County v. ACLU of Kentucky*, 545 US 844 (2005).

Someone has to make these hard decisions, and they are best made in a nonthreatening, relatively apolitical environment. The panoply of freedoms that we as Americans have come to enjoy, religious and otherwise, depend entirely on our understanding that judges, not politicians, have the final say in interpreting the laws—as Chief Justice Marshall rightly pointed out more than two centuries ago.

Religion in the Public Square

Congress shall make no law respecting an establishment of religion, or prohibiting the free exercise thereof

Patriotism Surge Raises Questions about Flags in Sanctuaries[1]

The events of September 11 have spawned a profusion of patriotism and flag waving—more than I have ever seen. From highway overpasses, to car antennas, to homes (including mine) and suit lapels, Old Glory is everywhere. American flags also adorn most Baptist church sanctuaries.

During the past six weeks, we have had a flood of inquiries about the propriety of flying the American flag in church. Should American flags be displayed in Baptist churches? The short answer is yes, but only in certain places and at special times.

Of course, this practice does not constitute a constitutional violation. The First Amendment's establishment clause bars government endorsement of a religious message; it does not prohibit a church from endorsing a patriotic symbol. The objection to the routine display of an American flag in the sanctuary is that it represents an act of "civil religion" that, for some, including me, raises serious theological concerns.

At worst, the placement of an American flag at the front of the sanctuary can result in "flag worship"—a form of idolatry. At best, when the American flag is placed alongside the Christian flag, it signals equivalence between the Kingdom of God and the kingdom of Caesar. Christians know this is not the case. We are citizens of two kingdoms. We are to respect our governmental institutions and pray for our governmental leaders, but that must always be secondary to our commitment to and love for God. Faith in God is superior to love of country; allegiance to God transcends all nationalism.

In any case, displaying the American flag in the sanctuary in Baptist churches in America diminishes our ability to reach out to non-Americans. This is particularly true in places like Washington, DC, where citizens from other countries routinely attend and worship with us. It sends a terrible signal to believers and unbelievers alike from around the world that

---

[1] *Report from the Capital* 56/21 (October 24, 2001): 3.

somehow the Kingdom of God and the United States of America are either the same or are on equal footing.

Even if it is not advisable to display the flag routinely in the worship center, there are other opportunities to show and celebrate the flag. Here are several ideas:

It is quite appropriate to display the flag, even in the sanctuary, on special occasions. These include the day of worship closest to the Fourth of July when we celebrate our independence, Religious Freedom Day when we express gratitude for the freedom we enjoy as Americans, and yes, even in times of national crisis and mourning. However, even then, the flag should be positioned in a way that does not signify equivalence with the Kingdom of God.

It is also fitting to display the American flag along with flags from other countries. This would be an appropriate gesture, for example, on World Communion Sunday or during a global missions emphasis. The symbolism would signify unity with Christians throughout the world.

Finally, the flag can be displayed routinely in other parts of the church campus not specifically devoted to the worship of God. This could include the fellowship hall, assembly rooms, the vestibule, and other places where it can be seen and appreciated, but where it does not threaten to displace the cross as the quintessential symbol of Christianity.

In this connection, Tim Turnham has recognized the symbolism involved in displaying the flag in the vestibule. He writes, "We would see the flags in the foyer as an indication that we go in to worship God and go out to live our lives as God's people in a community where we have chosen to live."

A healthy sense of patriotism is good, but we are Christians first and Americans second. When these words are used together, "Christian" is the noun and "American" is the adjective. Our symbolism in worship should reflect that theological truth.

National Prayer Day Not an Occasion for Government to Push Piety[1]

Earlier this month, we observed the 55th annual National Day of Prayer. In 1952, the Congress passed a joint resolution, signed by President Harry Truman, setting aside one day a year for prayer. Presidents since then have entered proclamations urging prayer, as had many going back to George Washington.

This year's day of prayer was marked by public events in our nation's capital. On the west steps of the Capitol, where presidents since Ronald Reagan have been inaugurated, a Bible reading marathon was held—90 hours long! According to media reports, 350 gathered in the Cannon Caucus Room to hear James Smith, Chief Justice of Mississippi, lament the total domination of secularism over our culture. Dana Milbank of the *Washington Post* observed the irony of this assertion—given three hours of prayer in a government building, complete "with a military band, a color guard, the House chaplain, a senior military commander, several congressmen and a member of the president's Cabinet."[2] At the other end of Pennsylvania Avenue, worshippers prayed and listened to remarks by the president that sounded more like a preacher's sermon than a president's speech.

What's wrong, if anything, about these activities and a National Day of Prayer? There's nothing wrong with people getting together to pray on a designated day, even public officials. Indeed, every day should be a day of national prayer. The rub comes when the government declares it to be such and exhorts its citizens to engage in a religious exercise, then leads the way by example. In 2002, then-chaplain of the Senate, Lloyd Ogilvie, even composed a prayer for us to use! (How many times did Roger Williams and John Leland roll over in their graves?)

---

[1] *Report from the Capital* 62/5 (May 2007): 3.
[2] "Dozens of Heads Were Bowed," Dana Milbank, Washington Post. May 4, 2007. A02.

Not all presidents have issued prayer proclamations. Thomas Jefferson, author of Virginia's Bill for Establishing Religious Freedom, refused to issue a thanksgiving proclamation because he believed it was both unconstitutional and unwise. In an 1808 letter, Jefferson voiced his concerns:

> I consider the government of the United States as interdicted by the Constitution from intermeddling with religious institutions, their doctrines, discipline, or exercise.... Certainly, no power to prescribe any religious exercise, or to assume authority in religious discipline, has been delegated to the General Government.... Fasting and prayer are religious exercises; the enjoining them an act of discipline. Every religious society has a right to determine for itself the times for these exercises, and the objects proper for them, according to their own particular tenets; and this right can never be safer than in their own hands, where the Constitution has deposited it.[3]

James Madison, Jefferson's successor and cohort in liberty, was no less opposed to such proclamations. Madison did issue several prayer proclamations during his tenure as president, apparently bowing to political pressures. Years later, however, he recanted. Madison gave five reasons why a religious pronouncement should not be handed down from civil magistrates—even presidents. First, the sword of civil government can never enforce a declaration of a religious holiday. "An advisory Gov't is a contradiction in terms," Madison wrote. Second, the government is not in any sense entitled to act as an ecclesiastical council of synod with the moral authority to "speak to the faith or the Consciences of the people." Third, such proclamations tend "to imply and certainly nourish the erroneous idea of a national religion," an idea Madison condemned as anathema. Fourth, such declarations inevitably use the terminology and theology of the dominant religious groups and are, to that extent, majoritarian in their flavor. Fifth, such proclamations carry the grave risk of using religion to serve the political ambitions of the moment.[4]

---

[3] Anson Phelps Stokes and Leo Pfeffer, *Church and State in the United States* (New York: Harper & Row, Inc., 1964) 88.

[4] Edwin S. Gaustad, *Faith of Our Fathers* (San Francisco: Harper & Row, Publishers, 1988) 55–56.

As church-state controversies go, a congressional resolution and a presidential proclamation establishing a National Day of Prayer is not a cataclysmic breach. After all, there is little (if any) actual coercion of anyone's conscience. But actual coercion has never been the standard for judging whether government has overstepped its bounds in endorsing religion. Also, it is helpful to understand that two of our most influential founders—Jefferson and Madison—either opposed religious pronouncements in principle or refused to issue them in practice.

Exhorting our country to repentance and prayer on designated days is altogether proper. Who would argue we don't need it? But it's more appropriately called for by the preachers, priests, and prophets among us—not civil magistrates, the Congress, or even an American president.

President's Words Should Show
Understanding of Religious Diversity[1]

The president's speeches and public pronouncements over the past several months—laced as they have been with evangelical religious rhetoric—have caused some to question the propriety of politicians associating their policy aims so closely with one religious point of view. From talking heads on television to radio call-in programs to the newsprint media, commentators and the public thoroughly aired the topic. For better or worse, it clearly belies the mistaken assertion that we have a "naked public square" when it comes to religion.

My take on it is that we must grapple with the tension created by our understanding that we have a separation of church and state in this country, but not a divorcement of religion from politics.

American politicians do not have to check their religious beliefs at the door when they enter public office. Nor should they have to mute their expression of that faith in words and conduct. I respect Mr. Bush and other American politicians.

But Mr. Bush was elected to serve as a *political* leader, not a religious leader. He is the political leader of the *whole* nation, not one segment of the religious community. His pronouncements should reflect the understanding that he is president of all the people in this religiously diverse, religious-freedom-loving nation.

In short, this should cause the president to temper his religious rhetoric and exercise more of that old-fashioned Christian virtue of humility—something he said he would do when he ran for office.

This by no means discounts the president's role as something of a "comforter-in-chief." From the Oklahoma City bombing to September 11 to the *Columbia* tragedy, presidents of both parties have led the nation in this way. When offered with sensitivity and a broad view, religious themes can unite and comfort the nation. However, when done to excess and from a

---

[1] *Report from the Capital* 58/5 (March 5, 2003): 3.

narrow theological perspective, they are divisive and discomforting for many Americans.

It only exacerbates the problem to use religious language without referring to it as such—to use code words to address a religious message to a particular religious community. For example, in his State of the Union Address, the president spoke of the "wonder-working power of the…faith of the American people." As I was sitting in the galleries that evening and heard those words roll out, the hymn I have sung a hundred times in church—"There Is Power in the Blood"—rang in my ears. I'm sure millions of evangelical Protestants across the country reacted the same way. Of course, the hymn is not about the public spirit of the American people; it is about salvation in Jesus Christ. The hymn goes on to say: "there is pow'r, pow'r, wonder-working pow'r in the blood of the Lamb." President Bush's use of the phrase clearly was intended to appeal to a particular political/religious constituency.

The impending war with Iraq ups the ante on all of this. Some have called it a "holy war." To his credit, the president has said the war should not be about religion, but the cumulative effect of his public theological verbiage contradicts that claim. If anything, one would think he would go out of his way to *avoid* suggesting that God is on our side—as something of a cheerleader for American foreign policy.

Again, I'm not saying that religious beliefs should not inform the president's decisions. In many ways, it is more a question of degree, style, and rhetoric. But I do believe that it is wrong to baptize one's policy aims in the sacred water of divine approval. If the policy turns out badly—and they all fail to some extent—God is left with much of the blame.

It is true, as Justice Douglas once pointed out, that Americans are a "religious people."[2] Public discourse should reflect that fact. However, we live in a constitutional democracy, not a theocracy, with a dizzying religious diversity along with millions of citizens who are nonbelievers.

The president should appreciate that he leads all Americans, not just those with whom he goes to church.

---

[2] *Zorach v. Clauson*, 343 US 306, 313 (1952).

Pledge Controversy Serves as Reminder that Civil Religion Pales Next to Authentic Faith[1]

The United States Supreme Court is being asked to decide whether teacher-led recitation of the Pledge of Allegiance in public schools violates the First Amendment's establishment clause. The Court should rule that it does not. Here's why.

First, the Pledge of Allegiance is not a religious exercise. Clearly, any attempt by the government to demand or even urge participation in a prayer or act of worship would violate the establishment clause—particularly in the public schools. But ours is a secular pledge that, when taken as a whole, is intended to inspire patriotism. It does not have the purpose or primary effect of advancing religion. At most, it is an acknowledgment of this nation's religious roots and the fact that we continue to be a "religious people," to use Justice William O. Douglas's phrase.[2]

Second, this reference to America's religious character is nonsectarian. A pledge to "One nation, under Jesus" or "under Buddha" would be difficult to defend. True, the word "God" implies a certain monotheism, and the phrase "under God" is not a perfectly nuanced reflection of this nation's religious pluralism. But, as my former colleague, Buzz Thomas, has said, this is a pledge—not an essay. It's hard to come up with a more inclusive phrase than this one.

Third, students cannot be compelled to recite the Pledge—with or without the words "under God." The Supreme Court ruled eleven years before "under God" was added in 1954 that students have the right to forgo pledging allegiance to the flag.[3] Students who object to reciting the Pledge cannot be compelled to say it or disciplined for not participating.

Finally, there is a practical reason. If the Court strikes the words "under God" from the Pledge, there would be an immediate groundswell to

---

[1] *Report from the Capital* 59/2 (February 2004): 3.
[2] *Zorach v. Clauson.*
[3] *West Virginia v. Barnette*, 319 US 624 (1943).

amend the Constitution. Although constitutional amendments are difficult to adopt, this one would most likely pass and, in the process, open the door to more far-reaching establishment clause mischief. Having said all this, what is legal and constitutional is not always helpful or wise. For theological and policy reasons, I would be happier if the words "under God" were not included.

Civil religion in its various forms has long been a pervasive part of American political culture. According to sociologist Robert Bellah, "civil religion is about those public rituals that express the nexus of the political order to divine reality." In its most benign forms, civil religion serves as a unifying, cultural balm that reminds us of our religious roots as a nation, but it can easily and often morph into an idolatry of nationalism, or, at the very least, result in the trivialization of religion.

Simply stated, civil religion is not the same as heartfelt, vital religion. Ceremonial religion is not life-altering, world-changing religion. "Ceremonial deism," as it is sometimes called, is a pale substitute for authentic faith in a personal God whom we call "Abba Father."

Indeed, one of the traditional arguments in favor of the constitutionality of this and other forms of ceremonial deism (such as "In God We Trust" on coins) is that, through long use and rote repetition, the words have lost any religious import they might have had. In short, what is commonplace becomes mundane.

As my friend, Derek Davis of the J. M. Dawson Institute of Church-State Studies, has written,

> The God of American civil religion is a God stripped of his real essence and instead becomes a God used to advance national interests, be it anticommunism in the 1950s when the phrase "under God" was added to the pledge, or in the 2000s, as the God of the bumper sticker "God Bless America" whom America calls upon to fight the war on terrorism. God becomes a watered down deity, a supreme power called upon only to bolster patriotic sentiment and advance national goals.

The vitality of religion in America is thus diminished—not enhanced—when we conflate our penultimate allegiance to Caesar with our ultimate allegiance to God.

This explains why the Baptist Joint Committee—along with many other religious organizations—declined to file a friend-of-the-court brief in this case. The Court can only rule on the legal issue, and our concerns are more theological, political, and practical. However, we will continue to speak out publicly about how this issue is something of a tempest in a teapot and about the dangers that attend a pervasive civil religion.

No One Can Claim Divine
Authority on Public Policy Issues[1]

Much was written and said during the run-up to and aftermath of the so-called "Justice Sunday: Stop the Filibuster against People of Faith"—or as Bob Edgar of the National Council of Churches called it, "Just-Us" Sunday[2]—pointing out the arrogant presumption that the organizers of the event are right and godly and those who disagree are not only wrong but hostile to people of faith.

The Baptist Joint Committee weighed in full force with an early media statement and helped organize a counter press conference the Friday before. Many thanks to our friends Joe Phelps, pastor of Highland Baptist Church in Louisville, and Reba Cobb, a Baptist Joint Committee board member, for leading that effort. Along with pastors from seventeen Louisville-area churches, Joe and Reba stood and delivered, telling the assembled press corps that the organizers of Justice Sunday do not speak for all Christians or even all Baptists. (Statements from the press conference are posted on the Baptist Joint Committee's website.[3]

Cary Clack, writing for the *San Antonio Express-News*, penned one of the most cogent op-eds about what was objectionable about Justice Sunday.[4] I think Mr. Clack hit the nail right on the head. His basic point was this: what was wrong about the Justice Sunday extravaganza was not its *purpose* but its *premise*.

The purpose of the rally was fine: to allow people of faith to speak out on the important issue of whether the filibuster should be used in the US Senate to oppose judicial nominations. Although the event was shrouded in unmistakable *partisan* wrapping, reinforced through a video pitch by the

---

[1] *Report from the Capital* 60/5 (May 2005): 3.

[2] John Dart, "Judicial Posts: for justice or 'just us'?" *Christian Century*, May 17, 2005.

[3] www.bjcpa.org/news/docs/050422_filibuster_phelps.pdf.

[4] Cary Clark, "Holier-than-thou attitude has no place in judicial filibuster debate," *San Antonio Express-News*, April 27, 2005.

Senate's majority leader, it was entirely appropriate for those with strong views to speak out in the public square.

The problem with Justice Sunday, as Clack points out, was the *premise* that those who oppose judicial nominees are carrying out a vendetta against people of faith or are motivated by some kind of religious bigotry.

This premise is hopelessly flawed. It was a shameful abuse of religion to suggest that God has taken up sides in this debate. Whatever our differences on the filibuster and on judicial nominees, there are people of faith on both sides, and neither has God in their hip pocket. An unintended consequence of Justice Sunday was to highlight the vast number of people of faith in this country who are willing to stand up and publicly oppose the narrow self-righteousness that was revealed at the rally on Sunday night. It is clearly as wrong to sacralize secular policy issues as it is to try to banish religious voices from the debate in the first place.

As Clack aptly points out,

> In the political realm, people of faith can be opposed to other people of faith on given issues without either side being condemned to the fires of hell. Being a Christian isn't synonymous with being a political conservative. That there is a Christian right and Christian left is a testament to how people find different interpretations and inspirations in the same sacred text. But there is something wrong with never having spoken to a person, not even knowing their middle name but purporting to know the condition of their soul. Who, not even knowing the contents of the other person's prayers, has the right to judge their relationship with God?

Moreover, I see no concerted effort to deny anyone a judgeship based on his or her religion. Debate about whether a nominee is fit to serve as a judge is not only legitimate but goes to the heart of the confirmation process. No one should be denied the right to serve based on some religious litmus test, but policy positions and legal philosophy are fair game for public scrutiny—however motivated by religious conviction they may be. Religious belief does not give anyone a free pass to the bench or any public office.

Yes, the Baptist Joint Committee defends the right of people of faith and religious organizations to advocate with their religious voices in the public square and to serve our country as public officials. But, at the same time, we must discourage claiming divine authority on behalf of public policy issues, characterizing political opponents as anti-God, and lying about their motives.

It Is a Myth that Christians are
Handicapped in Political Arena[1]

In the spring 2004 issue of *Southwestern News*, a publication of Southwestern Baptist Theological Seminary, Malcolm B. Yarnell III seeks to correct "nine modern myths" he says handicap Christian political involvement.

Some of the article's "myths" are not myths. Some tell only part of the story. And some that are myths are not seriously promoted. Judge for yourself:

Myth 1. "Politics is concerned with that which theology or religion is not."

Politics and religion are different. One gravitates around the kingdom of God; the other is around the kingdom of Caesar. This is not to say that religious ethics cannot have an effect on public policy. Jesus' admonition about rendering to Caesar and rendering to God does not mean that people of faith cannot take their rightful place in the public square and the marketplace of ideas.

Myth 2. "Morality must not be confused with law."

Yes, it is impossible to divorce morality from law. And we should not want to. There is a sense in which morality can be legislated. However, under our constitutional system, laws must have a secular justification and not have a primary effect that advances religion. The moral grounding must be broadly based.

Myth 3. "The U. S. Constitution demands a strict separation of church and state."

The First Amendment certainly mandates a separation of church and state. No, it should not be hostile to religion. Yes, it ensures the free exercise of religion as well as non-establishment. However, full religious liberty requires a decent distance between the institutions of government and religion, and neither should commandeer the other to do its work.

Myth 4. "Preachers should not speak about politics."

---

[1] *Report from the Capital* 59/4 (April 2004): 3.

I don't know many who peddle this "myth." Of course, when speaking for themselves, preachers can address politics, including electoral politics. Even when speaking for the church, preachers can endorse candidates if the church is willing to risk its tax-exempt status. Finally, preachers can speak prophetically on the great moral issues of our day, even from the pulpit.

Myth 5. "Jesus was not political, and therefore, Christians must not be political."

Yes, Jesus challenged some of the religio-political structures of his day, but Jesus' kingdom was not of this world. He did not advocate the forceful overthrow of government or try to use government to support his ministry. That said, it is a myth that "Christians must not be political." The problem is, I don't know many who believe it.

Myth 6. "The Christian doctrine of the priesthood of all believers demands that individual rights must be paramount."

This is no myth. The Baptist notion of "soul freedom" and the Reformation concept of a "priesthood of all believers" argue forcefully for the primacy of individual conscience and direct access to God. That is not to deny the importance of the church. It means that out of our individual freedom we live with and are held responsible by other believers and that we voluntarily assume the role of "priesting each other."

Myth 7. "The basis of political democracy is freedom and freedom demands a lack of religious judgment."

It's no myth that freedom is the baseline of a democracy. However, freedom is not the same as license. Freedom must certainly be exercised responsibly as Paul reminds us in Galatians 5. Freedom and responsibility must always go together.

Myth 8. "Freedom of religion entails a neutral state with regard to all religious beliefs."

This is no myth either. The state must be neutral with regard to religion. Just because, as Yarnell argues, the state sometimes limits certain religious practices—pursuant to an overriding compelling interest in ensuring health and safety—does not mean that the state is not neutral. Neutrality requires that the state apply the same standard to all religions and otherwise treat all religions evenhandedly.

Myth 9. "Christian political theology is ultimately triumphal."

True, it should not be; but it often is. I agree with Yarnell that "lashing our politics to the meaning and example of the cross will keep Christian political activity from becoming triumphal in attitude and action." But too many have not learned this lesson. Those who enter politics with a religious enthusiasm should also exhibit that classic Christian virtue of humility.

A real myth is the article's thesis that Christians are somehow handicapped in their political involvement—except to the extent the handicap is self-imposed.

Issues, Yes—Candidates, No[1]

It's another election year. Calls are already coming in about whether, and to what extent, churches can become involved in political campaigns. Thus, it's a good time to review the provisions of the Internal Revenue Code concerning political activity by tax-exempt organizations, including churches and religious institutions.

The tax code provides that exempt organizations cannot "participate in, or intervene in…any political campaign on behalf of (or in opposition to) any candidate for public office." If they do, they risk losing their tax-exempt status. Two recent cases against Jimmy Swaggart Ministries and Jerry Falwell's Old Time Gospel Hour, resulting from their respective political activity, show that the IRS is serious about enforcing this provision.

The bottom line is this: Churches and religious organizations may engage in a limited amount of lobbying and are free to take public positions on public *issues*, but they may not support or oppose candidates for elected office without jeopardizing their tax-exempt status. Here are a few dos and don'ts. Churches may become involved in several legitimate voter-education (issue-oriented) activities.

(1) Voting record and candidate questionnaire. Exempt organizations can distribute the voting records of candidates and the results of candidate questionnaires if they include a wide variety of subjects and provided the form and content of the distributed material is unbiased and accurate.

(2) Public forum and debates. Exempt organizations may sponsor non-partisan forums or debates if all *bona fide* candidates are invited to participate. The moderator should be neutral, and the exempt organization should state clearly its non-endorsement of any candidate.

(3) Individual political action. Ministers and employees of churches, of course, may become involved in politics as *individuals*. If they do, it should be made clear that they are not representing the church. A minister who speaks at a political gathering should not be introduced in his official capacity as representing the church.

---

[1] *Report from the Capital* 49/11 (May 31, 1994): 3. This summary of a complicated body of law is not intended to be legal advice governing all conceivable issues.

A church will be well advised not to engage in the following activities if it is interested preserving its tax-exempt status.

(1) Political endorsement. Candidates for public office should not be endorsed either directly or indirectly whether through a sermon, church bulletin, or other official organ of the church. If this happens, the church should issue a disclaimer in the same or similar form indicating the organization does not support or oppose candidates.

(2) Financial support. Financial or other support should not be provided to a campaign or to a candidate. In the same vein, a church may not provide volunteers, lists, free use of facilities, and the like, unless it is made available to all on an equal basis.

(3) Partisan campaign literature. Partisan campaign literature should not be distributed or displayed on church premises. This, generally speaking, includes the parking lot.

(4) Political action committees. Do not organize or become involved in a political action committee.

Even if tax exemption were not jeopardized by political activity, it's a risky venture. Explicit support of a political candidate by a church will almost always cause dissension in the congregation and water down the church's prophetic witness. By all means, speak out on political issues on which your congregation can agree, but steer clear of endorsing political candidates.

Testimony on Hostility to Religious Expression in the Public Square[1]

I. Introduction

Thank you, Mr. Chairman and members of the subcommittee, for this opportunity to speak to you on this important matter.

The BJC serves fourteen Baptist bodies, focusing on public policy issues concerning religious liberty and its constitutional corollary, the separation of church and state. For sixty-eight years in our nation's capital, the BJC has pursued a well-balanced, sensibly centrist approach to church-state issues. We take seriously *both* religion clauses in the First Amendment as essential guarantors of God-given religious liberty. It is, indeed, our "first freedom."

II. General Principles

The first sixteen words of the First Amendment to the Bill of Rights provide, "Congress shall make no law respecting an establishment of religion, or prohibiting the free exercise thereof." The wise architects of our republic fashioned these twin pillars—no establishment and free exercise—and placed them first in the Bill of Rights to protect what many of them believed to be the God-given right of religious freedom.

The establishment clause is designed to keep government from promoting, endorsing, or helping religion. The free exercise clause is intended to prevent government from discouraging, burdening, or hurting religion. The two, taken together, call for what Chief Justice Warren Burger called a "benevolent neutrality" on the part of government.[2] The religion clauses require government to accommodate religion without advancing it, protect religion without promoting it, and lift burdens on the exercise of religion without extending religion an impermissible benefit. These twin

---

[1] Testimony before the Subcommittee on the Constitution, Civil Rights, and Property Rights of the Committee on the Judiciary, United States Senate, regarding "Beyond the Pledge of Allegiance: Hostility to Religious Expression in the Public Square," June 8, 2004.

[2] *Walz v. Tax Commission*, 397 US 664, 669 (1970).

pillars buttress the wall of separation that is critical to ensuring our religious liberty. The best thing government can do for religion is to leave it alone.

The separation of church and state is relatively modern and distinctively American. True, it enjoys some biblical warrant. The notion that our relationship to God should be voluntary supports it; Jesus' admonition to "render to Caesar the things that are Caesar's and unto God the things that are God's" foreshadows it; the early church's refusal to seek help from Herod or shekels from Caesar models it.

Nevertheless, throughout most of the history of Western civilization, there was little, if any, affection for the separation of church and state. But the painful lessons of history teach that when government takes sides in religion—for or against—someone's religious liberty is denied and everyone's is threatened.

Our nation's founders had a decidedly different vision. The Constitution never mentions Christianity. It speaks of religion only once in article VI, and then to ban a religious test for public office. With the adoption of the religion clauses in the First Amendment two years later, our founders made it clear that the state must not take sides in matters of religion, and one's status in the civil community would not depend on a willingness to espouse any religious confession.

Our founders understood existentially that government and religion are both better off when neither tries to do the job of the other. When the state and the church are tied together, the church tends to use civil power to enforce its brand of religion and the state palms off the name of God to support its stripe of politics. But when the two are separated, religion tends to flourish, and the state is required to respect religious diversity. Far from encouraging hostility to religion, it has been indispensable in ensuring the greatest measure of religious liberty the world has ever seen.

The constitutional requirement of keeping church and state separate, however, does not call for the divorcement of religion from politics. The metaphorical wall of separation does not block metaphysical assumptions from playing a role in public life. Religious people have as much right as anyone else to vend their beliefs in the marketplace of ideas and (with some limits) to allow their religious ethics to influence public policy by preaching, teaching, organizing politically, and even running for office. Far from being prohibited, as a Baptist Christian I would say it is required. This is consistent with Jesus' call in the Sermon on the Mount to be "salt" and "light."[3]

Church-state separation and religious liberty are not opposing ideas engaged in a philosophical tug of war. Instead, separation is the means by which we ensure that liberty for everyone. The doctrine has never meant that church and state should be sealed off from each other with the state tending to important public affairs and the church shunted to the backwaters of private religion. Nor does it mean that religious people, when motivated to do so by their religious convictions, cannot speak out on public policy issues along with the rest of the political community. Religious people are not second-class citizens.

Thus, the BJC has always been committed to two goals: (1) the institutional and functional separation of church and state as an essential constitutional hedge protecting our religious freedom; and (2) the right of people of faith to express their religion freely and to engage in the political process the same as everyone else. While at first glance these goals may appear contradictory, in reality they are not. We affirm both a robust role of religion in public life and the institutional and functional separation of church and state. Indeed, the latter protects the former.

Religious expression pervades American culture, the media, and our politics. Anyone who has traveled abroad can see and feel the difference. We have come a long way since 1976 when Jimmy Carter announced he was a "born again" Christian and the Washington press corps—and most of the country for that matter—responded with befuddled amusement. They really did not know what he was talking about and were stunned that he spoke so freely and publicly about his faith.

Today, religious themes saturate the candidates' speeches and the public square generally. Religion animates most of the divisive current issues—from same-sex marriage, to abortion, to faith-based initiatives, to governmental posting of the Ten Commandments, to the Pledge of Allegiance. *Larry King Live, Crossfire, Hardball*, the *O'Reilly Factor*, the *Today Show, Real Time*, and the evening news—they cannot seem to stop talking about religion.

We have come a long way over the past quarter century, as speaking of God seems now to be a mandatory (not just a permissible) part of our political rhetoric. And our willingness as a culture to talk openly about

---

[3] Matthew 5:13–16.

religion belies any claim that we have a naked public square. Religious speech in public places by government leaders, the media, and private citizens abounds—bumper stickers, billboards, John 3:16 end-zone signs, post-game prayer huddles, cover stories on national news magazines, and religious programming on television and radio. And clearly the Mel Gibson movie, *The Passion of the Christ*, has taken this to a new level.

No, we do not and should not have a naked public square. Religious speech in public places by private citizens is commonplace; candidates for office routinely voice religious themes and language; and even public officials revel in various forms of civil religion with near impunity. In fact, far from a naked public square, it is actually dressed to the nines.

The following are helpful guidelines as we seek to honor the separation of church and state, while affirming the relevance of religious values to public life. We must defend the right of individuals and organizations to speak, debate, and advocate with their religious voices in the public square, as well as stand firm by the principle that government action without a secular purpose or with a primary effect that advances or inhibits religion violates the separation of church and state. Similarly, we should discourage efforts to make a candidate's religious affiliation or nonaffiliation a campaign issue and discourage the invoking of divine authority on behalf of candidates, policies, and platforms and the characterizing of opponents as sinful or ungodly.[4]

III. Examples of Application
Three contemporary issues provide good illustrations about how these general privileges play out in American life.

A. Religion in the Public Schools
A variety of church-state disputes commonly arise in the context of our public schools in ways that require a balancing of both no establishment and free exercise principles. The general rule is clear: the public schools must refrain from sponsoring religious exercises or otherwise promoting religion; but they should, and sometimes must, accommodate the free exercise rights of students. Voluntary, student-initiated prayer, for example, ordinarily

---

[4] The American Jewish Committee, Baptist Joint Committee, Interfaith Alliance Foundation, National Council of the Churches of Christ in the USA, Religious Action Center of Reform Judaism, *A Shared Vision: Religious Liberty in the 21st Century* (Washington, DC: 2002) 8.

should be permitted, but school-sponsored prayer must not be allowed. Public schools may *teach about* religion in history, social studies, comparative religion, and Bible-as-literature courses, but school officials should not *teach* religion in ways that would proselytize or promote a religious point of view.

The most recent Supreme Court case involving religion in the public schools, *Santa Fe Independent School District v. Doe* (2000), addresses the more difficult issue of student religious speech in the context of pervasive state sponsorship.[5] This case involved student-delivered prayers at football games in Texas. The Court, in a 6-3 vote, struck down the practice as unconstitutional. The Court reasoned that the student prayer was so shrouded in government sponsorship that it amounted to a state endorsement of religion. The school district adopted a pro-prayer policy; it conducted and supervised the election of the student to give the prayer; the prayer was delivered in the midst of a school-sponsored event (i.e., football game); and the school provided the microphone over which the prayer was to be broadcast. Finally, the Court reasoned that granting the student body the power to elect a speaker to pray is problematic. The very practice of voting whether to have a prayer before football games, and who the "prayer" would be, inevitably favors the majority religion in a given school district.

The focus of much of the current debate and developing case law is directed toward defining the proper contours of student-initiated religious expression. "Guidance on Constitutionally Protected Prayer in Public Elementary and Secondary Schools," issued by the United States Department of Education in 2003, addresses the issue in the context of school assemblies, athletic events, and graduation. It provides that where students are selected on neutral criteria and retain "primary control" over what they say, that expression will not be attributed to the school, and, therefore, cannot be restricted because of its religious content. The guidelines go on to suggest that, to avoid misunderstandings, school officials may make "appropriate disclaimers" to clarify that the speech is that of the student and not the school's. The guidelines supplement a more comprehensive set of guidelines issued by the United States Department of Education in 1995 by the Clinton administration.[6]

---

[5] *Santa Fe Independent School District v. Doe*, 530 US 290 (2000).
[6] http://www.ed.gov/Speeches/08-1995/religion.html.

The bottom-line, common-sense approach requires that we seek to balance the no establishment principle (i.e., no government-sponsored religion) with the free exercise principle (i.e., accommodating the rights of students to exercise their religion without interfering with the right of other students not to participate).

B. Ten Commandments

The posting of the Ten Commandments demonstrates how religious expression by politicians and government officials can turn into a violation of the establishment clause. While religious expression by public officials is ordinarily permitted, there are constitutional limits.

The Alabama Ten Commandments case is illustrative of a governmental official expressing his own religious views in a way that clearly crossed constitutional boundaries, and the federal courts were correct in so holding.[7] Sitting as the highest judicial officer in the state of Alabama, Chief Justice Roy Moore (1) singled out one favored religious tradition, (2) chose the preferred Scripture passage, and (3) displayed it in a way that created nothing less than a religious shrine. While so doing, he made theological judgments throughout. Which commandments? The ones found in Deuteronomy 5 or Exodus 20? Is it an English Old Testament version or the Hebrew Bible or maybe the Septuagint in Greek? If English, is it a Catholic or Protestant one? If Protestant, which translation—King James, New International Version, or Revised Standard Version? These are fundamentally religious decisions that government officials are uniquely ill suited to make. How strange it is to create a graven image out of a document in which God says we are not supposed to have any graven images!

It is critical to acknowledge the difference between *government* speech endorsing religion, which the establishment clause prohibits, and *private* religious speech, which the Constitution protects, to paraphrase Justice Sandra Day O'Connor.[8] Religious speech by private citizens, even in public places, is not forbidden; it is protected and commonly practiced.

There are unlimited ways in which the Ten Commandments can be expressed in public without the help of government. For example:

1. They can be posted in front of every church and synagogue in the land at the edge of the property in full public view.

---

[7] *Glassroth v. Moore*, 229 F.Supp.2d 1290 (M.D. AL 2002).
[8] *Board v. Mergens*, 496 US 226 (1990).

2. The Ten Commandments can be displayed even on *public* property if that property is dedicated as a free-speech forum.

3. One can hold up a sign reading "Exodus 20" or "Deuteronomy 5," instead of "John 3:16," in the end zones of televised football games.

4. Taking a lesson from the prophet Jeremiah, we can write the commandments on our "hearts" instead of on stone, thereby providing a living witness to the principles embodied in those teachings in a way that truly makes a difference.

In sum, the question is not whether the Ten Commandments embody the right *teachings*; the question rather is who is the right *teacher*—American politicians, public officials, and judicial officers, or parents, religious leaders, and families? The answer is the latter; they do not need the help of the former. As a Baptist minister, I can think of little better than for everyone to read and obey the Ten Commandments; as a constitutional lawyer, I can think of little worse than for governmental officials to tell us to do it.

Finally, even public officials are not prohibited from considering the Ten Commandments in the proper context. For example:

1. Schools may teach *about* the Ten Commandments in a Bible-as-literature course.

2. Schools may instruct students in the ethical precepts embodied in the last five commandments in a proper character education program.

3. The commandments can be depicted as an integral part of a historical/educational exhibit such as on the frieze in the US Supreme Court courtroom.

C. Pledge of Allegiance

The case presently pending before the Supreme Court, in *Elk Grove v. Newdow* (no. 02-1624),[9] illustrates a practice that may be constitutional, but represents a form of civil religion that vitiates vital religion. In my opinion, teacher-led recitation of the Pledge of Allegiance does not violate the establishment clause for several reasons.

First, the Pledge of Allegiance is not a religious exercise. It is a secular pledge that, when taken as a whole, is intended to inspire patriotism. It does not have the purpose or primary effect of advancing religion. At most, it is an acknowledgment of this nation's religious roots.

---

[9] *Elk Grove Unified School District v. Newdow*, 542 US 1 (2004).

Second, this reference to America's religious character does not play favorites. A pledge to "one nation, under Jesus," or "under Buddha" would be difficult to defend. True, the word "God" implies a certain monotheism, and the phrase "under God" is not a perfectly nuanced reflection of America's religious pluralism. But it is hard to come up with a more inclusive phrase than this one.

Third, students cannot be compelled to recite the Pledge—with or without the words "under God." The Supreme Court ruled eleven years before "under God" was added to the Pledge in 1954 that students have the right to refuse to pledge allegiance to the flag.[10] Students who object to reciting the Pledge cannot be compelled to say it or disciplined for not participating.

That said, what is legal and constitutional is not always helpful or wise. One wonders if including the words "under God" in the Pledge has done religion any favors. Civil religion in its various configurations has long been a pervasive part of American political culture. In its more benign forms, civil religion serves as a unifying, cultural balm that reminds us of our religious roots as a nation, but it can easily and often morph into an idolatry of nationalism or, at the very least, result in the trivialization of religion.

Simply stated, civil religion is not the same as heartfelt, vital religion. Ceremonial religion is not life-altering, world-changing religion. "Ceremonial deism," as it is sometimes called, is a pale substitute for authentic faith. Indeed, one of the traditional arguments in favor of the constitutionality of this and other forms of ceremonial deism is that, through long use and rote repetition, the words have lost any religious import they might have had. In short, what is commonplace becomes mundane.

The vitality of religion in America is thus diminished—not enhanced—when people of faith conflate our penultimate allegiance to Caesar with our ultimate allegiance to God.

IV. Conclusion

We must catch the vision of our nation's founders—religious freedom for all, unaided and unhindered by government—and make it a reality in our day. We must commit ourselves to protecting religious expression in public places—even sometimes from the mouths of public officials—without

---

[10] *West Virginia v. Barnette*, 319 US 624 (1943).

allowing government officially to promote religion or to pick and choose among religions.

Two founders succinctly expressed this aspiration. Daniel Carroll, a Catholic from Maryland, captured the pith of the free exercise principle when he said, "The rights of conscience are of particular delicacy and will little bear the gentlest touch of government's hand."[11] On the other side of the Potomac, Virginia Baptist John Leland expressed the rationale for the no establishment principle when he exclaimed, "The fondness of magistrates to foster Christianity has done it more harm than all the persecutions ever did."[12]

The stirring words of Carroll and Leland call for government neutrality in religion and highlight the importance of protecting the rights of conscience of every human being. They reflect the bookends for a well-balanced view of a free church in a free state.

---

[11] *Annals of Congress*, ed. J. Gales (Washington, DC: Gales and Seaton, 1834) 757.

[12] C. F. Green, ed., *The Writings of the Late Elder John Leland* (New York: Arno Press 1970) 278.

The Religious American Citizen

Matthew 22:17-21; Romans 13:1-5; Acts 4:13-20

Perhaps to a greater degree than any other time in history, the subject of religion and politics fills our political culture and public discourse. We've come a long way since 1976 when Baptist Jimmy Carter announced he was a "born again" Christian and the entire Washington press corps—and much of the country—responded with befuddled amusement. They really didn't know what he was talking about and were stunned that he spoke so freely and publicly about his faith.

Today, God-talk saturates politicians' speeches and debates. Religion animates most of the divisive issues from same-sex marriage, to abortion, to faith-based initiatives, to the Ten Commandments, to the Pledge of Allegiance, to support for and opposition to war. Additionally, media outlets like *Larry King, Daily Show, Hardball, Real Time, O'Reilly Factor, Today Show*, the evening news can't seem to get enough of it.

Yes, we've come a long way over the past thirty years; I would say we've overshot the mark, as God-talk is now a mandatory (not just a permissible) part of our political rhetoric (a practical "religious test"). Our willingness as a culture to talk about religion openly belies any claim that we have a "naked public square." Religious speech in public places by government leaders, the media, and private citizens abounds—bumper stickers, billboards, truck signs, John 3:16 end-zone signs, post-game prayer huddles, cover stories in national news magazines, and religious programming on TV and radio. And movies too—*The Passion of the Christ*, last year's *The Lion, the Witch, and the Wardrobe*, and this year's *The DaVinci Code*—carry that tradition forward.

These days the public square is not naked; in fact, it is "dressed to the nines." We are one of the most religious and certainly the most religiously diverse nation on this planet!

I.

How do we honor our Baptist and American commitment to separation of church and state, while affirming the relevance of religious ethics to politics? How do we have a public conversation about religion without dragging it through the mud of political campaigns? How do we give religion its due without promoting a watered-down "civil religion" that in its extreme morphs into an idolatry of nationalism or trivializes genuine faith?

We need to think clearly about our duties as citizens of faith and our responsibilities to the two kingdoms of which we are a part—the United States of America and the kingdom of God. How we define and respond to those two allegiances is a difficult and often divisive question.

New Testament scriptures give us some guidance but no easy answers. Jesus said to "render unto Caesar the things that are Caesar's and unto God the things that are God's" (Matt. 22:15-22). He affirmed the two kingdoms and our dual allegiance, but he didn't tell us what belonged to whom. He did not say how many taxes to pay to Caesar!

Then we turn to the writings of Paul. In Romans 13 he speaks glowingly of the state. Paul affirms not only allegiance to the state, but he plainly says that the authority of the state is divinely ordained. Civil government is good. God created it to keep order and to provide for the general welfare. And if Paul's teachings applied to the heavy-handed Roman rule in the first century, how much more should they apply to us living in a robust constitutional democracy? This is the passage we love to read on the Fourth of July.

But then we turn over to Acts 4 and see the encounter of Peter and John with the Sanhedrin. The Sanhedrin was a high court with some civic as well as religious jurisdiction. The Sanhedrin was exercising the same kind of authority Paul spoke of so approvingly in Romans 13. When they order Peter and John not to preach anymore in Jesus' name, we get a decidedly negative picture of government. The disciples repudiated civil authority because it sought to interfere with their proclamation of gospel. There are others too—such as Revelation 13 and 17—where the state is called a blasphemous beast and a great harlot. We turn to these passages for comfort on April 15!

So we have both of those strains in the Bible. The state is good, but not the ultimate good! That should not surprise us. The Bible is full of tensions and seeming paradoxes on a variety of scores. These two views of the state also pick up on the theme of "priest" versus "prophet" that we see throughout Scripture.

Sometimes religious citizens are called to be priests to the government—like Elisha, pasturing, cajoling, and comforting Naaman (2 Kings 5). Sometimes we provide a pastoral word to government. (This is hardest to do when your political opponents are in office.) Modern political philosophers, including many of our nation's founders and others since then, have recognized the value of religion to a stable, democratic government. Civic virtue grounded in religion is part of the glue that holds us together as a society. We should do no less than to pray for our leaders.

But our citizenship demands more. It should also drive us to be prophets. Sometimes it requires us to be prophetic—like Nathan calling upon David to repent from his sinful ways and to toe the line of righteousness. Religion doesn't exist just to prop up government, but to challenge government and call it to judgment. (This is hard to do when you like those who control the reins of power.)

So, again, how as American citizens of faith do we strike the appropriate balance? We can look to history, as well as Scripture. The wise founders of our republic fashioned a Constitution that outlaws any religious test for public office and protects the freedom of religion and the rights of conscience. Informed by centuries of religious persecution that always occurred when political power and religious zeal came together, the founders took the radical step of separating church and state—forbidding government from taking sides in matters of religion.

As a minister, I know the separation of church and state is good—not bad—for religion; and as a lawyer I know it is good for government, too. When we separate the two, religion tends to flourish and flower, and the state is freed from the daunting task of making decisions about religion—something it doesn't do well. You don't have to take my word for it, and it's not a modern notion. James Madison—the father of the Constitution—recognized its value when he reflected on this audacious experiment in the 1820s: "The number, industry and morality of the priesthood, and the devotion of the people have been manifestly increased by the total separation of church and state."[1]

---

[1] Robert S. Alley, ed., *James Madison and Religious Liberty* (Buffalo: Prometheus, 1985) 80–81.

Separation does not require a segregation of religion from politics or God from government. Religious people have as much right as anybody else to seek to vend their convictions in the marketplace of ideas and (with some limits) to convert their religious ethics into public policy by organizing, speaking out, voting, getting involved, and even running for office. Candidates for office need not shed their religious beliefs or keep silent about them. Not only is this not prevented, but as a Christian I would say it is required. This is consistent with Jesus' call in the Sermon on the Mount to be "salt" and "light."[2]

A critic once took the late nineteenth-century preacher Dwight Moody to task for his involvement in political and social affairs. "Are you not a citizen of heaven?" the detractor asked. "Yes, someday I shall be," Moody responded, "but right now I'm registered to vote in Cook County, Illinois." The same is true for us.

We need not limit our piety to the church house or to acts of private devotion, nor do we have to concede the public square to others. We must speak out, become involved, and transform our culture in part through the political process.

II.

We hear a lot of talk these days about the Ten Commandments. We'd be better off if we took Jeremiah seriously and wrote them on our hearts instead of carving them in stone. I want to set out five, not ten, commandments for us to follow as we enter the fray of political life.[3]

1. *Thou shalt acknowledge the limited scope of thy perspective, exercising much humility.* Any foray into politics with focused religious motivation should be tempered with a good dose of humility and self-criticism. Blaise Pascal reminded us that "men never do evil so completely and cheerfully as when they do it from religious conviction."[4] We need to understand that, however sure we think we are of our position, the other person at least has something to say and maybe in the final analysis is right. This reflects the main problem I have with the bombastic broadsides that we hear mainly from the religious right in recent years. As James Dunn has said, "What they say is

---

[2] Matthew 5:13–16.

[3] Based on Randall Frame and Alan Tharpe's *Ten Commandments of Moderate Political Behavior* (Grand Rapids MI: Zondervan, 1996).

[4] Pensèes, no. 813, ed. A. J. Krailsheimer; no. 895, ed. Brunschvieg (1670, trans. 1688), rev. A. J. Krailsheimer (1966).

not totally false; it is falsely total." It often lacks a note of self-evaluation, of tentativeness, of humility that one needs to bring to bear on a public policy message based squarely on one's religious conviction. This goes for fundamentalism on the religious left as well. We all "see through glass darkly."[5]

Barbara Jordan, our Baptist sister, had it right. At a meeting of the Baptist Joint Committee twenty years ago, she was asked how properly to articulate Christian values in government. Her response went something like this: "You would do well to pursue your causes with vigor, while remembering that you are a servant of God, not a spokesperson for God and remembering that God might well choose to bless an opposing point of view for reasons that have not been revealed to you."[6]

Some humility is called for here.

2. *Thou shalt acknowledge that thy brother and sister may disagree with thee and yet deserve thy respect.* Any attempt to elevate "my" view on an issue to the status of "the Christian" or "the godly" position, to the exclusion of others, should be held in check. Religious persons of good will can (and usually do) disagree over how their religious convictions play out in the public arena. As Carl F. H. Henry once said, "there is no direct line from the Bible to the ballot box."

We even see this in Baptist life. Bill Moyers, in his own inimitable way, paints a portrait of Baptists in history and contemporary culture:

> Baptists have been to the left of the American establishment—and to the right. Jesse Jackson is a Baptist; so is Jesse Helms. Baptists defended slavery, and Baptists agitated to end it. Some black Baptists churches are precincts of the Democratic Party, while in some white churches GOP stands for God's Own Preserve. Some Baptists read the Bible as if it were a AAA road map to Armageddon: others find it a spiritual codebook to the mysteries and miracles of the Kingdom within. Millions of Baptists see American culture as the enemy. Millions of others proclaim that we are part of the show. On-lookers shake their heads at how people so disputatious could be defined by a common name; those of us who

[5] 1 Corinthians 13:12.

[6] Address, Baptist Joint Committee 50th Anniversary Celebration, First Baptist Church of the City of Washington, DC, 1986.

wear it shrug our shoulders at the anomalies and schisms and go on punching (usually each other).[7]

We need to stop trying to convince each other we've got God in our hip pockets. God is not a Republican or a Democrat, nor even an American for that matter. God's precinct is the universe. To paraphrase Abraham Lincoln's famous pronouncement about the Civil War, the question is not whether God is on our side, but whether we are on God's side. God is not aligned with any political party, but is able to work within and through all political movements and nations to accomplish ultimate purposes.

We will not always agree on issues of public policy or vote the same way.

3. *Thou shalt speak and act in a way that does not undercut thy witness, resisting the temptation to stereotype.* This means at least that we don't lie about our opponents, distort their positions, or resort to violence. It means that we speak forcefully to be sure but also truthfully, directly, and lovingly—always paying proper attention to nuance. Charles Colson has warned conservatives and liberals alike "to cool the incendiary rhetoric." He says the so-called culture war will "never be won by waving placards in the faces of supposed enemies or whacking them with leather bound Bibles."[8]

Bumper stickers, sound bites, and clever sloganeering do little to advance the commonweal. Shrill examples fill and often debase our politics: (1) Those who are pro-choice are not "pro-abortion"; they mostly don't want government to invade the sanctity of a woman's body. Those who are pro-life are not necessarily "anti-choice"; they simply move the time for choosing back to the act of conception. (2) Those who favor same-sex marriages or civil unions may not be as much "pro-gay" as they are pro-equal protection and civil rights for all. Those who oppose such measures are not always "homophobic bigots," but people who are trying to be faithful to their understanding of biblical truth. (3) Those who oppose government hanging of the Ten Commandments in public places are not "anti-Ten Commandments"; they simply don't want government officials picking the preferred religion and Scriptural passage endorsing the message, "I am the Lord your God...You shall have no other gods before me." (4)

---

[7] Ibid.

[8] Charles Colson, "Sweet Reason and Holy Outrage," *Christianity Today*, July 19, 1993, p. 64.

Those who oppose the war in Iraq may not be the least unpatriotic, but serious disciples of the "prince of peace" and against preemptive war except in the face of dire necessity. (5) Those who decry the policies of the religious right are not all "Christian bashers." Those who rail against the coarsening and secularization of our culture are not all "benighted reactionaries."

Yet, these outlandish diatribes against one another continue. We need to debate our differences vigorously. However, we must speak and act in a way that sheds light, not heat, on the important issues of our day.

4. *Thou shalt not fall into the civil religion trap.* Though our debate should be civil, our religion shouldn't be. I have argued for the constitutionality of many forms of civil religion; now I want to mention theological and ethical qualms about its overuse. Robert Linder defines it as "that generalized form of national faith that mixes…piety with patriotism and traditional religion with national life until it is impossible to distinguish between the two."[9] It's often the blend of a murky Judeo-Christian consensus with uncritical, flag-waving Americanism. Former Senator Mark Hatfield adds that civil religion "distorts the relationship between the state and our faith. It tends to enshrine…national righteousness while failing to speak of repentance, salvation and God's standard of justice."[10]

Civil religion results when we fail properly to distinguish between God and government. It happens when we go too long on the pastoral and too short on the prophetic. When we fail to keep that healthy distance from government, we can get captured by government and used for political purposes. We can become "cheerleaders" instead of "referees."

Civil religion in its extreme form amounts to an idolatry of nationalism. We need to place our faith in the biblical God of justice and righteousness, not the puny deity of civil religion.

5. *Thou shalt not involve thy church in electoral politics.* While our duties as citizens of faith require individuals to become involved, churches and religious organizations must be more circumspect. First, being politically involved can jeopardize the nonprofit's tax-exempt status. The tax code is clear that, while churches may take position on public *issues*, they may not support or oppose *candidates* for public office. This includes outright

---

[9] R. V. Pierard and R. D. Linder, *Civil Religion and the Presidency* (Grand Rapids MI: Academie Books, 1988) 23.

[10] [CITE?]

endorsement, financial support, distributing campaign literature, and joining political action committees.

Churches, of course, may encourage good citizenship and promote voter education by distributing voting records of candidates and unbiased results of candidates' questionnaires on a range of issues, holding a public forum and debate (as long as all candidates are invited), and spearheading voter registration drives. Ministers and other church leaders may become involved in politics as long as it's clear that they are doing so as individuals, not representing the church.

Even if you don't care about the tax-exempt status of churches, it's still not a good idea for a church to become involved. It can be dangerous and highly divisive and turn our pulpit prophets into political puppets. We must be careful about the activities of the church in the arena of political campaigns.

III.

Richard Niebuhr wrote a thoughtful book years ago called *Christ and Culture*.[11] It outlined five different ways Christians can (and do) relate to the surrounding culture: (1) Christ against culture, (2) Christ of culture, (3) Christ above culture, (4) Christ and culture in paradox, and finally, the one Niebuhr liked best, (5) Christ transforming culture—for the church to so penetrate culture that it converts the world around it through its public presence and witness. At the end of the book Niebuhr gives this parting advice to guide our decision making as we try to transform culture: "[We] make our decisions in faith...[and] make them in view of the fact that no single [person] or group or historical time is the church; but there is a church of faith in which we do our partial, relative work.... [We] make them in view of the fact that Christ...is not only the head of the church but the redeemer of the world. [We] make them, in view of the fact that the world of culture—man's achievement—exists within the world of grace—God's Kingdom."[12]

So religious American citizens move in both realms—the Kingdom of God and the kingdom of Caesar, and we are at the proper time both pastoral and prophetic. We speak our piece and advance our cause with humility, not expecting that others will agree or claiming to know for sure the mind of

---

[11] H. Richard Niebuhr, *Christ and Culture* (New York: Harper, 1951).
[12] Ibid., 256.

God. We behave responsibly and with integrity knowing that unworthy means are never justified by even the worthiest of ends.

Respecting Religion,
Respecting Liberty

Congress shall make no law respecting an establishment of religion, or prohibiting the free exercise thereof

Showing Proper Respect[1]

Efforts by government officials to display the Ten Commandments on public property is one of the most divisive church-state issues experienced in the United States for the past twenty-five years. Perhaps second only to state-sponsored prayer in the public schools, the posting of the Ten Commandments has spawned widespread debate throughout the nation and its courts. How ironic that a sacred text that millions regard as the word of God should be the source for so much discord.

The United States Supreme Court will consider two cases challenging Ten Commandments displays under the First Amendment's establishment clause this term. One case, *Van Orden v. Perry* (no. 03-1500),[2] involves a Ten Commandments monolith donated in 1961 by the Fraternal Order of Eagles and displayed with the authorization of the Texas legislature on the grounds of the Texas capitol. The Fifth US Circuit Court of Appeals upheld the constitutionality of this display. The court ruled that the monument has a secular purpose of teaching about our legal system and denied that any reasonable observer would view it as an endorsement of religion. The second case, *McCreary County v. ACLU of Kentucky* (no. 03-1693),[3] involves displays in courthouses in two Kentucky counties. There the Sixth Circuit ruled that these displays do not have a sufficiently secular purpose and have the primary effect of endorsing religion. These cases are expected to be decided before the end of the Court term in June 2005.

Media tend to present the dispute as a clash between forces of secularism trying to ban religion from the public square and people of faith bent on promoting morality through the offices of government. This dichotomy is unfortunate and misleading. Many people of faith and religious organizations oppose government endorsements of the Ten Command-

---

[1] *Liberty* 100/3 (May/June 2005): 9. The Baptist Joint Committee, along with the Interfaith Alliance Foundation, has filed friend-of-the-court briefs in both cases discussed in this article. I express gratitude to Professor Douglas Laycock, of the University of Texas School of Law, and K. Hollyn Hollman, general counsel of the BJC, for writing and editing these briefs.

[2] *Van Orden v. Perry*, 545 US 677 (2005).

[3] *McCreary County v. ACLU of Kentucky*, 545 US 844 (2005).

ments for reasons having everything to do with religion and religious liberty. Everyone's religious liberty is denied when government officials select the preferred religion, pick out a particular passage of sacred text, and display it in a way that carries with it the full endorsement of the state. Opposition to government-sponsored displays of the Ten Commandments is buttressed by several rationales. Such displays are often unconstitutional, based on bad theology, predicated on a misreading of history, and contrary to notions of fundamental fairness.

Government is presumed to endorse the message it communicates in its official displays. It is possible to negate affirmatively the appearance of an endorsement, but none of the governmental bodies in these cases did so. Although the capitol grounds in Austin contain seventeen different monuments, they are spread out over nearly 20 acres. Thus the Ten Commandments monument is essentially freestanding, and none of the other monuments have anything to do with religion or bear a religious text. The content of this Ten Commandments display is undeniably religious.

The Ten Commandments displays in Kentucky, though less dramatic in size and presented on the walls of courthouses, amount no less to an endorsement of religion. After the litigation began, Kentucky officials added some secular documents, but the message endorsing the Decalogue remained clear.

Supreme Court precedent supports the unconstitutionality of these endorsements of sacred texts. In *Stone v. Graham*, the Court ruled that the posting of the Ten Commandments by the state of Kentucky in public school classrooms violated the establishment clause. The Court reasoned,

> The Ten Commandments are undeniably a sacred text in the Jewish and Christian faiths, and no legislative recitation of a supposed secular purpose can blind us to that fact. The Commandments do not confine themselves to arguably secular matters.... Rather, the first part of the Commandments concerns the religious duties of believers: worshipping the Lord God alone, avoiding idolatry, not using the Lord's name in vain, and observing the Sabbath Day.... If the posted copies of the Ten Commandments are to have any effect at all, it will be to induce the schoolchildren to read, meditate upon, perhaps to venerate and obey, the Commandments. However desirable this might be as a matter of

private devotion, it is not a permissible state objective under the Establishment Clause.[4]

There are also important theological reasons that many people of faith object to government posting and endorsing of holy writ. It puts government officials in the role of priests, making fundamentally theological determinations that they are ill suited to make. How can they speak to questions such as the following: Do we post the commandments of Deuteronomy 5 or Exodus 20? Is it an English Old Testament version, the Hebrew Bible, or maybe the Septuagint in Greek? If in English, is it Catholic or Protestant? If Protestant, which version—King James, New International, Revised Standard? All of these translations and versions vary in language and theological import. For example, the Hebrew Bible translates a word in one of the commandments "murder," while the various English versions render the word "kill." The Catholic version says nothing about "graven images," but has two commandments on "coveting." There are many "Ten Commandments," not just one, and government officials are not competent to pick and choose from among them. These decisions are best left to families, churches, and synagogues.

Moreover, one cannot properly interpret a sacred text without considering the context. The Ten Commandments, including the first one—"I am the Lord your God.... You shall have no other gods before me" (Exodus 20:2, 3)—are part of a covenant between God and the Hebrew people. The text is betrayed when Moses and the Israelites are replaced with politicians and American citizens. One has to wonder why some Christians are so intent on posting the Ten Commandments. The commandments emphasize law and rules, leaving out crucial Christian concepts such as God's grace, faith in Christ, personal conversion, and New Testament ethics. The commandments, while foundational in their teachings, fail to capture the full hope of Christianity.

Finally, the Ten Commandments are often posted with the idea of making them a talisman—something of a good-luck charm—to help protect our culture from the influences of secularism. This risks violating the first commandment against having other gods and the second commandment against making graven images. How strange it is to violate two of the commandments by endorsing all ten!

---

[4] *Stone v. Graham*, 449 US 39 (1980).

Governmental attempts to post the Ten Commandments are also based on bad history. Proponents often argue that such postings are justified because the American system of law is predicated on the Ten Commandments. Indeed, the United States Department of Justice has filed a brief in the Supreme Court claiming as much.

Although there is a vague sense in which a Judeo-Christian ethic underpins our legal system, the connection is too attenuated to justify government officially endorsing that religion's sacred text. Only some of the commandments—such as killing, stealing, and bearing false witness—are the proper subjects of secular law. The others are demonstrably religious. American law is based on the common law of England, but these prohibitions were already a part of Anglo-Saxon jurisprudence before England was Christianized. The fundamental notion that it is wrong to murder, steal another's property, or bear false witness was already well ensconced among the Saxons before they ever heard of the Ten Commandments.

Moreover, documents that have directly influenced our legal system—the Magna Carta, English Bill of Rights, Mayflower Compact, Declaration of Independence, Federalist Papers—say little about religion and nothing about the Ten Commandments. Most important, our Constitution—the civil compact that governs our public life together—mentions religion only once, in article VI, and then only to disallow a religious test for public office. Further, the First Amendment makes clear that the federal government is not permitted to advance or inhibit religion. In sum, although the Ten Commandments—along with many other ancient secular and sacred legal codes—stand in the backdrop to American law, that alone does not justify government officials endorsing this one distant precursor.

Last, posting of the Ten Commandments by governmental officials violates common notions of fair play. It is simply unfair for government to endorse this one expression of faith. Nothing is more basic to our sense of fairness than the golden rule. People of faith and no faith embrace it. How does the golden rule play out in church-state relations? In this way, I cannot ask government to promote my religion if I don't want government to promote someone else's religion. I cannot permit government to ignore someone else's religion in order to promote my religion.

In our pluralistic nation, one of the worst things government can do is to take sides in matters of religion. One of the reasons we have had precious little religious strife despite our dizzying diversity is that government has generally remained neutral in such matters. Those who follow religious traditions other than Judaism and Christianity can rightly question why their sacred text is ignored and that of the dominant religious tradition is acknowledged and approved.

Finally, although governmental endorsement of the Ten Commandments is unconstitutional, theologically suspect, predicated on faulty history, and fundamentally unfair, there are ways in which government may deal with the Ten Commandments.

First, the Decalogue sometimes can be included as part of a cultural and historical display. For example, the frieze encircling the ceiling of the courtroom at the Supreme Court shows a Moses figure holding tablets with several Hebrew letters. However, along with Moses, the frieze depicts seventeen other great lawgivers of history, including the likes of Hammurabi, Confucius, Justinian, Muhammad, Charlemagne, William Blackstone, and John Marshall. The overall effect of the frieze is not to endorse Judaism, Christianity, or even religion in general. Rather, it is simply an architectural depiction of law in history.

Moreover, the Ten Commandments can be taken up in our public schools in an effort to teach *about* religion in a course on comparative religion or on the Bible as literature, as long as it serves an educational rather than a devotional purpose. The contents of the "second table" of the Ten Commandments, dealing with our relationships to one another rather than with God, can be advanced by government, even in the public schools. School officials, of course, can teach students that it is wrong to kill, steal, or lie.

Finally, nothing prohibits *private* citizens from displaying the Ten Commandments in *public* places. Justice Sandra Day O'Connor has repeatedly emphasized the crucial difference between government speech endorsing religion, which the establishment clause prohibits, and private religious speech, which the Constitution protects. The Ten Commandments can be posted in front of every church and synagogue in the land in full public view. They can be displayed by private citizens, even on public property, if the site is open to all forms of expression. Best of all, we can take a lesson from the prophet Jeremiah and write the commandments on our hearts instead of on stone or on paper, thereby providing a living witness to the principles embodied in those teachings.[5]

In conclusion, the debate is not about whether the commandments teach sound theology or wholesome ethics—particularly for Jews and Christians. The question is who is the right *teacher*—politicians or parents, public officials or pastors, government committees or families? As a Baptist minister I can think of little better than for everyone to obey the Ten Commandments, but as a constitutional lawyer I can think of little worse than for public officials to tell us to do it.

---

[5] Jeremiah 31:31–34.

Respecting Religious Diversity
During the Holiday Season[1]

Are "Christian haters" and "professional atheists" engaged in an all-out war on Christmas, as *FOX News* anchor John Gibson claims? I don't think so—unless one is prepared to say that President Bush and the First Lady are leading the effort. This year's White House greeting card extends "best wishes for a holiday season of hope and happiness." No mention of "Merry Christmas" from the First Family.

Between Thanksgiving and New Year's, various religious groups observe about a dozen holy days. For decades we have been confronted by the "December dilemma" of how to acknowledge and celebrate winter religious holidays, usually in the context of the schools, in a way that is constitutional and culturally sensitive. People of good faith, including the Baptist Joint Committee, have worked long and hard to develop guidelines that comply with the Supreme Court's interpretation of the First Amendment's religion clauses and respect the amazing religious diversity in this country.

There is widespread agreement that

1. Holiday concerts in the public schools can and should include religious music along with the secular, as long as the sacred does not dominate.

2. Religious dramatic productions can be presented in the public schools as long as they do not involve worship and are part of an effort to use religious holidays as an occasion to teach about religion.

3. Freestanding crèches, as thoroughly religious Christian symbols, should not be sponsored by government, but Christmas trees and menorahs are sufficiently secular to allow their display without a constitutional problem.

Having settled many of the legal issues, some are now bent on fighting battles in a culture war against an enemy that does not exist. Some on the religious and media right lament political correctness run amok, such as

---

[1] *Report from the Capital* 60/10 (November/December 2005): 3.

calling a Christmas tree a "holiday tree" and extending "seasons greetings" instead of "Merry Christmas." In fact, they have threatened lawsuits to rectify such indiscretions and, in the private sector, encouraged a boycott of merchants that fail to use the right words.

What irony and how sad—to pick a fight over what to call a season that for many celebrates the coming of the Prince of Peace. We would all do well to take a deep breath and exercise some common sense as we think and talk about this season.

Christmas is Christmas and a tree is a tree. There's nothing wrong with calling it what it is: a Christmas tree. And it is perfectly appropriate to extend a specific holiday greeting such as my Jewish friends do when they wish me a "Merry Christmas," and I return a "Happy Hanukkah."

Often, though, it's quite appropriate to wish another "happy holidays" or "season's greetings." It's just a matter of good manners and common courtesy. If I am talking to a person whose religious affiliation I do not know, I will employ the more general greeting, and the same goes for merchants who advertise goods to Americans of many religious traditions who may or may not celebrate Christmas.

None of this disparages Christmas one iota or diminishes my enjoyment of it in the least. Why are these culture warriors bound to start a brouhaha in the midst of the love, joy, peace, and hope of Advent?

It's part of a concerted effort to affirm the mythical "Christian nation" status of the United States. (By the way, the Puritans and many other religious people well into the nineteenth century refused to celebrate Christmas because they thought it was unchristian and not supported by Scripture). In the words of the title of the Beatles song, "I, Me, Mine," it's all about *me* and the brash assertion of *my* supposed right to impose my religion on others. Moreover, and I hope it is not a too-jaded thought, these bombastic diatribes about a war on Christmas attract publicity and make for good fundraising. Truth be known, the Christmas spirit is threatened more by runaway commercialism—beginning just after Halloween—than by any supposed cultural hostility to a holiday that more than 90 percent of our citizens celebrate.

No, we do not need government promoting our religious holidays to the exclusion of others. Nor do we need a corps of purity police trying to dissuade our efforts to respect the religious diversity that is the hallmark of this country.

To all of our readers, then, Merry Christmas, Happy Hanukkah, and a Joyous Kwanzaa, Martyrdom Day of Guru Tegh Bahadur, Bodhi Day, Maunajiyaras Day, Beginning of Masa'il, Nisf Sha'ban and Yalda Night, Yule and Shinto Winter Solstice, and Ramadan! Or simply happy holidays!

Gentle Breeze of Freedom in China
Allows Churches to Move Forward[1]

The state of religious liberty in China has been and should be the subject of much discussion. Despite welcome economic and social reforms, China is no paragon of Jeffersonian democracy. Freedom in China is more like a gentle breeze than a gusty gale.

Religious liberty is sometimes repressed, particularly by provincial governments. That's the bad news. The often overlooked good news is that the conditions are far better than critics of the Chinese government often claim, and China is far ahead of where it was twenty—even ten—years ago! What I observed during an eight-day trip to that amazing and ancient land gave me hope for the future about religious liberty in China. But you should judge for yourself.

Chen Mei Lin, executive associate general secretary of the China Christian Council (CCC), spoke with pride of China's churches and the way in which the CCC strives "to render unto Caesar the things that are Caesar's and unto God the things that are God's." The group's credo is "Love country/ love church—glorify God/serve people." Stated another way, they want to be good citizens and good Christians at the same time. Sound familiar? Chen Mei Lin spoke with great elation when she surveyed the Christian movement in China. In 1979, there were approximately 600,000 Christians in China; today there are more than 16 million, and that doesn't count millions of Christians who are not associated with the CCC.

Rev. Yu Xin Li, general secretary of the Beijing Christian Council, was relegated for twenty-two years to harvesting rice during the Cultural Revolution. He returned to pastor the Gang Wa Shi Church—the first church in Beijing to reopen—in 1980. A gregarious man, he regaled us with sermons and stories over a gourmet meal. Sitting at the same table was the studious dean of the seminary in Beijing, who was a member of the Red Guard in his younger years. Wow! A former persecutor and victim sharing table fellowship.

---

[1] *Report from the Capital* 8/14 (September/October 2003): 3.

Our visit to the Eastern China Theological Seminary and the Jiangsu Bible School revealed a fecund climate of theological education—eighteen seminaries—training pastors to serve in rapidly burgeoning Chinese churches. The CCC and private donations support the seminaries. Tuition is free. There is no direct financial support from the government, although seminaries, like churches, are often given good deals on land. They operate openly and above ground.

We worshipped on Sunday morning at the Mo Chou Road Christian Church in Nanjing. The sanctuary was already rocking when we arrived early for the 8:30 service. The entire congregation had come early, as it always does, to "practice" the hymns. A female lay leader, Zhang Fenglin, delivered the forty-minute sermon. I did not understand a word but enjoyed every minute of it. Chinese Christians come to worship early, stay late, and long for the next opportunity to gather.

On Wednesday, we attended prayer meeting at the Gang Wa Shi Church, also at 8:30 a.m. Again, the place was packed and the worshippers raring to go. Led by a female pastor, Du Fengying, the church has grown over the past 20 years to more than 5,000 people. Multiple services are needed to accommodate the congregation.

These worship services were conducted openly and with full knowledge—even blessing—of the government. Even so-called "underground" churches (ones that are not affiliated with the CCC and not "registered" with the government) typically worship without interference. It is said that what is reputed to be the largest "underground" church in all of China meets on the second floor of a building that houses the police station on the first floor!

The state of church-state relations in China is too complex and multifaceted to be explored adequately in this space. China continues to struggle with human rights and religious liberty, but the situation is far better than many suppose. Some of the stories of persecution—particularly outside the urban centers in the East—are credible. As Bill O'Brien has observed, in a country of 1.2 billion, anything that can be said about China is true somewhere in China. But, to criticize China for failing to replicate in 25 years American constitutional constructs and culture that have germinated for 250 years seems unfair and unrealistic. Lest we be too smug, even in this country we still struggle to get it right and often fail to secure religious liberty for all.

When we sing or pray "God bless America," let's remember also to thank God for the progress China has made as we continue to pray for China and for freedom throughout the world.

Unlike France, Religion-friendly Secular State Exists in US[1]

In the aftermath of the utterly inane response to France's refusing to support the war in Iraq—you know, "freedom fries" instead of "French fries," etc.—we now have cause to complain about how the French government is planning to deal with an issue of religious expression.

In France, a government-appointed committee recently proposed a measure that would ban public school students from wearing conspicuous religious garb and symbols such as head scarves, yarmulkes, crosses, and turbans. A law is currently being drafted to implement the recommendation.

President Jacques Chirac has endorsed the proposal, claiming it is needed to preserve the secular French state and required to "fight against Xenophobia, racism and anti-Semitism." Another governmental official was quoted as saying the law banning religious attire in the public schools is necessary "to protect French democracy."

Leaving aside the almost laughable disconnect between these laudable ends and dubious means, the French proposal would obviously stifle religious freedom. In the name of promoting state secularity and its independence from the institutions of religion, the French law would exhibit outrageous hostility toward public expressions of religion, and, in the words of syndicated columnist E. J. Dionne, Jr., "push religion to the margins of public life."

A comparison of the French proposal with the way religious garb issues are typically addressed in the United States illustrates an important point. The American concept of a secular state and the separation of church and state means that government should not dominate, control, or become entangled with religion, but should accommodate or at least not obstruct religious choices of its citizens, including public school students.

In short, the American idea of secularity does not mean hostility; it means neutrality. Church-state separation does not mandate a naked public square; it means often a rowdy, raucous, even religious one. This specific

---

[1] *Report from the Capital* 9/1 (January 2004): 3.

debate in the United States typically centers on whether teachers should be permitted to wear religious garb or exhibit symbols of faith. This is where the debate should occur. Teachers are state actors and while acting in that capacity their right to endorse religion is quite properly limited, but students are usually free to express religious sentiments and sport religious attire with precious few restrictions.

Supreme Court cases and federal Department of Education guidelines make clear that public schools are not religion-free zones. One of the federal guidelines issued by the Clinton administration provides, "Schools may not single out religious attire in general, or attire of a particular religion, for prohibition or regulation. Students may display religious messages on items of clothing to the same extent that they are permitted to display other comparable messages. Religious messages may not be singled out for suppression, but rather are subject to the same rules as generally apply to comparable messages."[2] Voluntary student religious expression is permitted so long as it is not disruptive or done in a manner that indicates state sponsorship.

It is risky to presume to tell another country how to deal with perceived challenges presented by burgeoning religious pluralism. I'll be the first to admit we in the United States sometimes fall short of the mark. For example, there is no federal constitutional right to a religiously based exemption from neutral, generally applicable dress codes. Nevertheless, this comparison illustrates that the American tradition of church-state separation is intended to create a secular but religion-friendly state that accommodates the claims of conscience and protects the free exercise rights of all citizens.

When right-wing radicals bash the wall of separation between church and state and lament the supposedly naked public square, they speak more of the religion-hostile French understanding of these concepts than the more religion-friendly version that exists under the First Amendment in the United States. Don't let them get away with it.

By the way, the only reason not to eat French fries is if you have high cholesterol.

---

[2] www.bjconline.org/resources/pubs/pub_relinpubschools.htm.

Sometimes a Helping Hand
Does More Harm than Good[1]

One of the great heresies of our time is the claim that separation of church and state is bad for religion. This charge fuels the Istook amendment,[2] animates school voucher proposals, and energizes the push for charitable choice. But it is a lie. The separation of church and state has resulted in more religious liberty and a more visibly religious culture in this country than anywhere else I know.

Church-state separation has always been a core principle of the Baptist Joint Committee, but sometimes we fail to appreciate it fully. Recent encounters with people living in two European democracies drove this point home to me like never before.

Last month, I was interviewed by Urdur Gunnarsdottir, a journalist from Reykjavik, Iceland, who writes for *Morgunbladid*, one of Iceland's oldest newspapers. She was in this country for several weeks to research a piece on religion in America and its influence on politics. She wanted to find out what makes Americans tick and to see firsthand what these people called "Baptists" are all about.

After we talked for a while, she became intrigued by how there could be so much public discussion, debate, and religion talk in a country that preaches the separation of church and state. She told me that, in Iceland, religion is hardly ever discussed in public. People there keep their religion to themselves. More than 95 percent of Icelanders are Lutheran. Lutheranism is the preferred religion and enjoys considerable state support. Despite this religious dominance, religion is seldom, if ever, discussed or employed by politicians to inform their positions on public policy. In short, there is little evidence of religiosity in Icelandic culture.

I responded, yes, that is precisely the point. The separation of church and state does not mean a divorcement of religion from politics or God from

---

[1] *Report from the Capital* 53/5 (March 10, 1998): 3.
[2] Istook seeks to amend the First Amendment to allow greater government support for religion.

government. In fact, it allows and encourages religion to inform political debate. In Iceland, ironically enough, the opposite is true. The merger of church and state, far from promoting public religiosity, encourages its absence.

This week I had the pleasure of talking to a friend from Poland named Tadeusz Zielinski, a member of the Polish Parliament. He has the distinction of being the only Baptist M.P. in all Poland. He is an accomplished scholar and a Baptist to beat all Baptists. In fact, he just published a book in Poland about Roger Williams. His signal accomplishment, I think, is getting elected as a proud, professing Baptist in a country that is overwhelmingly Catholic and where fewer than 100 Baptists live in his district of 1.5 million people. It would be like a Buddhist getting elected to Congress from Biloxi, Mississippi. I wondered how he got elected.

Dr. Zielinski shot me an incredulous look. It was no great mystery to this Baptist scholar. For people in Poland, religion is a private matter and does not play much of a role in predicting Polish voting behavior. Then he reminded me, "That's exactly what you would expect when you don't have a separation of church and state."

So, to prove the benefits of separation, one does not have to point to theocratic regimes or repressive countries like the Sudan where there is outright persecution. Even constitutional democracies can kill religion when they try to give one religious tradition, or religion in general, a helping hand.

I guess Elder John Leland had it right when he said more than two centuries ago that "the fondness of magistrates to foster Christianity has done it more harm than all the persecution ever did."[3] He was exactly right then, and he's still right today. The best thing government can do for religion is to leave it alone.

---

[3] Cf., Green, ed., *The Writings of the Late Elder John Leland* (New York: Arno Press, 1970) 278.

National Tragedy a Test for America's Faith Groups[1]

Our lives have been changed forever. Americans have suffered the most hellish act of aggression against civilians on our native soil, at least since the British burned the Capitol and White House on an August day in 1814. No longer will the perennial question be the one my parents asked: "Where were you when Pearl Harbor was bombed?" Nor will it be my generation's query: "What were you doing when President Kennedy was assassinated?" For this generation of Americans, it will always be, "Where were you when the hijacked commercial airliners crashed into the World Trade Center and the Pentagon and thousands died?"

While watching the ghastly events in Manhattan on my office television, I gazed out the window past the Capitol dome and saw the smoke billow from the Pentagon several miles to the west. As the Baptist Joint Committee staff prepared to leave the building, we paused to pray for the unfolding situation that turned out to be even worse than we knew.

It is still hard fully to fathom the enormity of that day. In a sense, I wonder what more can be said given the media saturation of news reports, opinion pieces, and talking heads reflecting on what happened that awful day. In another sense, I wonder if we are not still too close to the tragedy to appreciate its implications fully. I simply cannot get my mind around it.

We certainly need to continue to pray for those who have lost family members and loved ones, for the heroic rescue workers and other support personnel, and for President Bush, members of Congress, and other policymakers.

As we respond to this horrific tragedy, personally and nationally, we have important choices to make. We can put our arms around each other, commiserate in the loss of innocence, and, as Franklin Roosevelt said, bask in the "warm courage of our national unity."[2] As we do, we should support

---

[1] *Report from the Capital* 56/19 (September 26, 2001): 3.
[2] From his first inaugural address delivered March 4, 1933.

efforts to seek justice, punish the wrongdoers, and prevent this kind of thing from ever happening again.

However, we also need to be careful not to compound the tragedy by sowing seeds of hate, casting blame where it does not belong, or seeking vengeance rather than justice and thus adding names to the list of innocent victims.

We have already witnessed threats and acts of violence against Muslims and their houses of worship and against many other Arab Americans. This is wrong. Those who perpetrated this evil do not speak for or act on behalf of Islam, any more than the hateful venom of the Ku Klux Klan can be attributed to all Christians. Muslims and Arab Americans perished along with people of other nationalities and religions. They grieve along with us. America must continue to protect the religious liberty of all of its citizens; we must not engage in religious and ethnic stereotyping.

We see other forms of scapegoating and casting blame, not on the Muslim community, but on political and cultural adversaries. Even while the fires still clouded the Manhattan and Washington skylines, Jerry Falwell and Pat Robertson engaged in a hair-raising conversation on national television.[3] They blasted the American Civil Liberties Union, People for the American Way, abortionists, feminists, and gays and lesbians for the events of September 11. The implication was that God allowed this to be perpetrated to punish all Americans for the views and lifestyles of these groups and people. At best, it is preposterous to purport to know the will of God with such breathtaking certainty. At worst, it is demagogic to use a national tragedy as a tool to castigate those with whom one disagrees. In any case, it again plays directly into the hands of terrorists to foster hatred, strife, and fear. Although both men have issued apologies, those remarks stand as a stark reminder to measure our words carefully in a time of crisis.

In addition, it is important that we not overreact to the point of compromising our commitment to civil liberties. To fall prey to that temptation would be fundamentally to alter what it means to be America. Of course, we need to protect our citizens and our national sovereignty. We will have to tolerate the added inconvenience of increased security at airports and other public places. We may even be forced to tolerate (even applaud) marshals on passenger planes and other extraordinary law enforcement measures. But, as E. J. Dionne, Jr., wrote in his syndicated

---

[3] Interview on *700 Club*, Thursday, September 13, 2001.

column, "our nation can be both tough and democratic...we can guard both public safety and liberty."[4] Both/and, not either/or.

So, as we Americans come together enjoying a welcomed sense of heightened patriotism, let's all fall to our knees in prayer to God, respecting each other and appreciating our differences, take the necessary steps to punish the wrongdoers without foregoing our way of life, and remember that being free is at the core of what it means to be American Baptist Christians.

---

[4] E. J. Dionne, "To Go on Being Americans," *Washington Post*, September 14, 2001.

Feeding the Hungry? Not in My Backyard![1]

When Jesus decided to feed the 5,000, it was a good thing that he lived in Galilee under the heavy hand of Herodian rule instead of in the capital of a modern democracy dedicated to religious liberty. Otherwise, the lad's two fish and five loaves might never have been eaten.

Last April, when Western Presbyterian Church in Washington, DC, moved to new quarters a few blocks from its old location, it immediately faced a zoning prohibition designed to stop it from feeding the homeless. "The concept of feeding the hungry is rooted in Jesus' ministry itself," said John Wimberly, pastor of Western Presbyterian. "To prohibit us from feeding the homeless is almost like closing down our congregation."

What had been permissible a short walk from the White House and just off the George Washington University campus suddenly was not allowed a few blocks away, in the shadow of the Kennedy Center, Watergate complex, and other pricey abodes in fashionable Foggy Bottom. Though the church's new neighbors said they favored feeding the homeless in principle, they didn't want it in their own backyard. "The key here is safety," said Barbara Kahlew, a member of the Foggy Bottom Association. "We are a community of women. [Our residents] are terrified to go outside."

At the association's urging, the DC zoning administrator—under the guise of enforcing the city's zoning laws—sought to prevent the church from continuing its ten-year homeless ministry. The city argued that at the church's old location, zoned for commercial use, the feeding program was permissible, but at the new location—called "special purpose district" and designed as a buffer between commercial and residential areas—the feeding ministry was not allowed as a matter of right. Instead, it would require a variance.

The need for a variance in the situation was outrageous. The law states that in zones in which churches are permitted, other "ancillary" activities are allowed when conducted on the same premises. Thus, daycare centers, playgrounds, counseling centers, coffeehouses for college students, parking

---

[1] *Liberty* 90/4 (July/August 1995): 6.

lots, radio antennas, homeless shelters, and even feeding ministries have been permitted.[2]

The ordinance in Washington acknowledges that ancillary uses are permitted if "customarily incidental and subordinate to the principal use, and located on the same lot with principal use."

What could be more integrally related to the religious use of the premises than feeding the hungry? The Bible is replete with admonitions to feed the hungry and care for the less fortunate (see Ezekiel 18:5-9; Matthew 25:34-36; James 2:14-17). Nevertheless, the zoning administrator ruled that the feeding program was not covered by this provision of DC law, and the Board of Zoning Adjustment (BZA) upheld the zoning administrator's decision that feeding the homeless was not a "customary" activity. "I see," said one board member, "nothing customary about feeding people in a church."

On the eve of its move to 2401 Virginia Avenue, the church got an injunction in federal court against enforcement of the zoning ordinance. Although the church argued the "accessory use" doctrine and its constitutional rights under the First Amendment, it relied primarily on the Religious Freedom Restoration Act of 1993 (RFRA), signed by President Clinton in November 1993. RFRA restores the high level of protection that the courts had historically accorded to the free exercise of religion. Under RFRA, if a church's religious liberty is substantially burdened by the state action, then government must show that it is pursuing a "compelling state interest" and that it adopted the "least restrictive means" of doing so.[3]

Clearly the zoning board substantially burdened Western Presbyterian's religious liberty. The church regards feeding the homeless as a religiously motivated calling that goes to the core of ministry. "We feed

---

[2] A New Jersey court has ruled that a church providing meals and overnight lodging for homeless people in its basement is an ancillary use of the church (*St. John's Evangelical Lutheran Church v. City of Hoboken*, 479 A. 2d 935 [NJ Sup.Ct. 1983]). In New York a church sought to open an emergency homeless shelter on its premises. A New York court ruled that a program providing food and shelter to homeless people was a protected activity (*Greentree at Murray Hill Condominium v. Good Shepherd Episcopal Church*, 550 N.Y.S. 2d 981 [NY Sup. Ct. 1989]). The court reasoned that "it has long been held that a church or synagogue may be used for accessory uses and activities which go beyond just prayer and worship." The court concluded that the church's shelter was a permissible "accessory use" of the church and was protected under the zoning laws (ibid., 985).

[3] 42 USC §2000bb.

the hungry because we have been called to do it," said Wimberly. "Would we even be a church, or Christians, if we did not?"

The question then became whether the city would show a compelling interest and whether it had adopted the least restrictive means of accomplishing the interest.

No doubt government has a compelling interest in enforcing laws designed to ensure the health, safety, and welfare of its citizens. But the city had no compelling interest sufficient to justify shutting down the feeding ministry. In response to the neighbors' highly speculative and unsubstantiated fears of attracting undesirables, visual blight, and rising crime, the church pointed to its uneventful, unblemished, ten-year record at its old location. Because none of the feared problems happened there, what made anyone think they would happen at the new location? The city at the injunction hearing conceded, in fact, that it had no compelling interest.

Similarly, even if there were a compelling state interest, the city's outright ban would not be the "least restrictive means." Less intrusive ways of ensuring against neighborhood disruption abounded. "The church itself," said Wimberly, "voluntarily agreed to limit the numbers that would be fed, require the chow line to be indoors, have a clean-up crew afterward, and disallow any loitering around the church before and after breakfast is served."

The court ruled that the city both substantially burdened the church's free exercise rights and failed to demonstrate compelling state interest.[4] It concluded that "this well-run and necessary effort to minister to the less fortunate residents of this city ought not be arbitrarily restricted and relegated to the less desirable areas of the city because of the unfounded or irrational fears of certain residents." On September 9, 1994, the court made the injunction permanent.

Certainly, zoning laws are important. A landfill should not be allowed next to a restaurant, nor an X-rated theater in the midst of a residential neighborhood. But zoning laws should be applied judiciously and in a way that respects the constitutional rights of those whom they seek to regulate.

In retrospect, why wouldn't Washington, DC—with a horrendous homeless problem and all but bankrupt—welcome, even encourage, churches to render a service that the city would otherwise have to perform?

---

[4] *Western Presbyterian Church v. Board of Zoning Adjustment of the District of Columbia*, 862f.Supp. 538, 547 (DC Cir. 1994).

The answer, of course, is that landowning voters have more political clout than dispossessed street people. Nevertheless, churches must always fight intrusive attempts on the part of government to interfere with their call to "be salt and light" to the world, especially through such a basic ministry as providing a few loaves and fish to the hungry.

American Pluralism and
Lunchbox Evangelism[1]

Galatians 5:1; 1 Peter 3:15

America—now 300,000,000 strong and counting—is an astonishingly diverse country. Our national motto is *E Pluribus Unum*, and, for better or for worse, we are more *pluribus* than *unum*. Our other motto is "In God We Trust." In our nation we have citizens who trust in many different gods, and some trust in no god at all. With all the deep splits and disagreements that divide us, particularly over religion and politics, it's important that we try to find common ground—or at least figure out a way to live together with our differences without disparaging the other person's rights of citizenship or religious beliefs.

I'm reminded of a *Peanuts* cartoon in which Sally tells Linus, "I would make a good evangelist."

"Oh, yeah? How come?" Linus responds.

"You know that boy who sits behind me in the classroom?" Sally continues.

"Yes."

"I convinced him that my religion was better than his."

"How'd you do that?"

"I hit him over the head with my lunchbox."[2]

This is what I'm talking about. We need to avoid hitting each other over the head with our cultural, political, and religious lunchboxes or calling judgment down on those who are different. The recent remarks of certain evangelical leaders—like Franklin Graham and Pat Robertson—disparaging Islam is exactly the wrong way to go. Who can forget the words of a former president of the Southern Baptist Convention several years ago, calling the prophet Muhammad a "demon-possessed pedophile"?[3] I wonder how he

---

[1] Unpublished sermon.

[2] *Peanuts*, Charles Schulz.

[3] Rev. Jerry Vines, sermon at Southern Baptist Convention Pastors Conference, St. Louis MO, June 13, 2002.

would like it if a fundamentalist Imam were to call Jesus a homeless wine-bibber who hung out with prostitutes and publicans. That's a charge that easily can be proof-texted in the New Testament.

The plush pluralism we see today was in the cards from the beginning. It started at least by the 1630s in Massachusetts Bay Colony when the Massachusetts moral majority declared, "you must believe and behave as we say." The Puritans came to these shores to find religious freedom, but when they got here they turned around and denied it to everybody else. Still, the voices of others could be heard over the shouting saying, "We answer to God alone on spiritual matters, not to the magistrate."

One who spoke such words was a young Puritan preacher by the name of Roger Williams. Called by some the "apostle of religious liberty," he came to these shores from England preaching and teaching "soul freedom"—the notion that faith cannot be dictated by any civil or ecclesiastical authority, but must be nurtured freely and expressed directly to God without human interference. He spoke out forcefully about voluntary religion and liberty of individual conscience. The Puritan theocrats in Massachusetts were not amused with his wild-eyed heresy. When they had heard enough, they booted Roger Williams out of their colony.

He began the long journey south to a new land—slogging on foot through snow and surviving the frigid New England winter only with the help of the Narragansett Indians. Searching for a place where he could be true to his beliefs, where his conscience would remain unmolested by civil authority, Roger Williams and others settled in a place he called "Providence" because he figured that God's providence had led him there. He gave birth to what would become the colony of Rhode Island. Its guiding principle, its reason for existence, its claim to fame, was complete and absolute religious liberty. Williams began what he liked to call a "livelie experiment" and, in 1638, founded the first Baptist church on North American soil.

As a result, Rhode Island became a safe haven for all sorts of religious misfits—people who would not allow the government to decide spiritual issues or meddle in matters of faith. Sure, Rhode Island had its blind spots by modern standards. Catholics—though unmolested in their worship—were not allowed to hold public office, and Jews were denied full-fledged citizenship. But Rhode Island was light years ahead of its time.

Rhode Island was a fussy place. It was a messy place. It was a "sectarian free-for-all" for every stripe of theological expression. As historian Ed

Gaustad has reminded us, part of the problem of inviting people to a haven for conscience is that, sooner or later, everybody is going to come. And come they did! The sects and denominations competed mightily for the hearts and souls of the people. Roger Williams himself engaged in heated debates with the Quakers, one on one. But the government was not allowed to take sides in those religious disputes. Williams had, in his words, successfully erected "a hedge or wall of separation between the garden of the church and the wilderness of the world."[4]

Despite the urging of Williams and successive generations of Baptists, complete religious liberty was slow in coming. Centuries of religious intolerance were firmly ingrained, and old habits died hard. All but four colonies (Rhode Island, Pennsylvania, Delaware, and New Jersey) had officially established churches and varying degrees of persecution and intolerance. All but two colonies (Virginia and Rhode Island) had religious qualifications for public office; five denied basic civil rights to Catholics; and in Vermont, blasphemy was a capital offense.[5]

But the wise founders of our republic had a different idea in mind for the new country. They took the bold step of separating church and state in civil society. They provided in article VI of the new Constitution that there would be no religious test for public office. These able architects of the new nation further decided that the federal government would not be permitted to make any law "respecting an establishment of religion, or prohibiting the free exercise thereof." These initial sixteen words of the Bill of Rights erected "twin pillars" protecting the freedom of religion and upholding the wall of separation between church and state. These two clauses, when taken together, require government to remain *neutral* toward religion—turning it loose, leaving it to flourish or flounder on its own.

For the first time in human history, a nation denied to itself the right to become involved in religious matters or violate the consciences of its citizens. One's status in the civil community would not depend on a willingness to profess any religious belief.

Some of my friends who do not believe in church-state separation want to appeal to the "original intent" of the founders. I welcome that debate because I think I can win it. Our founders were mostly religious men, some

---

[4] Edwin S. Gaustad, *Liberty of Conscience: Roger Williams in America* (Grand Rapids MI: Eerdmans, 1991).

[5] Douglas Laycock, "'Nonpreferential Aid' to Religion: A False Claim about Original Intent," *Wm. & Mary L Rev.* 27 (1986): 875, 916.

more devout than others, but they chose to enshrine religious liberty for all, not ensconce their own religious views, in the constitution they drew up.

James Madison, the father of our Constitution, was a devout Anglican and studied theology at a Presbyterian college that would later become Princeton University. He thought diversity was essential to the success of our new form of government. He foresaw political factionalism and, to use his words, a "zeal for different opinions concerning religion."[6] He hoped that, as the factions competed for the minds and souls of the people, this pluralism would prevent any one of them from dominating the political and cultural landscape. Madison penned these prophetic words in the *Federalist Paper* #51:

[S]ociety itself will be broken into so many parts, interests and classes of citizens that the rights of individuals, or of the minority, will be in little danger from interested combinations of the majority. In a free government the security for civil rights must be the same as that for religious rights. It consists in the one case in the multiplicity of interests, and in the other in the multiplicity of sects. The degree of security in both cases will depend on the number of interests and sects; and this may be presumed to depend on the extent of country and number of people comprehended under the same government.

It should come as no surprise to any of us more than two centuries later—given the disestablishment of religion, the explicit constitutional protection for religious freedom, and the endorsement by Madison of a robust pluralism—that we have developed this dizzying diversity of religion. Ed Gaustad was right. If you say, "y'all come," and offer to protect religious diversity, then that's exactly what's going to happen, and come they did.

Whether you like it or not, pluralism abounds today to an extent that I'm sure even Madison did not fathom. Estimates reveal nearly 1,000 Christian denominations and sects, and more than 650 non-Christian groups. We have nearly as many Jews as Episcopalians and as many Muslims as members of Assemblies of God churches. The dominant faith in Hawaii is Buddhism, and in Utah it is Mormonism. And in most towns of any size in America, the skyline is outlined by mosques, temples, and synagogues, as well as steeples and crosses. In their new album, the Dixie Chicks sing a

---

[6] "Federalist #10," in *The Federalist Papers*, James Madison.

song titled "Lubbock or Leave It," with a line referring to a "crucifix skyline."[7] But even Lubbock, Texas, has these other houses of worship.

I want to join Madison in proclaiming that pluralism is positive. Not only was it expected, not only did we see it coming, but pluralism is positive. I'm not endorsing an "anything goes" moral relativism. One can hold firmly to his or her own beliefs while according the other person, seen and unseen, the right to think differently and to come to a different conclusion about his or her spiritual destiny.

Nor do respect for pluralism and religious freedom rule out the right to bear witness and to share our faith. In fact, they encourage and make real evangelism possible. The incredible freedom we enjoy as Baptists and Americans allows us to talk about our faith with others. We are all painfully aware of places in the world where speaking the name of Christ gets you killed or thrown in jail. Baptists historically have valued missions and evangelism along with freedom. Respecting the other person's soul freedom doesn't mean you cannot share your faith with that person; it does mean, however, that you respect and honor his or her right to tell you no. We must fight to ensure against others doing, or the church doing, or the government doing what even God will not do—violate conscience or force faith.

Moreover, religious freedom and resulting pluralism has in a real sense brought the world to us. No longer do we discharge the Great Commission to take the gospel to "the ends of the earth" only by sending foreign missionaries; no, the "world" is now next door, down the street, in the enjoining cubicle, in the classroom. It has been estimated that a new immigrant arrives every thirty-one seconds! Living side by side allows us to get to know and understand other people and their religious points of view. Ideally, "with-nessing" should precede "witnessing." Getting to know individuals makes what we say so much more effective and credible, and it allows us to learn from the Hindu, the Buddhist, the Jew, and the Jain. As Christians we believe we know the *ultimate* truth in the person of Jesus Christ, but we do not presume to know *all* the truth. We can learn a lot from our brothers and sisters regardless of their religious tradition.

Finally, all of this means that we live with and work with the "other," trying to find common ground where we can and disagree agreeably when we must. A good example of this is the work that we at the BJC do in the

---

[7] From the 2006 album with Sony titled *Taking the Long Way*.

ecumenical context in Washington. We work in broad coalitions of widely diverse religious groups from the Far Left to the Far Right, Jewish and Muslin, evangelical and liberal, and Catholic and Protestant. We are able to do this despite our deep differences over religion and other policy issues, and we do so as we stand on common ground and seek to influence policy goals that will expand the religious liberty of all of us.

This is biblical, too. Paul announced the clarion call of freedom in Christ to the Galatians when he said "for freedom Christ has set us free, do not submit again to the yoke of slavery."[8] Paul was a freedom guy, but there was no greater evangelist in the early church than the apostle Paul. His embrace of freedom did not detract from but *added to* his enthusiasm for sharing the gospel. Then, his counterpart, Peter, tells us in his first letter that we must "always be prepared to make a defense to anyone who calls you to account for the hope that is in you, yet do it with gentleness and reverence."[9]

This is not, I submit, what is happening today. There is nothing gentle and reverent about some of the preaching we hear—the scathing attacks we witness against other religions, especially Islam. I think we would do better to follow the advice of Chuck Colson, who is no friend of liberal Christianity. He said we will never evangelize the world or win the culture war by "waving placards in the faces of supposed enemies or whacking them with our leather-bound bibles." (I am sure Colson would have used the lunchbox metaphor if he had thought of it!) Rather, Colson tells us the best thing we can do is "to live as a holy community embodying the love of Christ, demonstrating Christianity's benefits to the culture at large."[10]

Our evangelism must always be done in the context of our amazing pluralism and remarkable freedom and be bathed with the grace of God, the love of Christ, and the fellowship of the Holy Spirit. With a nod to Charles Schultz, we should share our lunches with a hungry world, but refrain from wielding our lunchboxes as weapons of hate and intolerance.

---

[8] Galatians 5:1.
[9] 1 Peter 3:15.
[10] Charles Colson, "Sweet Reason and Holy Outrage," 64.

Index